The Milk-free Kitchen

Beth Kidder

Henry Holt and Company

New York

THE
MILK-FREE
KITCHEN

Living Well Without
Dairy Products

Copyright © 1988, 1991 by Beth Kidder
All rights reserved, including the right to reproduce
this book or portions thereof in any form.
Published by Henry Holt and Company, Inc.,
115 West 18th Street, New York, New York 10011.
Published in Canada by Fitzhenry & Whiteside Limited,
195 Allstate Parkway, Markham, Ontario L3R 4T8.

Library of Congress Cataloging-in-Publication Data
Kidder, Beth.
The milk-free kitchen : living well without dairy products /
by Beth Kidder.—1st ed.
p.   cm.
"A small portion . . . appeared previously as Cooking
without milk . . . in 1988"—T.p. verso.
ISBN 0-8050-1255-9 (alk. paper)
1. Milk-free diet—Recipes.   I. Title.
RM234.5.K53   1991
641.5'63—dc20   90-35314
CIP

Henry Holt books are available at special discounts
for bulk purchases for sales promotions, premiums,
fund-raising, or educational use. Special editions
or book excerpts can also be created to specification.
For details contact:
Special Sales Director, Henry Holt and Company, Inc.,
115 West 18th Street, New York, New York 10011.

First Edition

Designed by Kate Nichols

Printed in the United States of America
Recognizing the importance of preserving the written word,
Henry Holt and Company, Inc., by policy, prints all of its
first editions on acid-free paper. ∞

1   3   5   7   9   10   8   6   4   2

A small portion of this book was previously published as
Cooking Without Milk by Beth Kidder in 1988.

*Dedicated to good home cooks everywhere,
and especially to those who cook
around food allergies.*

Contents

Contents

Preface

When my son came home for the summer after his first year at college and announced that he was allergic to milk, I refused to believe him at first. He's big, he's active, and he burns a lot of calories; plenty of milk and baked goods (usually made with milk) had helped keep him fed. He needs so much more food than the rest of us do that it's important to keep snack foods around for him. He had been drinking a half gallon of milk each day. Until I learned to bake without milk products this allergy meant lots of peanut butter sandwiches and fruit juice for him. When he was home the whole family now needed to have milk-free meals, since we wished to eat together. At first this meant a very limited diet, but our choices became less restricted as I developed more recipes. Guests don't realize that our meals are milk-free unless we mention it.

At first I thought there was some simple substitute for milk in baked goods; for instance, X tablespoons of sugar and Y tablespoons of egg in one cup of water would be the equivalent of one cup of milk. Or, perhaps some product sold at health-food stores would solve the problem. I found out that although milk-free cooking is easy when you know how, there is no simple substitute for milk. Each recipe has to be reinvented, and all react a little differently. I worked out milk-free recipes for the foods we usually eat, and after a year or two both children (our daughter, who is older, was now allergic to cows' milk) said that my recipes were much better than those they had been able to find anywhere else, and that there was a greater variety of them. They urged me to write them down, so, here is the collection. I hope my book will help you.

I would like to thank the following people, who have helped me immensely:

My children, Marjorie and Douglas, for their encouragement and interest.

My husband, George, for his patience in eating a great many experimental meals; and for his help when I don't understand the computer that we use as a word processor.

My mother, Betty Lewis, who raised me on good food well prepared.

Alan White-Rogers, who does business as "The Cheese Man" in Ellsworth, Maine; for generously sharing his knowledge of cheeses with me.

Dr. Ting Wang, for discussing the material with me.

Introduction

Milk is an excellent source of high quality protein and calcium but, as Beth Kidder explains, there are many people who cannot safely or comfortably digest milk. One medical survey suggests that milk intolerance may affect 6 percent of the adult population to some degree. The two most common causes of intolerance to milk are a lactase deficiency and a milk allergy. If either disorder is considered likely from solid clinical and laboratory evidence, it may be important to be certain that milk be totally eliminated from the diet, but persons with either diagnosis may be able to eat or drink small quantities of milk products without apparent ill effects.

Lactase Deficiency

Milk sugar, lactose, is split into two simpler sugars, glucose and galactose, by an enzyme called lactase. This enzyme is present in cells on the surface of the small intestine. Once formed, the simple sugars are easily absorbed by the body. If this crucial enzyme is absent or deficient, most of the lactose will be digested instead by bacteria to create much gas, abdominal swelling, and diarrhea.

Persons with this problem are often mistakenly said to have an irritable bowel or a nervous stomach. Indeed, many lactose-intolerant persons are irritable and difficult to live with, simply because they feel so poorly. A correct diagnosis of their problem can dramatically alter their lives for the better. A simple breath test or a blood test called the lactose intolerance test can easily establish the diagnosis, but marked improvement with the elimination of milk from the diet, or with the addition of lactose-free milk, may be adequate to establish a diagnosis.

Lactose intolerance may be congenital, but the symptoms may only begin to appear during teenage years. Sometimes inflammation in the gastrointestinal tract from a disease such as regional enteritis may cause a secondary deficiency of the lactase enzyme with the same effects as the inherited form of this disorder. As I have noted, some persons may be able to tolerate reasonable amounts of milk in which most of the lactose has already been digested by the addition of the enzyme lactase in tablet form. Others may need to eliminate almost all milk to feel well.

Milk Allergy

A true milk allergy is a more complex problem. It may be more difficult to diagnose and our knowledge of the immunologic mechanisms is still incomplete. There can be a large array of symptoms involving more than the gastrointestinal tract. Though a milk allergy occurs in adults, it is more common in infants and children. Some milk-allergic children may, as they grow older, be able to drink milk without trouble, but this is not always true.

What do we mean by a milk allergy? It is an immune response by antibodies or white blood cells to one or more milk proteins that, instead of being protective to the body, may cause tissue damage, physical discomfort, or even serious risk to the sensitive person.

Milk allergy can show itself in a variety of ways. It may cause a sudden reaction throughout the body with vomiting, severe abdominal pain, diarrhea, as well as a rash, respiratory obstruction, and even circulatory collapse. More often a target organ, the gastrointestinal tract, may be predominantly involved.

Or a milk allergy can be more subtle. It may worsen a chronic skin rash, called atopic dermatitis or eczema, or it may occasionally be one trigger for asthma or chronic nasal congestion, called chronic allergic rhinitis.

A fortunately rare severe allergic reaction to milk may cause the bowel to be unable to absorb almost all foodstuffs, and it can provoke bleeding from the bowel, leading to an iron-deficiency anemia. This most often occurs in infants. They may also have a pulmonary disease associated with the milk allergy.

The majority of persons with a milk allergy will have evidence of other food or respiratory allergies. Members of the immediate family may also be affected with allergies. Most though not quite all persons with a true milk allergy will have a positive immediate skin test to milk proteins. A blood test called a RAST test can give similar information. However, positive skin tests or the RAST test do *not* provide conclusive evidence of a clinically important allergy to milk. There are persons with positive skin tests who can drink milk safely. Most persons with negative skin tests or a negative RAST test do not have a milk allergy, although there are exceptions.

Someone exhibiting only gastrointestinal complaints, for whom a lactase deficiency or other gastrointestinal disease has been excluded, may show dramatic improvement with the exclusion of milk and milk products from his or her diet. Conversely, the patient may show a recurrence of symptoms when these foods are reintroduced into the diet. This may be the best evidence that a problem exists.

The key to making the right diagnosis is to make sure that bias or preconception does not influence judgment. If there is doubt about the reliability of the clinical findings, a double blind challenge may be helpful. With this test neither the person with the suspected milk allergy nor the doctor must know when milk is being taken by mouth. This is not an easy task. Sometimes opaque capsules can be filled with powdered milk, while sugar-filled capsules serve as the matching placebo. If the expected symptoms appear only when the milk-filled capsules are swallowed, the diagnosis is confirmed. Usually this kind of challenge is not necessary when milk can produce an observable skin rash or asthma.

Introduction

A number of controversial tests for food allergies have been shown not to be valid. One example is a sublingual test or subcutaneous injection of food extracts to provoke symptoms. Another is to look for damage to white blood cells under the microscope when milk proteins are mixed with the cells. Many complaints have been attributed to food allergies, including arthritis and all types of neurologic and psychiatric disorders, even schizophrenia. Food allergies have almost never been conclusively shown to cause these problems.

Once a milk allergy is established with confidence, treatment is elimination of the allergen. Mrs. Kidder's book will prove invaluable to all those who need to eliminate milk and milk products from their diets.

Harold M. Friedman, M.D.
Chief of Allergy
Dartmouth-Hitchcock Medical Center

The Milk-free Kitchen

Living with Allergies

People with allergies live in a somewhat different world from the ordinary. Whereas a heart patient can have occasional small amounts of saturated fat without any ill effects, someone who is allergic to a food will know soon and painfully if he or she ate the wrong thing.

Living with food allergy implies a whole different way of looking at food. Constant vigilance becomes second nature. People with food allergies have difficulty at buffet meals and learn either to eat beforehand or else contribute a dish. Scrutinizing salads and examining unfamiliar stews become automatic.

If you are sensitive to nuts and you mistakenly eat some, your reaction to this accidental dose will range from a mildly upset stomach to something that sends you to the emergency room and might even kill you. Milk presents essentially the same problems as nuts do, except that milk is more widely used in western food than are nuts, *and* once food has been stirred the milk disappears from sight. I have learned these things as the wife of a man who is severely allergic to nuts and as the mother of two children who became severely allergic to cows' milk in their late teens, and it has colored the way I think about food.

With most allergies all you need to do is avoid the offending substance—eliminating nuts or chocolate from your diet, or keep-

1

ing away from dogs, or staying indoors during ragweed season, isn't going to hurt you. However, in our culture milk is the main source of valuable nutrients such as calcium and phosphorus (not getting enough of them *will* hurt you) and you must find out how to deal with this. You will probably need to take calcium pills. It is important for you to get advice from a physician or dietitian.

Living Well Without Milk
or Milk Products

A certain amount of reeducation of the taste buds takes place in the person with a newly discovered allergy. Any liking for milk products vanishes when you realize that they can cause painful symptoms.

Most people who deal with food intolerance day in and day out become pretty good "scratch" cooks. Since allergists and other physicians very seldom cook for a family, don't be surprised if your physician thinks that he's helped you enormously by giving you a list of foods to avoid and a booklet given to him by a manufacturer of milk-free infant formula. I wrote this book as an all-occasion cookbook. The idea is to give you lots of choices.

This book is focused on all the things you *can* have.

The idea behind every recipe here is that the food should taste good. I hope you will enjoy your milk-free meals and that you and the people with whom you share them will not feel deprived or "different."

All of the recipes here can be used by someone who is allergic to cows' milk (and only cows' milk). Since a few of the recipes use cheese made from goats' or sheep's milk, someone who is lactose-intolerant may not be able to use these few recipes; however, such a person may be able to add some yogurt or well-aged cheese instead.

Since many people who are allergic have allergies to more than one thing, I devised a wide variety of recipes for this book and have suggested ways to vary the ingredients wherever possible. For example, there is a special list of recipes for egg-free baked goods on pages 438 to 441 for those who are allergic to eggs.

Warning: It has recently been shown that many raw eggs carry Salmonella, a bacterium that causes food poisoning if you eat the eggs raw or undercooked (still runny). Thoroughly cooked eggs are safe. Eggs that contain Salmonella do not look or smell any different from other eggs; it requires laboratory testing to tell the difference.

A few recipes in this book, such as those for best salad dressing (page 207), mayonnaise (page 114), and rum frosting (page 398) are made with raw egg. If you wish to use any of these recipes, either choose another recipe or use eggs that you know to be safe. Lightly cooked foods containing raw eggs, such as lemon meringue pie (page 322), boiled frosting (page 402), orange sauce (page 409), and even french toast (page 158) may also be unsafe to eat. I developed these recipes before undamaged raw eggs were known to be carriers of disease, and have left them in the book because I hope the day will come when raw or undercooked eggs may once again be safely eaten.

Some recipes are for foods such as beef stew, or hummus, or eggplant dip, all normally made without milk products, to give you a wide variety of choices when planning a meal. There are recipes for items such as meat loaf that are often prepared with milk; the uncooked meat may be mixed with milk or with bread crumbs from a loaf made without milk. I use rolled oats instead of bread crumbs and leave out the liquid altogether. I developed some recipes to replace recipes that depend on milk or cream. For example, try chicken with bacon and sherry (page 91) as a substitute for chicken sautéed with mushrooms, wine, and cream.

The recipes for baked goods were the most difficult of all to develop, as the lack of milk affects texture and keeping qualities as well as flavor. In creating these I had to change the proportions of all of the ingredients in order to come up with milk-free foods that have good flavor, texture, appearance, and keeping qualities.

I rely for the most part on foods that have been only lightly processed and are in a relatively natural condition—for example, plain wheat flour, but not cake mix.

I try to keep the salt and fat content of foods down but have certainly not eliminated either from my diet or from the book. This means that I trim fat from meat, use mayonnaise and cooking oil sparingly, and balance a rich dish with one or several that are low in fat. I use eggs and sugar in moderate quantities. I believe that sugar is bad only if eaten to the point at which it replaces other foods or stimulates overeating. If you like doughnuts, an occasional one won't hurt your body and will benefit your immortal soul.

Some Special Cases

The Allergic Child

The allergic child presents special problems once he or she is old enough to toddle about and accept cookies and other snacks. Later on when the child is older he or she will want to behave exactly as "everybody else" does and eat cheese pizza with friends.

Your first step is to alert any adults who may feed your child to the problem, and ask for their cooperation. Grandparents, neighbors, and the school dietitian are a good beginning. Since most people aren't aware of what foods contain milk or are milk products, you should go into some detail: "Jenny can't have milk or any milk products; this means cheese, butter, margarine, ice cream, most baked goods, and many candies. Yes, even a very little milk makes her quite sick."

School lunches should be avoided. Furnish your child with a brown-bag lunch. After-school snacks are best provided by you. Fresh fruit, pretzels, peanuts, little boxes of raisins, homemade cookies, lollipops, apple cider, and lemonade are a few possibilities.

Birthday parties are difficult because cake and ice cream will be on the menu, and such foods as hot dogs or pizza may be served. Call up the parent of the birthday child, explain the difficulty, and offer to supply Tofutti and milk-free cake for your child.

Summer camp or boarding school can be very difficult. You

should ask about the possibility of a special diet for your child if you're thinking of having him or her live away from home.

When You're Invited to Dinner at Somebody's House . . .

Explain your problem to the hosts when you accept the invitation, and discuss the menu. Usually you'll do just fine with simple changes that can be made only to your serving—cooked vegetables set aside for you before a cream sauce is added, your salad prepared with plain oil and vinegar dressing. You might offer to supply anything you'll eat that would be different from what everybody else is eating, and you can present the party-giver with some milk-free margarine to use in cooking. If everybody else will be having ice cream, bring some Tofutti or plain fruit sorbet.

Potluck suppers are easy. You will of course be bringing a delicious contribution, and you can eat that plus anything else on the table that appears to be milk-free, such as pretzels, pumpernickel bread, clear gelatin salad. You can bring both a dessert and a main dish. When contributing food to a potluck dinner at which some milk-intolerant guest will be present, I label my milk-free contribution "Made without any milk products." Otherwise it will be ignored by the allergic person it's intended to help.

Our experience has been that it is wise to decline brunch invitations.

Sometimes when dining out you will accidentally eat a milk product. You should carry with you any medication that will help to overcome your symptoms.

If you can avoid milk products for months or years, you may become so sensitive to milk's flavor that you can test an unknown food by tasting a tiny amount.

Eating in Restaurants

My son, Douglas, eats a great many business meals in restaurants. Here are some of his suggestions.

When ordering, tell the waiter or waitress that you must not eat any milk, cream, butter, cheese, or margarine because you are allergic to them. Ask questions about all the foods you plan to order.

Choose Asian foods or an Asian restaurant whenever possible; people from the Far East use little or no milk in cooking. However, some trendy Chinese restaurants use milk products, and dim sum and other appetizers may contain butter or cream cheese.

Truly kosher fleishig restaurants are an excellent choice. A kosher restaurant will serve only fleishig or only milchig food so if the restaurant serves meat (fish is pareve and doesn't count), it will be safe for you to eat there. Kosher-style is not the same thing as kosher, it is imitation kosher. See pages 15 to 16 for an explanation of kosher food.

In good Mexican restaurants—not the fast-food variety—the cheese or sour cream will usually be clearly visible and therefore easily avoidable. Beans, especially refried beans, may be prepared with a milk product. Fajitas are a good choice.

You should avoid French and Italian restaurants, although good Italian restaurants may use olive oil instead of butter if requested to do so.

Indian restaurants are not a good choice. They use a great deal of yogurt and ghee (clarified butter) in cooking, and since the dishes are very complex, it is nearly impossible to tell by inspection what's in them.

Plain American cooking is a good bet. If there is milk or cheese in a main dish, you will often be able to see it. Fruit pie is usually milk-free in less expensive restaurants, but a good restaurant or home cook may use milk products in the crust or dot the filling with butter before putting on the top crust. Avoid "French" or "Dutch" fruit pies.

Grill restaurants or the grill side of a menu are good choices. Ask the waiter to have your meat, fish, or chicken cooked with oil instead of butter or margarine. However, you *must* ask questions. Local cooking tradition may dictate that the chicken or fish be soaked in milk before it's grilled or fried.

Fast-food places are poor choices for people with food allergies. The person who serves you may not know what is in the food. Generally speaking, the hamburgers are milk-free but the hamburger buns are made with milk.

Dark beer may cause problems for you. Some mixed drinks are made with cream, and so are some liqueurs.

Breads served in restaurants are usually milk-free, and rye bread is nearly always milk-free. Whole-grain breads are more apt to be milk-free than are white breads. Avoid muffins and other quick breads.

Pass up appetizer dips, and stick to nuts or pretzels. Many restaurants stir sour cream into their guacamole. Since many sheep's- or goats'-milk cheeses are made partly with cows' milk it is best to avoid them, but see the list on pages 17 to 18.

Clear soups are usually a good choice; of course you should avoid cream soups, chowders, and French onion soup with cheese floating on top. Although homemade bean soups are usually made without milk, restaurant bean soups often contain milk products.

A salad of mixed greens is probably safe for you to eat; any bits of cheese should be easy to see if you look closely. Beware of croutons since they may have been flavored with cheese or fried in butter. Ask to have the dressing served on the side so that you can take a small taste, or ask for a bottle of oil and one of vinegar to dress the salad yourself. Or omit the dressing entirely and sprinkle a little salt and pepper on the greens; undressed, lightly salted salad is surprisingly good.

Avoid fried foods that have been rolled in crumbs or dipped in batter. Avoid complex dishes such as stews, meatballs, pasta, and any other sauced dishes. Steak or roast beef or boiled ham served plain probably holds no milky surprises.

Sandwiches made on rye bread or French bread are usually a good choice. Avoid any sort of salad sandwiches and choose instead ham, pastrami, or other plain meat. Pasta salad often contains milk products. Potato salad is usually milk-free but may be unsafe at restaurants. Be wary of coleslaw.

Some items labeled nondairy, such as coffee whitener, contain milk products, so read labels carefully.

It is a good idea to skip dessert, unless plain fruit is available.

Airlines will supply a milk-free meal if you request it. Since this meal is apt to consist mostly of lettuce with a few carrot sticks, it is very dull indeed. Choose instead chopped steak (hamburger) or chicken and scrape off any coating or stuffing. Avoid fish.

It is nearly impossible to avoid milk products in college dining halls because they are likely to buy food preprocessed in large containers. The best solution might be for you to live someplace off campus where you can do your own cooking.

Cooking Without Milk

Substitutes for Milk
and Milk Products

Cooking is fun, and cooking around a milk allergy can be an interesting challenge. Here are suggestions for substitutions so that you can adapt recipes to make them milk-free.

Instead of milk, use water, fruit juice, wine, liqueur, soy milk, coconut milk (see page 17), canned or fresh tomatoes (in soups or stews), beef broth, chicken broth. In baked goods use water plus egg plus sugar, or milk-free infant formula.

Instead of cream, use fruit juice, wine, liqueur, a dessert sauce, a milk-free nondairy creamer. In baked goods or frostings try egg or milk-free margarine.

Instead of whipped cream, use softened tofu-based ice cream substitute, fruit cream (page 294), a milk-free nondairy whipped topping, a dessert sauce.

Instead of cream cheese or sour cream, use soft tofu beaten with a little lemon juice and mayonnaise, milk-free margarine, mayonnaise.

Instead of butter, use oil or milk-free margarine (see page 16). Do not use oil for baking except as specified.

Instead of ice cream, use tofu-based ice cream substitute (like Tofutti or Tofulicious), milk-free sherbet, fruit cream (page 294).

If you can't find a substitute for an ingredient, sometimes the opposite of what the recipe calls for can be used; for instance, chicken broth or wine instead of cream in beef strogonoff. Cream thickens and smooths a sauce; wine or broth will thin it and sharpen the flavor. I was happy to find my milk-free recipe for beef strogonoff an improvement over the traditional version using sour cream.

First the Bad News . . .
Foods to Avoid

You may not recognize some of these milk products, such as whey, or sodium caseinate, which are not sold as such at your local supermarket. They are contained in processed foods like bread, TV dinners, or chocolate chips. The only reliable way to find out whether a food contains them is to read the label on the package.

Butter
Butterfat
Buttermilk
Cheese, but see pages
   17 to 18.
Curds
Cream
Ghee
Ice cream
Ice milk
Milk
Milk fat

Milk solids
Nonfat dry milk
Simplesse, the new artificial
   fat substitute, is made of
   skim milk and egg whites.
   Watch for it as an ingre-
   dient in ice creams and
   other desserts.
Sour cream
Whey
Yogurt

Foods Usually Made with Milk or Milk Products

When buying food at a store, read all labels carefully; when eating at a restaurant or a party, ask questions.

Appetizers and dips
Au gratin foods
Batter-dipped fried foods
Beer, dark

Biscuits

Bread and rolls, except for the ones listed as not usually containing milk on page 15

Cakes

Candies

Casseroles

Cheesecake

Chicken, fried; sometimes this is soaked in milk before being cooked, and sometimes it's coated with milk-containing cracker crumbs or bread crumbs.

Chocolate (the hot beverage)

Chocolate, milk

Chocolate, semisweet or bittersweet; but sometimes not. Check the label each time you buy it; at least one manufacturer uses milk products at some seasons but not at others.

Chocolate, white; it is made from cocoa butter, sugar, and milk solids.

Chowder, except for Manhattan clam chowder, which is made with tomatoes instead of milk

Cocoa (beverage; hot cocoa). Powdered cocoa used in cooking is a chocolate from which most of the fat, cocoa butter, has been removed. It is safe for you to eat if it has not been mixed with milk products.

Coconut milk, sometimes (see page 17)

Cold cuts

Coleslaw

Cookies

Corn chips; many are flavored with cheese.

Crackers, some

Crêpes

Custard

Dips

Doughnuts

Eggnog

Fish, fried

Fritters

Gravy, especially gravy for fried chicken

Kosher food in which the heksher mark is either followed by
 a D or labeled "milchig"
Margarine, except for a few safe brands; some are listed on
 page 16.
Mashed potatoes
Mayonnaise; it is sometimes mixed with milk or cream.
Meatballs
Meatloaf
Muffins
Omelets
Pancakes
Pastries
Pies with a creamy filling, such as chocolate pie, lemon me-
 ringue pie, cream pies, pecan pie, pumpkin pie, squash pie,
 or sweet potato pie
Potato chips flavored with cheese or sour cream
Potato salad
Puddings
Salad dressings, especially creamy dressings
Sauces, creamy
Sausages, including frankfurters and lunch meat
Scalloped anything
Sherbet
Soufflés
Spaghetti sauce; it's often made with cheese.
Tortilla chips
Turkeys, self-basting (whether these turkeys contain milk
 products varies)
TV dinners and other convenience foods
Vegetables, cooked; they are often tossed with butter.
Waffles

*Highly Processed Milk Products That May
or May Not Be Safe*

These foods may be all right for you to eat; it depends on which
fraction of milk you are sensitive to and on how sensitive you are
to it. You will find them listed on the labels of such foods as breads,

cold cuts, and salad dressings. They are used as fillers, to improve flavor or texture, or to prolong the shelf life of foods. The only way to find out whether one or these compounds bothers you is to carefully eat a little of a food product that contains it.

Calcium or any other sort of lactate
Casein
Lactalbumen
Lactic acid
Lactoglobulin
Lactose
Sodium or any other sort of caseinate

And, two really sneaky items:

Pills sometimes have a milk-product filler. Ask your druggist or your doctor.

Monosodium glutamate (MSG), an additive used by some Chinese restaurants to enhance flavor, often has a lactose filler.

Now the Good News . . . Foods You Can Eat

Milk-Free Foods

The following foods are usually milk-free. If in doubt, always check.

Angel food cake
Bagels
Breads: French, Italian, pumpernickel, rye
Candies, hard
Carrot cake, unfrosted
Crackers, plain
Fish, broiled or plain baked
Ketchup
Kosher (or kashruth) foods labeled "fleishig" or "pareve"
    (parva, parve). Because observant Jews believe that milk

and meat must not be eaten at the same meal, kosher meat products are milk-free. Pareve foods like fish, fruits, and vegetables are neither meat nor dairy. You can identify kosher products by looking for a kosher symbol (heksher mark) on the label. One of the most commonly seen is the U inside a circle, the mark used by the Union of Orthodox Congregations of America. If the heksher mark is followed by a D, this means that the food is considered a dairy product. If the mark is followed by a P, this means that it is kosher for Passover, and does not mean that the food is pareve.

Margarine, a few brands. Most margarines are made with milk, and since manufacturers do change their formulas from time to time you should always read the label. I have found the following widely distributed brands to be reliably milk-free: Fleischmann's Sweet Unsalted stick margarine, Mazola Sweet Unsalted stick margarine, Shedd's Spread Country Crock tub margarine (but *not* their stick margarine), Weight Watcher's Reduced Calorie Margarine, either tub or stick form. Kosher, pareve margarines are also free of milk products.

Mayonnaise when not mixed with milk or cream

Meat, broiled or roasted

Mustard

Nondairy creamer, but check the label

Nondairy whipped topping, but check the label

Pasta: noodles, spaghetti, and the like. However, pasta sauces are often made with butter, cream, or cheese.

Pies, plain fruit, unless the crust was made with butter or nonmilk-free margarine, or cream or butter was added to the fruit.

Poultry, broiled or roasted, unless it's a self-basting bird (see page 100)

Pretzels

Shortenings based on vegetable oil, such as Crisco or Spry

Sorbet, plain fruit; but read the label

Tofu

Tofu-based ice cream substitutes such as Tofutti, Rice

Dream, and others. Look for these at health-food stores or displayed beside regular ice cream at supermarkets.

Be careful of anything labeled nondairy. It's surprising how many of these foods are made with milk products.

Manufacturers will sometimes change the ingredients of their products—perhaps adding milk where they didn't before—so, check labels regularly, even on foods you buy often.

Cereals, dried beans, grains, fruit, and vegetables are all safe unless cooked with milk products.

Non-Milk Products That Sound Like Milk Products

Cocoa butter

Coconut cream. This is sold in cans, and is meant to be mixed with alcoholic beverages. It is a mixture of coconut meat with various additives, which are usually nondairy, but read the fine print on the label to be sure.

Coconut milk. This is the liquid found in the center of a fresh coconut and is a plant product; however, you *must* be careful of it, because many cooks soak coconut meat in cows' milk and call the result coconut milk. Your local supermarket may not carry coconut milk but you should be able to buy the real, noncow product in cans at a specialty food store or at an oriental grocery store.

Cream of wheat

Cream-style canned corn

Head cheese

Peanut butter

Soy milk

Cheeses Made from Sheep's or Goats' Milk

If your problem is an allergy to cows' milk, not lactose intolerance, you may be able to use milk from other animals such as sheep or goats. This is because your allergy may be to milk from cows and the milk from sheep or goats may be different enough not to bother you. Buffalo and water buffalo are so closely related to cows that you will probably react to cheese made from their milk as you would to cheese made from cows' milk. The following cheeses are usually made from sheep's or goats' milk; however, many people in this country dislike the sharp taste of goats' milk, so these cheeses when domestically produced are often adulterated with cows' milk. A cheese made from sheep's milk in one country may be made from cows' milk in another.

Some new soy-based cheeses are milk-free. Many of them have a lot of casein, and some people are sensitive to this.

Buy cheese only from a good health-food store or from a specialty cheese shop. Ask questions of someone, a clerk or the manager, who is really sure of the composition of the store's various cheeses. Never buy these cheeses from an ordinary supermarket.

I would like to take this opportunity to once again thank Alan White-Rogers, who is the source of most of my information about cheese.

Brebis
Bucheron
Buchette
Caprella
Capricorne
Caprine
Chèvre
Chevrette
Chevrotin
Ekte gjetost, but not plain, or any other gjetost
Etorki
Feta, imported from Bulgaria, Greece, or Romania. U.S. feta uses cows' milk.
Kashkaval
Kasseri, Greek; domestic kasseri is made from cows' milk.
Lingot
Montrachet
Ricotta salata
Ricotta sheep's milk
Romano
Roquefort
Sheep Pyrenee

Romano cheese can substitute for Parmesan cheese. Kasseri is very good for cooking, and can be used in place of provolone or of Swiss cheese.

Bibliography

If you're interested in more information about food allergy or lactose intolerance, you might be interested in reading the following:

Carper, Steve. *No Milk Today: How to Live with Lactose Intolerance.* New York: Simon & Schuster, Inc., 1986.

Frazier, Claude A., M.D. *Coping with Food Allergy,* rev. ed. New York: Times Books, 1985.

Hunter, John, M.D., Jones, Virginia Alun, M.D., and Workman, Elizabeth, R.D. *Food Intolerance.* Tucson, AZ: HPBooks, Inc., 1986.

Zukin, Jane. *Milk-free Diet Cookbook.* New York: Sterling Publishing Co., Inc., 1982; *Dairy-free Cookbook.* New York: St. Martin's Press (Prima Publications), 1989.

Appetizers

Tofu Base for Dips
  Jalapeño Dip
Tapenade
Hummus
Eggplant Dip
Guacamole
Chopped Liver
Deviled Eggs
  Eggs Stuffed with Crab
Cocktail Sauce
Spiced Nuts
Toasted Pumpkin Seeds

Tofu Base for Dips

This is good by itself, but is most useful as a base for other dips like clam dip, bacon-horseradish dip, or the following jalapeño dip. Use it in place of the sour cream, cream cheese, and cottage cheese called for in most dip recipes. It's very creamy and tastes like milk products; do try it!

> ¾ pound soft tofu
> 2 tablespoons mayonnaise
> 2 teaspoons lemon juice or vinegar

Drain the tofu, rinse it briefly with water, and drain thoroughly in a sieve or colander for 5 minutes. Beat all of the ingredients for a few minutes in a food processor or blender, until smooth. Vary the amount of mayonnaise and lemon juice or vinegar to please yourself.

Stir in minced clams, or onion and herbs, or anything else you might like to add to the dip

MAKES ABOUT 2 CUPS.

Jalapeño Dip

> 1 recipe Tofu Base for Dips
> 1 clove garlic
> ¼ teaspoon salt
> About 2 teaspoons green jalapeño sauce

Put everything except the jalapeño sauce into a food processor or blender, and process until quite smooth. Add the jalapeño sauce and process for a few seconds longer, just enough to mix the peppers into the dip.

MAKES ABOUT 2 CUPS OF DIP.

Tapenade

Sometimes called poor man's caviar, this is a lovely vegetable dip or cracker spread. Since it's strong-flavored, make it thin so that only a little clings to the vegetable dipped into it.

2-ounce can rolled
  anchovy fillets with
  capers
9 dry-cured ripe olives,
  pitted

One 4-ounce can pitted
  ripe olives
2 cloves garlic, peeled
3/4 cup olive oil
1 teaspoon lemon juice

Drain the anchovies and the olives. Put half the olives and all the other ingredients into a blender or food processor and run the machine until you have a smooth, thin paste. Add more garlic to taste. If the tapenade is too thick, add a little more olive oil. If it is too thin, add more olives. To see whether the dip is the right strength and consistency, try some on a vegetable stick or cracker.

Dry-cured olives vary a lot in their potency, and people vary a lot in how strongly flavored they like their dips; you can add more olives at this point if desired. Pitted olives will make the dip milder.

MAKES ABOUT 1 1/4 CUPS OF DIP.

Hummus

A classic dish from the Arab countries. Serve this at room temperature, with plain crackers or pieces of toasted pita bread.

1/2 pound (1 cup) dried
  chick-peas or two 1-
  pound cans chick-peas
Juice of 1 lemon (2
  tablespoons)
1 or 2 cloves garlic,
  peeled

1/2 cup sesame oil or
  olive oil
2 tablespoons water
1/2 teaspoon salt
1/8 teaspoon pepper

Cook the chick-peas: Soak them overnight in about 4 cups of water; drain them, and cook in fresh water for about 3 hours, or until tender. Drain; you should have about 3 cups.

If you use canned chick-peas, drain and rinse the peas well. Use only a little salt, or none at all, and mix in 3 or 4 tablespoons of water.

Put the chick-peas, lemon juice, garlic, ¼ cup of the oil, water, salt, and pepper into the bowl of a food processor and process until smooth, using the steel blade. Add more oil and water as needed to make a fine smooth paste; add more salt and pepper if needed. If making this in a blender, you will need to do it in several batches.

MAKES ABOUT 4 CUPS OF HUMMUS.

Eggplant Dip

Another good dish from the Middle East. This version uses baked eggplant, so it has a lot less oil than one made with fried eggplant. Serve with crackers or toasted pita bread.

> 2 medium-sized eggplants, about 1 pound
> each

Scrub the eggplants, prick them all over with a fork, set them in a baking pan, and bake at 350° for 1 hour, or until the eggplants are quite soft.

Remove the eggplants from the oven and allow them to cool a bit. Scoop out the pulp, and discard the skin. Measure the pulp; the two eggplants should yield about 1 cup total.

For each cup of eggplant, you will need:

1 small clove garlic, peeled	1 tablespoon lemon juice
2 teaspoons grated onion	¼ teaspoon salt
¼ cup olive oil	Dash of black pepper

Whirl all the ingredients together in a blender or food processor until smooth; add more seasoning if needed. Let set an hour or so to blend the flavors. Refrigerate the dip if not using immediately. Serve at room temperature.

MAKES ABOUT 1 CUP.

Guacamole

The real California kind. Usually served as a dip with nachos, this is also good spread thickly on cooked hamburgers.

1 ripe avocado
1 teaspoon lemon juice
1 teaspoon grated onion
1/8 teaspoon chili powder
1/4 teaspoon salt
1 teaspoon olive oil, if needed
1/2 tomato

Peel the avocado and remove the pit; mash the flesh with a fork. It should not be smooth. Add the lemon juice, onion, chili powder, and salt and mix well. Add oil if the guacamole seems dry. Slice the tomato, and cut the slices into little squares; this can be difficult with a nice ripe, juicy tomato, but do the best you can. Stir in the chopped tomato, or arrange it around the edges of the guacamole.

MAKES ABOUT 2/3 CUP.

Chopped Liver

Another classic, similar to a pâté. This is liver for people who think they don't like liver.

1 tablespoon margarine or rendered chicken fat	1 hard-boiled egg
	1/2 teaspoon Worcestershire sauce
1 small onion, peeled and chopped	Salt and pepper
1/3 pound fresh chicken livers	6 thin slices of bread, toasted

Melt the margarine or chicken fat in a small frying pan and sauté the onion until it is limp and starting to turn golden. Remove the onion from the pan and sauté the livers until cooked through. Let them cool a little. Cut any tough bits off the liver.

At this point, you can prepare the dish in either of two ways; either put all ingredients except the bread into a blender or food processor and make a smooth paste, or chop the ingredients together to make a rather coarse mixture. A smooth paste is more traditional, but I prefer the coarsely chopped version.

To make a smooth paste, cut the liver and the egg into pieces. Put them into the blender or food processor and then add the onion, Worcestershire sauce, salt, and pepper. Process until the mixture forms a smooth paste. If it seems a little dry, add more margarine or chicken fat. Adjust the seasoning.

For the chopped version, cut the egg and the cooked liver into pieces about the size of raisins; mix in the onion and seasonings.

Cut the 6 pieces of toast diagonally to make 24 triangles, and spread them with the chopped liver. Serve immediately.

MAKES 24 SPREAD TOASTS.

Deviled Eggs

12 hard-boiled eggs
2 tablespoons
    mayonnaise
2 teaspoons grated onion
1 tablespoon lemon juice
    or vinegar
3/4 teaspoon
    Worcestershire sauce

1/8 teaspoon salt
Dash of pepper
Hot paprika (optional)
Powdered sage or dried
    dill leaf (optional)

Peel the eggs and cut them in half lengthwise. Put the yolks into a small bowl and mash them well with a fork. Add the mayonnaise, onion, lemon juice or vinegar, Worcestershire sauce, salt, and pepper; mix well, and pile the mixture into the egg whites, mounding it up attractively.

Sprinkle half the eggs with dill or sage, and the other half with paprika.

MAKES 24.

Eggs Stuffed with Crab

Follow the preceding recipe for deviled eggs, but omit the Worcestershire sauce and add:

1/2 pound cooked fresh crabmeat

Flake the crabmeat well with your fingers, picking out any bits of shell or membrane. Mix the crabmeat with half the seasoned yolks (set the rest of them aside for another use; crumble them over a green salad or cooked asparagus, for instance). Pile the mixture into the egg whites. Sprinkle each egg with a little paprika or dill, and chill until serving time.

MAKES 24.

Cocktail Sauce

Spicy. Serve it with chilled cooked seafood.

1/4 cup ketchup
1 tablespoon horseradish
1/2 teaspoon grated onion

1/4 teaspoon grated fresh
  ginger, or a pinch each
  of basil and thyme
Dash of black pepper

Stir all the ingredients together, adjust the seasoning to your taste, and serve.

MAKES 1/3 CUP OF SAUCE, ENOUGH FOR ABOUT 1/2 POUND OF SHRIMP.

Spiced Nuts

These are hard to resist.

2 teaspoons margarine
1 cup (6 ounces) almonds, pecans, or other nuts
1 teaspoon Worcestershire sauce
1/4 teaspoon salt
Dash of cayenne pepper

Preheat the oven to 325°. Melt the margarine in a glass pie plate or other baking dish in the oven.

Remove the baking dish from the oven and tip it so that the margarine coats the bottom, then add the rest of the ingredients. Stir briefly, and return the dish to the oven.

Bake for about 25 minutes, or until the nuts just begin to brown. Once or twice during the cooking period, remove the baking dish from the oven and stir the nuts.

Let the nuts cool in the pan, then store them in a covered jar. They're even better if left to mellow for a day or so.

1 CUP SPICED NUTS.

NOTE: In hot weather I prefer to season the nuts on top of the stove. Use a frying pan (not an iron one, which may flavor the nuts) and stir the nuts gently over medium heat just until they begin to brown.

Toasted Pumpkin Seeds

When you carve a jack-o'-lantern, save the seeds and toast them to use as a snack.

Remove the seeds from your pumpkin. Discard the membrane, and rinse the seeds in a big bowl of water. Spread only the plump seeds in a large pan lined with paper towels, and set the pan in a warm place to dry for a few days. The top of the hot water heater or a cupboard above the oven are both good places.

Preheat the oven to 325°. Remove the paper towel from the seeds. Sprinkle the seeds with salt and bake them for about half an hour, shaking the pan once or twice during baking so that the seeds will brown evenly. (You can add 2 or 3 tablespoons of margarine to the pan before toasting the pumpkin seeds, but it isn't necessary.)

Cool the seeds and store them in a covered jar.

Soups

Carrot Soup
Green Pea Soup
Eggplant Soup
Corn Soup
Onion Soup
Leek Soup
Clear Mushroom Soup
Chicken Vegetable Soup
Beet Soup
Beef Soup with Winter
   Vegetables
Lamb Soup with Barley and
   Mushrooms
Turkey Soup
Fish Chowder
Split Pea Soup
Lentil Soup
Black Bean Soup
   Vegetarian Black
   Bean Soup

About Making Soup . . .

Soups are easy to make if you know one or two tricks. Some soups are just a few vegetables cooked in broth, homemade or any good commercial brand.

The starting point of many soups is meat—usually with some bone—simmered slowly in plenty of water for several hours, until the broth is rich and the meat falls apart. If you have a particularly tough piece of meat, you can cut down on the cooking time by adding to the cooking water something acidic like tomatoes, wine (especially an acidic red wine), or vinegar. If you start with cooked meat, like the leftovers from a roasted chicken, you only need to simmer the meat and broth for half an hour to an hour. Let it cool to room temperature; remove and discard the bones, skin, and gristle. Separate the meat from the broth, then chill both. Defatting the chilled broth is easy: skim the hardened fat off the surface with a spoon and discard it. (Defatting hot broth is no simple task, and you never can get it all.) Refrigerate or freeze the broth until you need it.

When you are ready to finish the soup, return the broth to a soup pot, add the other ingredients, and finish cooking. This usually takes less than an hour, depending on the other ingredients.

If you are using dried beans (navy beans, kidney beans, and so on), rinse and soak them ahead of time and add them to the soup before any other vegetables as they take quite a long time to cook. Lentils and split peas don't need to be soaked.

Tomatoes, peas, summer squash, and most other fresh vegetables cook very quickly and can be added to the soup at the last minute.

Check your soup as it cooks, and add more water if it gets too thick. It is impossible to give the exact amount of liquid needed for soup; you just have to stir, and taste, and decide for yourself. How much water a soup or stew will lose during cooking depends on how tightly the lid fits and how high the heat is. If you find there is too much liquid, you can cook the soup over high heat with the lid off for a while to reduce it. To add flavor, stir in a bouillon cube. (Remember that bouillon cubes contain a lot of salt.)

The following soup recipes are ones that we like, but I hope you will try out your own combinations, too. Soup is an accommodating sort of dish, and can be very good indeed when made with whatever you have around the kitchen; a few peas, an extra tomato, a handful of rice . . . it's fun to experiment.

Carrot Soup

A cold soup, to be served before the main course. The hint of curry powder brings out the flavor of the carrots.

1 small onion, peeled
and chopped
1 tablespoon margarine
½ pound carrots,
skinned and cut into
thin rounds (about
1¾ cups)

1 small potato, peeled
and sliced thin
One 10-ounce can
condensed chicken
broth
⅛ teaspoon curry
powder

Sauté the onion in the margarine until it is limp and turns golden. Add the sliced carrots and potato, the chicken broth, and the curry powder; cover and simmer gently until the vegetables are tender, about 10 minutes.

Save some carrot slices for garnish, and purée the rest of the soup in a blender or food processor until smooth. Thin the soup with a little water if it's too thick.

Chill the soup. Decorate it with the reserved carrot slices before serving.

MAKES 2½ CUPS; SERVES 4.

Green Pea Soup

A first course soup; serve either hot or chilled.

1 tablespoon margarine
1 small onion, peeled
and sliced thin
1 small potato, peeled
and sliced thin
1½ cups water

One 10-ounce package
frozen green peas, or
2 cups shelled fresh
green peas
½ teaspoon sugar
½ teaspoon salt
Dash pepper

Sauté the onion in the margarine just until it begins to turn golden. Add the potato and the water, cover and simmer until the potato is tender; about 5 to 10 minutes. Add the remaining ingredients and cook until the peas are done, about 2 to 5 minutes after the soup has begun to boil again.

Purée the soup in a blender or food processor. Push the puréed soup through a sieve if necessary to remove any unwanted bits of skin.

MAKES ABOUT 2 CUPS; SERVES 4.

Eggplant Soup

A summer soup made with beef broth. Serve very cold.

1 clove garlic, peeled and
  minced
2 tablespoons olive oil
1 medium eggplant,
  about 1½ pounds,
  skinned and cut into
  1-inch cubes
2 stalks celery, scrubbed
  and cut into thin
  crosswise slices
1 or 2 green peppers,
  scrubbed and cut up
2 tomatoes, scrubbed
  and chopped
One 10-ounce can
  condensed beef broth

Sauté the garlic in the olive oil just until it begins to brown. Add the rest of the ingredients, bring the soup to a boil, cover and simmer gently until vegetables are tender, about 15 minutes. Season with salt and pepper if you like. Chill before serving.

MAKES ABOUT 4 CUPS OF SOUP; SERVES 6 TO 8.

Corn Soup

A milk-free version of corn chowder. Serve hot.

One 10-ounce can condensed chicken broth
One 1-pound can salt-free cream-style corn
1 small potato, peeled and sliced thin
Dash of pepper

Combine all the ingredients in a saucepan, cover and simmer until the potatoes are tender, about 10 minutes. You will probably not need to add salt, as there is plenty in the chicken broth.

MAKES ABOUT 3½ CUPS; SERVES 2 AS A MAIN COURSE, 4 AS A FIRST COURSE.

Onion Soup

2 tablespoons margarine
   or olive oil
1 large onion
1 clove garlic
One 10-ounce can
   condensed beef broth
   diluted with 1 can
   water, or 2½ cups
   beef stock

1½ tablespoons dry
   sherry (optional)
2 teaspoons grated
   Romano cheese
   (optional)

Heat the margarine or olive oil in a heavy saucepan. Peel the onion and cut it once crosswise, then slice it thinly into the pan. Peel and mince the garlic and add it also. Over medium heat, sauté the onion until it is limp and slightly browned. Add the beef broth and water. Cover and simmer for 5 minutes.

Add sherry if you wish just before serving. Pass grated cheese at the table.

SERVES 2 OR 3 AS THE MAIN COURSE OF A LIGHT LUNCH, OR 4 TO 6 AS A FIRST COURSE.

Leek Soup

3 medium-sized leeks
1 tablespoon margarine
6 cups chicken broth
1 small potato, peeled
   and cut into ½-inch
   dice

½ cup sliced mushrooms
Salt to taste, and plenty
   of pepper

Remove the outermost leaf from each leek, cut off the root end, and slice the leek lengthwise. Fan each leek out in your hand and rinse it well under the tap, to get rid of sand.

Slice the leeks up into thick rounds, including plenty of the green part. Sauté them in the margarine in a saucepan until they're limp, then add the chicken broth, potato, and mushrooms. Cover and simmer until the potato is tender, season to taste, and serve.

SERVES 6 AS THE MAIN COURSE OF A LIGHT MEAL, OR 12 AS A FIRST COURSE.

Clear Mushroom Soup

A light beginning to a meal.

>   One 10-ounce can condensed beef bouillon diluted
>   with 1 can water, or 2½ cups beef stock
>   2 cups raw mushroom slices
>   1 tablespoon tomato purée or tomato paste
>   2 tablespoons sherry

Pour the beef bouillon and water (or the beef stock) into a saucepan. Add the mushrooms and the tomato purée or tomato paste. Cover and simmer until the mushrooms are cooked, about 5 minutes. Stir in the sherry, and serve hot.

SERVES 6 AS A FIRST COURSE.

Chicken Vegetable Soup

Good as a vegetable soup or enriched with cooked chicken meat. Serve hot.

1 small onion, peeled
1 large stalk celery with
  leaves, washed
1 tablespoon margarine
1 quart unseasoned
  chicken broth
1 carrot, peeled and
  sliced thin
One 10-ounce package
  frozen corn

½ cup cooked chicken
  meat (optional)
4 mushrooms, wiped
  clean and sliced
¼ teaspoon grated
  lemon rind (optional)
1 chicken bouillon cube
  (optional)
Salt and pepper

Slice the onion and the celery very thin, and sauté lightly in the margarine; do not let them brown. Add the chicken stock and carrot, cover and simmer for about 10 minutes, until the carrot slices are cooked. Add the corn, chicken, and mushrooms, and simmer for a few minutes. Season to taste with the lemon rind, the bouillon cube or salt, and pepper.

MAKES ABOUT 2 QUARTS SOUP; SERVES 4 AS THE MAIN COURSE OF A LIGHT MEAL, OR 8 AS A FIRST COURSE.

Beet Soup

Serve pumpernickel bread with this Russian-style soup. It's hearty and makes a good meal for cold weather.

2 pounds meaty beef bones	1 stalk celery, washed and cut up
1 medium onion, peeled and chopped	2 tomatoes, washed and cup up, or 8 ounces canned Italian plum
1 bay leaf	tomatoes with juice
3 or 4 carrots, peeled and cut into thick rounds	1 pound beets, fresh or canned
2 or 3 medium potatoes, peeled and cut into 1/2-in cubes	1/2 pound cabbage, coarsely chopped
	Salt and pepper

Cover the bones with about 2 quarts of water and boil gently for 2 or 3 hours, until the meat is very tender. Let cool for several hours, skim off the fat, and remove the bones.

About an hour before you plan to eat, add the onion, bay leaf, carrots, potatoes, celery, and tomatoes. If you are using fresh beets, peel them, cut them into cubes about 1/2 inch on a side, and add to the soup. Cover the soup and boil gently for about 30 minutes, or until the vegetables are cooked. Add the cabbage about ten minutes before the soup is done. If using canned beets, add with the cabbage. Season to taste with salt and pepper.

SERVES 6.

Beef Soup with Winter Vegetables

After you serve roast beef, slice off the remaining meat and refrigerate it for later use. Cook up the beef bones right away for this good soup. You can also make this with lamb.

Bones from a rib roast of beef
3 onions, peeled and chopped
1 bunch parsley, leaves only, or 1 tablespoon dried parsley
3 carrots, peeled and cut into thick rounds
1 small turnip, peeled and cut into ½-inch cubes
¼ cup uncooked rice
¼ cup uncooked lentils
1 stalk celery, scrubbed and cut up
2 tomatoes, washed and chopped, or ½ pound canned Italian plum tomatoes with juice
Salt and pepper

Cover the bones with 2 to 3 quarts water and simmer for about 1 hour. Let cool, and skim off the fat. Remove the bones and gristle; leave the meat in the broth.

About an hour before you wish to serve the soup, add the onions and parsley to the soup stock, cover, and simmer for about 10 minutes. Add the carrots, turnip, rice, and lentils; cook for 20 minutes. Add the celery and tomatoes and simmer for about 10 minutes more or until the lentils and rice are cooked. Add more water as necessary during the cooking. Season with salt and pepper, and serve. Add just a little more pepper than you might think necessary.

SERVES 4 TO 6.

Lamb Soup with Barley and Mushrooms

Serve this with muffins (page 261), a green salad, and apple pie (page 312).

1 or 2 pounds meaty
lamb bones, or the last
of a roast
1 bay leaf
1 pound tomatoes, fresh
or canned with juice
¼ cup barley

Beef bouillon cube
(optional)
10 medium-small
mushrooms, sliced,
about 1 cup
Salt and pepper

Cover the lamb with 1½ quarts water, add the bay leaf, and cover and simmer slowly for about 2 hours. Cool, skim off the fat, and remove the bones and the bay leaf. Add the tomatoes, barley and crumbled bouillon cube if desired, and cook for about 30 minutes, or until the barley is nearly done. Add the mushrooms and simmer for another 10 minutes or so, until the barley is cooked. Season to taste with salt and pepper, and serve.

SERVES 4.

Turkey Soup

A turkey carcass
Chicken bouillon cubes
(optional)
½ cup brown rice
1 carrot, peeled and cut
into rounds
2 stalks celery with
leaves, washed and
cut up

5 or 6 mushrooms,
cleaned and sliced
1 pound tomatoes, cut
up; fresh or canned
with juice
Shredded cabbage, about
1 cup
Salt and pepper

Simmer the turkey carcass in water (about 3 quarts for a medium-sized turkey) for an hour or so, until the meat falls off the bones. Cool a little, then remove the bones and skin; return the meat to the broth, and chill. Skim off the fat.

Make soup with about 6 cups of broth and meat; if you don't have this much, add water and a chicken bouillon cube or cubes to make up the difference. Bring the stock to a simmer and cover. Add the rice and simmer for 10 minutes. Add the carrot, celery, mushrooms, tomatoes, cabbage, salt, and pepper, and continue simmering for about 10 minutes more, until everything is cooked. Season to taste, and serve.

SERVES 6.

Fish Chowder

Fish chowder is more characteristic than clam chowder of certain parts of northern New England, including the area near Bangor, Maine, where my grandmother grew up. This is an adaptation of her recipe; she used milk, which is always an ingredient of New England chowders, but she didn't use bacon. To make a richer broth, do as she did and cook the fish in water in which you have poached a fresh fish head.

Serve the soup with old-fashioned accompaniments: a green salad, and plain crackers or freshly baked hot biscuits (page 271).

½ pound fillet of haddock or cod	2 slices bacon
2 cups water	1 small onion, peeled and sliced
1 medium potato, peeled and sliced	Salt and pepper
	1½ teaspoons margarine

Simmer the fish in the water just until it flakes easily, about 5 minutes. Remove the fish with a slotted spoon, and set it aside. Add the sliced potato to the water in which the fish cooked, cover and simmer just until the potato is cooked, about 8 minutes.

Meanwhile, cook the bacon in a small frying pan. When it's quite brown, set it aside. Gently cook the sliced onion in the bacon fat until lightly browned. Remove the pan from the heat, and crumble the bacon over the onion.

When the potatoes are tender, add the fish and the onions to them; season to taste with salt and pepper, add the margarine, and let set in a warm place for 15 minutes or so to "flavor," as the old-time cooks said.

SERVES 2.

Split Pea Soup

Served hot with corn bread (page 247) and a salad, this soup is a good cold-weather meal.

1 ham bone	1 stalk celery, washed
1 pound green split peas	and sliced (optional)
1 carrot, peeled and	Pepper to taste
sliced in rounds	Salt if needed
(optional)	

Remove all of the fat from the ham bone, and simmer bone in 3 quarts water for 2 or 3 hours to make a good stock. Chill overnight, and in the morning skim off the fat.

Rinse and pick over peas; add them to the stock, and cook for an hour or more until the peas are soft and the soup is thick. If you are using carrot or celery, add them when you first start to cook the peas. Add water if necessary to thin the soup.

Before serving, fish out the bones and break the meat up into small pieces. Add pepper. You will probably not need to add salt; usually the ham bone will give the soup plenty of salt.

This soup freezes beautifully.

SERVES 6 TO 8.

Lentil Soup

As bean soups go, this one is very quick-cooking; it needs to simmer for only 45 minutes. Good with popovers (page 269), coleslaw (page 194), and fruit.

1 pound lentils
One 10½-ounce can
  condensed beef broth
1 carrot, peeled and
  sliced
1 stalk celery with
  leaves, washed and
  sliced thin
3 slices uncooked bacon,
  cut in squares

1 teaspoon dried winter
  savory
½ teaspoon dried parsley
10 thin slices pepperoni,
  or 3 thin slices kosher
  salami
Salt and pepper
Horseradish
Lemon juice

Pick over the lentils, wash, and drain them. Add 6 cups water, the carrot, celery, bacon, savory, parsley, and pepperoni or salami. Bring to a boil, cover, and simmer for about 45 minutes or until the lentils are tender but not mushy.

If you wish, purée half of the cooked soup in a blender or food processor or by forcing the soup through a strong sieve, and then add it back to the pot before serving. Season to taste with salt and pepper.

Pass horseradish and lemon juice at the table.

SERVES 6.

Black Bean Soup

No need to precook the meat for this traditional New England soup.

1 pound black beans	1 tablespoon dried
1 pound stewing beef,	parsley
cut up	1½ teaspoons salt
3 slices bacon, cut into	¼ teaspoon black pepper
1-inch squares	Lemon slices or lemon
1 medium onion, peeled	juice (optional)
and chopped	
2 stalks celery, scrubbed	
and chopped	

Pick over the beans and rinse them in several changes of water. Soak them overnight in enough water to cover by about 2 inches. Drain the beans and put them in a large pot with 2 quarts water, the beef, bacon, onion, celery, and parsley. Bring the soup to a boil and simmer, covered, for 3 or 4 hours, or until the beans are cooked. After it has been cooking for a few minutes, skim the soup with a slotted spoon to remove scum. When the soup is cooked, purée all or part of it in a blender or food processor before serving. Season to taste with salt and pepper and place a slice of fresh lemon in each bowl before ladling in the soup, or pass a small pitcher of lemon juice at the table. Serve hot.

SERVES 6 TO 8.

Vegetarian Black Bean Soup

Omit the beef and the bacon, and reduce the water to 1½ quarts (6 cups). The cooking time can be reduced to about 1 hour.

SERVES 4.

Fish and Shellfish

Sautéed Fish
Baked Fish
Fish Cakes
Salmon Cakes
Tunafish Casserole
Seafood Stew
Sautéed Scallops
Steamed Clams
Boiled Lobster
Spicy Baked Shrimp
Scalloped Oysters

To cook fish, allow about 10 minutes' cooking time for each 1 inch of thickness; double this for frozen fish. This rule of thumb applies to baking, broiling, and steaming fish. You can easily test for doneness by poking the fish with a fork; if the meat has lost its transparent quality, it is cooked.

Sautéed Fish

The best and easiest way to cook a piece of good fresh fish.

Fresh fish, either whole or filleted, about 6 to 8
    ounces per person
Cornmeal seasoned with salt and pepper (optional)
Vegetable oil, margarine, or bacon fat to grease a
    skillet

Put the seasoned cornmeal on a plate and dip the fish in it to coat both sides. Melt some fat in a medium-hot skillet and cook until the fish just flakes easily when tested with a fork or the point of a knife. This will take about 8 to 10 minutes for the usual 3/4-inch-thick fillet, a little longer for a thicker fillet.

Serve immediately. Pass salt, pepper, and tartar sauce or lemon juice at the table.

Baked Fish

Fish fillets about 1 inch thick, 6 to 8 ounces per
    person
Bacon, 4 strips per pound of fish

Preheat the oven to 375° and grease a shallow ovenproof dish.

Cook the bacon until lightly browned but not crisp. Wrap the bacon around the fish, and lay it in the prepared dish.

Bake until just before the fish flakes easily, about 15 to 20 minutes. Serve immediately with salt, pepper, and lemon juice or tartar sauce.

Fish Cakes

This old-fashioned New England dish deserves a revival. It's delicious and easy to prepare, and is a good use for leftover cooked fish. The amounts given in this recipe don't need to be followed to the letter; they are only guidelines. Fish cakes used to be fried in deep fat, so this is a modern version.

1 cup mashed potatoes	2 teaspoons grated onion
1 egg	¼ teaspoon salt
3½ tablespoons vegetable oil or melted margarine	Dash pepper
	1 cup flaked cooked fish

Mix the potatoes, egg, 1½ tablespoons of the oil or margarine, onion, salt, and pepper. Stir in the fish.

Heat 1 tablespoon of fat in a heavy skillet, and drop large spoonfuls of the fish mixture onto it. Flatten the fish cakes a little. Cook until lightly browned and a crust has formed, about 5 minutes, then turn and cook the other side. Add oil or margarine as needed to keep the fish cakes from sticking to the pan. Serve hot, with pickles or ketchup.

SERVES 3.

Salmon Cakes

A good, quick main dish from your pantry shelf. Serve hot with pickle relish, mushroom sauce (pages 110–11), or horseradish sauce, and accompany with boiled potatoes.

¼ cup dry bread crumbs
1 egg
2 teaspoons grated onion
¼ teaspoon dried dill
Pinch of salt

Dash of cayenne pepper
One 8-ounce can salmon
1 tablespoon oil or
  margarine

Mix crumbs, egg, onion, dill, salt, and cayenne in a bowl. Drain the salmon, remove the bones and skin, and flake the meat into small pieces. Mix it into the bread crumb mixture.

Heat the oil or margarine in a frying pan. Form the fish mixture into 4 cakes, each about ½ inch thick. Sauté the cakes over moderate heat, turning once so that both sides are browned, for about 5 minutes.

SERVES 2.

Tunafish Casserole

Here is my version of a good old American standby and favorite of children. It is usually prepared with canned mushroom soup, which, of course, contains milk. Some people like green peas mixed with the tunafish, but I prefer to serve them on the side.

12 ounces uncooked egg
  noodles or pasta such
  as bowties or
  fettuccine
3 tablespoons margarine
5 large mushrooms,
  wiped clean and sliced,
  or one 4-ounce can
  mushrooms, drained

3 tablespoons flour
One 10-ounce can (1¼
  cups) double-strength
  chicken broth
One 7-ounce can good-
  quality tuna, drained
1 handful saltines or
  potato chips, crumbled

Cook the pasta or egg noodles in about 4 quarts of rapidly boiling salted water until just done.

Preheat the oven to 350° and grease a 2-quart baking dish.

Meanwhile, prepare the mushroom sauce: Melt the margarine

in a small frying pan. If you are using fresh mushrooms, sauté them in the margarine until just cooked. Remove the pan from the heat and stir in the flour; make sure all of the flour is moistened by the margarine. Stir in the broth, continuing to stir until it is well mixed and there are no lumps.

Return the pan to the heat and cook, stirring, until the mixture has boiled gently for 2 minutes. Stir in the tuna, breaking it up as you do so. If you are using canned mushrooms, stir them in now.

Drain the noodles or pasta and mix them into the sauce.

Pour the mixture into the baking dish and top with the crumbled crackers or potato chips.

Bake until heated through and bubbly around the edges, about 30 minutes.

SERVES 4.

Seafood Stew

This Mediterranean-style stew is good served with French bread, a green salad, and wine. It is even better the second day. If you increase the recipe, crab or lobster is a nice addition to the stew.

1 onion, peeled and chopped	¼ pound raw shrimp, in the shell
1 clove garlic, peeled and minced	½ pound haddock fillets
2 tablespoons olive oil	¼ pound scallops
½ green pepper, washed, cored, seeded, and chopped	½ pint raw, shucked clams
1½ cups water	1 large tomato, washed and chopped
1 pinch dried thyme	¼ cup white wine
1 bay leaf	Dash of cayenne pepper
	Salt and pepper

Sauté the onion and garlic in the olive oil until they're golden. Add the green pepper to the pan and sauté briefly until the pepper turns bright green. Set the vegetables aside.

Combine the water, thyme, and bay leaf in a saucepan. Simmer the shrimp in this water just until done, no more than 5 minutes. Remove them from the liquid and set aside to cool. Cook the haddock in the same water just until it flakes easily with a fork; set aside. In the same broth cook the scallops about 2 minutes until they turn opaque; remove immediately. Now cook the clams for about 5 minutes and remove them. Cook the tomato last and leave it in the broth. You can refrigerate the cooked fish and the broth at this point.

When you're about ready to serve dinner, shell the shrimp. Put all of the cooked vegetables and seafood into the broth, add the wine, and bring to a gentle boil just long enough to heat the stew thoroughly. Remove the bay leaf, season to taste with salt and pepper, and serve.

SERVES 3.

Sautéed Scallops

If cooking more than one pound of scallops, either do it in batches or use two skillets. If you use large sea scallops, cut them in halves or quarters before sautéeing.

1½ tablespoons margarine or olive oil
1 clove garlic, peeled and minced
¾ pound scallops
2 tablespoons dry white wine or water
Salt and pepper

Melt the margarine in a heavy skillet. Add the garlic and sauté it lightly; add the scallops and sauté over medium heat just until the centers have lost their pink color, and the scallops are white all the way through. Scallops vary greatly in size, so some batches will take longer to cook than others. It takes about 10 minutes to cook medium-sized sea scallops, much less time for tiny bay scallops.

Add the white wine or water to the pan and simmer briefly. Season lightly with salt and pepper. Serve immediately.

SERVES 2.

Steamed Clams

Steamed clams make a lovely informal meal or appetizer.

>2 quarts clams, in their shells
>⅓ cup margarine, melted (optional)
>Minced garlic (optional)
>½ cup clam liquor

Scrub fresh clams and put them into a pot with an inch or so of water in the bottom. Cover the pot and simmer gently for a few minutes, until the clams open up. I've been known to hang over the pot, removing the clams as they open; overcooking can toughen a clam. Discard any clams that don't open.

Drain the clams and serve them in their shells. To serve as a main course, heap all the cooked clams on a large platter in the center of the table; give each person a plate and two small bowls for dipping, one of melted margarine seasoned with garlic if desired, and one of clam liquor.

SERVES 2 AS A MAIN COURSE; ALLOW ABOUT 6 CLAMS PER PERSON AS AN APPETIZER.

Boiled Lobster

The lobster meat is mostly in the tail and claws; there is also a little in the legs. The meat will be easier to get at if you make a cut the length of the tail through the underside of the shell before serving the lobster. Nutcrackers are used for cracking open the claws.

>1 lobster, about 1½ pounds, per person
>Seawater or salted water
>Margarine
>Lemon juice (optional)

Raw lobsters are dull green in color; they turn bright red only when cooked. Since lobster, like other shellfish, spoils quickly once it dies, make sure your lobster is still alive before you start to cook it.

Look over your cooking pots; you need one large enough to contain the lobsters. You may have to cook only one or two lobsters at a time. Half fill the pot with seawater or salted water and bring to a boil. (An alternative method is to steam the lobsters in two inches of water.) Plunge the lobsters, head first, into the boiling water. It is smart to do this with the lobster in one hand and the lid for your cooking pot in the other, so that you can cover the pot immediately. When the water returns to the boil, cook for 15 to 20 minutes.

Serve immediately with melted margarine seasoned with lemon juice.

Spicy Baked Shrimp

A good company dish.

2 cloves garlic, peeled
 and minced
¼ cup margarine
1 cup fine dry bread
 crumbs
½ teaspoon dried thyme
½ teaspoon freshly
 grated orange peel

Pinch cayenne pepper
Dash salt
2 pounds shelled raw
 shrimp
3 tablespoons white
 wine

Preheat the oven to 350° and grease a shallow casserole.

Sauté the garlic in the margarine until it turns pale gold. Remove the cooking pan from the heat. Add the bread crumbs and seasonings, and mix thoroughly.

Spread the shrimp in the prepared casserole and sprinkle with the crumb mixture and then with the wine. Bake for about 15 minutes.

SERVES 6.

Scalloped Oysters

Usually prepared with milk, this dish is good made with water.

1/8 pound saltine crackers
1 pint fresh oysters in their own
    liquor
Salt and pepper
1 tablespoon margarine
1/4 cup water

Preheat the oven to 375° and grease a 1½-quart casserole. Crush the crackers; you should have enough to measure about 1¼ cups. Strew some of the cracker crumbs in the bottom of the casserole, and spoon half of the oysters over the crumbs, reserving the oyster liquor. Top with half of the remaining crumbs, and sprinkle with salt and pepper. Repeat the layers with the rest of the oysters and the rest of the crumbs; sprinkle with a little more salt and pepper.

Put small chunks of margarine over the top layer of crumbs and pour the oyster liquor and just enough water to moisten the cracker crumbs over the top of the casserole. Bake uncovered for about 45 minutes.

SERVES 2.

Meat

Roast Beef
Steak with Wine Sauce
Shish Kabob
Beef Stroganoff
Pot Roast
Beef Stew with Red Wine
Beef Stew with Onions
Beef Stew with Paprika
Sauerbraten
Sherried Beef Stew
Ragbag Stew (Ropa Vieja)
Meat Pasty
Meat Loaf
Meatballs
Filled Hamburgers
Sloppy Joes

Baked Ham
Roast Pork
  Roast Pork with Prunes
  Leftover Roast Pork

Spicy Pork Chops
Pork Stew with Apple
    Cider
Polish Stew
Pork Chops and Sauerkraut
Quick Pork Stew
Stir-fry Dinner

Roast Lamb
Herbed Lamb Chops
Marinated Lamb Chops
Satay

Meat

Meat for stew should be browned quickly in batches of three-quarters of a pound or less. If you crowd the meat when browning, it will steam.

When you have a tough piece of meat to cook, tenderize it by long, slow cooking with moist heat, as in a stew. Adding an acidic substance like vinegar, wine, lemon juice, or tomatoes will help tenderize the meat.

Hamburger or other ground meat like fresh sausage should be cooked and served within one day of purchase. Work gently when you prepare hamburgers or meatballs; hamburger meat becomes tough if it is handled too much.

If you double a recipe for a stew or similar meat dish, double the amount of meat and other major ingredients such as potatoes and onions, but use only one and a half times the amount of fat, liquid, and seasonings, unless you find you need more.

Cooked meat tastes stale if kept, even under the best of refrigerated conditions, for more than a few days. The fat develops a rancid taste, one good reason for cutting off the fat as quickly as possible.

Roast Beef

A standing 2-rib roast of beef, which will weigh about 3 pounds if the short ribs have been cut off, serves about 4 people. The meat is wonderful all by itself, and I cook it very simply. Our local butcher says that meat should always be roasted at 325° and no hotter, so that the meat will be tender and juicy; however, modern roasting meat is usually very tender anyway, and I'm too impatient to roast beef at that temperature.

Put your beef roast in a roasting pan (any cooking pan with shallow sides will do) and roast at 350° until a meat thermometer inserted into the center of the meat, but not near a bone, reads 110°

for rare, 130° for medium, or 150° for well done. For a 3-inch-thick 2-rib roast cooked to 110° degrees, this will take just slightly over 1 hour; longer of course for medium or well done, or for a thicker piece of meat.

Take the roast out of the oven just as soon as it is done to avoid overcooking. Put it on a serving platter and set it in a warm place (not the oven) for about 20 minutes before carving. (The internal temperature of the meat will often rise another 10 degrees while it waits.)

Meanwhile, make gravy in the pan, using the beef drippings, flour, and cooking water drained from the vegetables you will serve with the meal.

Serve the roast beef hot with oven-roasted or mashed potatoes (pages 183 and 182), gravy (page 109), and vegetables or salad. Or do as the English do, and accompany your beef with Yorkshire pudding (page 269). Use the leftover cold meat in sandwiches or make open-faced hot roast beef sandwiches by pouring a little hot gravy over slices of roast beef on bread slices spread with margarine. Simmer the bones to make soup stock. I usually cook more roast beef than I need, the leftovers are so good.

Steak with Wine Sauce

A good dish to prepare for a celebration when you haven't much time to cook.

1 pound boneless steak
such as beef fillet, or 1¼
    pounds bone-in steak
    such as porterhouse or
    sirloin
1 tablespoon margarine
    or olive oil, if needed

1 clove garlic, peeled and
    minced
⅓ cup red wine
1 teaspoon
    Worcestershire sauce
1 tablespoon tomato
    sauce or tomato paste

Pan-grill the steak on a very lightly greased frying pan until it's done as you like; set it aside in a warm place.

If little or no fat has cooked out of the steak, add the margarine to the hot pan and sauté the garlic just until it begins to brown. Add the wine (preferably some of the wine you are going to serve with the steak), and scrape up all of the browned bits from the pan; add the Worcestershire sauce and the tomato paste or sauce, cook over very high heat until about 3 tablespoons of liquid are left, and pour the sauce over the steak. Serve immediately.

SERVES 2 OR 3.

Shish Kabob

Serve these hot on groats or boiled rice. Pass salt and pepper at the table.

3 tablespoons olive oil
¼ cup lemon juice or
  wine vinegar
1 large clove garlic,
  peeled and sliced

Dash cayenne pepper
⅛ teaspoon dried
  oregano
1 pound beef (any tender
  cut) in 1-inch cubes

Mix the oil, lemon juice, garlic, cayenne, and oregano in a glass or pottery dish; add the meat, stir well to coat with the marinade, cover the dish, and let rest for about 3 hours at room temperature or overnight in the refrigerator. (It is okay if the olive oil congeals.) Stir every so often, to expose all sides of the meat to the marinade.

Thread the meat onto skewers, and broil just until done, 10 or 15 minutes. Overcooking the meat will make it tough.

If you wish to include some vegetables like mushrooms, chunks of peeled onions, or green peppers cut into squares, precook them first briefly before you thread them onto the skewers. Cherry tomatoes are colorful and do not need precooking. Spoon some marinade over the vegetables before broiling.

SERVES 2.

Beef Stroganoff

Stroganoff is usually made with sour cream; however, it is also good with the sour cream omitted, as it is here.

1 pound beef, sliced thin	1 clove garlic, peeled and
1½ tablespoons flour	minced
Pinch of pepper	1 beef bouillon cube
¼ cup margarine	Pinch dry mustard
6 large mushrooms,	½ cup water
sliced (about 2 cups)	3 tablespoons tomato
1 large onion, peeled and	sauce
cut up	3 tablespoons sherry

Put the beef slices into a paper bag with the flour and pepper, close the bag, and shake well to coat the meat with flour; set aside.

Melt 2 tablespoons of the margarine in a large skillet and sauté the mushrooms; remove the mushrooms from the pan and set aside. Sauté the onion and garlic together in the same pan, then set them aside with the mushrooms.

Add the remaining 2 tablespoons of margarine to the skillet, then add the meat. Cook, stirring constantly, until the meat is just done. Crumble the bouillon cube over the meat, add the dry mustard and the water, and stir while you bring the mixture to a boil and simmer for 2 minutes.

Add the reserved cooked onions and mushrooms, the tomato sauce, and sherry; stir briefly until just beginning to simmer. Usually you won't need to add any salt to this dish, as there is enough in the bouillon cube. Serve very hot over cooked noodles, rice, or groats.

SERVES 3.

Pot Roast

Pot roast makes a wonderful meal for company or family, and isn't difficult if you know how to go about it; this is a dish that takes a long time to describe, but is very little trouble to cook. Pot roast improves upon standing so it can be cooked a day ahead of time and reheated. Serve with carrots, boiled or baked potatoes, and a green salad.

2 cloves garlic
3½ pounds boneless beef; flank steak is best, but beef
    chuck or round will do nicely
1 or 2 tablespoons vegetable oil, if needed
1 cup water or red wine

Peel the garlic cloves and cut each lengthwise into 3 or 4 slices. With a small sharp knife, cut deep slits in the meat and insert a slice of garlic into each slit. Use about half of the garlic slices in one side of the meat, then turn it over and insert the rest of the garlic slices in the other side.

Preheat a heavy pot and brown the meat in it in a little oil. Add the wine or water, cover the pot, and turn the heat down to a gentle simmer. Cook the meat about 2 hours, or until very well done.

The secret to a really good pot roast is to let the meat boil *nearly* dry at a late stage in the cooking process; after this add just enough water to produce about a cup of pan juices. Pot roast that has been overcooked, or allowed to cook without any water for more than a minute or two, will be dry, even though there is enough fat. Meat cooked this way is very flavorful and does not really need seasoning, even pepper. Salt can be passed at the table; it doesn't take much. Pass a pitcher of the pan liquid when you serve the meat.

SERVES 6.

Beef Stew with Red Wine

Serve this good company dish with a green vegetable, a salad, and rolls.

1 ½ cups dry red wine
2 small onions, peeled and chopped
1 clove garlic, peeled and cut in half
1 bay leaf
¼ teaspoon dried thyme
Freshly ground black pepper

2 pounds stew beef
A piece of beef bone (optional)
3 strips bacon
3 tablespoons olive oil
1 leek, rinsed and chopped
¼ teaspoon salt

Start the stew a day ahead of time, to give the beef time to marinate. Mix the wine, one of the cut-up onions, garlic, bay leaf, thyme, and a dash of pepper in a nonmetal bowl. Add the meat and bone, turn it once in the marinade, cover the bowl, and refrigerate overnight. Turn the meat over occasionally to expose all sides to the marinade.

When you are ready to cook the meat, line a large plate with paper towels; remove the meat and onion from the marinade and set them on the towel to drain, turning once. If you omit this step, the meat will spatter a great deal when you brown it.

Heat a heavy pot and add the bacon and 1 tablespoon of olive oil; sauté until bacon is crisp. Remove the bacon and brown the meat cubes, a few at a time, in the hot fat. When all of the meat has been browned, add the remaining olive oil to the pan and brown the remaining raw chopped onion and the marinated onion lightly in it. Return the beef and bacon to the pan. Remove the garlic from the marinade and discard it; add the bone if using and the marinade to the pan, along with the chopped leek. Cover the pan, turn the heat down to a simmer, and cook until the meat is very tender, about 2 hours. Add a little water from time to time if the stew gets too dry. Season to taste with salt and pepper and serve hot.

SERVES 4.

Beef Stew with Onions

One version of classic American home-style stew.

¼ cup cornmeal or
  wheat flour
½ teaspoon salt
¼ teaspoon pepper
2 to 2½ pounds stew
  beef, in 1-inch cubes
3 tablespoons vegetable
  oil
1 cup water
6 to 8 onions (about
  1½ pounds), peeled
  and cut up

2 medium potatoes,
  peeled and cut up
  (optional)
3 or 4 carrots, peeled
  and cut in chunks
  (optional)

Mix the flour or cornmeal, salt, and pepper in a bag or on a large plate. Coat the beef cubes on all sides with the seasoned cornmeal.

Heat a large, heavy pot on top of the stove. Add 2 tablespoons of the oil to the heated pot. Brown half the meat in the oil; remove it, add the remaining oil, and brown the rest of the meat.

Return the meat to the pot, add the water, and turn the heat down so that the stew just barely simmers. Cover the pot and cook for about 2 hours, or until the meat is tender. Add more water from time to time if the stew threatens to go dry. Add the vegetables and cook for 20 or 30 minutes more, or until they are tender. Add more salt and pepper if needed, and serve.

SERVES 5.

Beef Stew with Paprika

You can make this Hungarian-style stew with pork instead of beef. Serve with noodles. It's a good dish for company because it can be made the day before and reheated before serving. Use a good grade of imported paprika, which will have a strong, distinctive flavor.

3 pounds stew beef
½ cup olive oil
4 large onions (about 1½ pounds), sliced
2 teaspoons Hungarian hot paprika

1 cup red wine
One 6-ounce can tomato paste
Salt and pepper to taste

Brown the beef, about ¾ pound at a time, in 2 tablespoons hot olive oil; as each batch is browned, remove it and set aside, adding more oil as needed with each batch.

Cook the sliced onions quickly, in just enough oil to keep them from sticking, until they are limp and beginning to turn yellow. Add the meat and paprika to the pot and stir well. Add the wine and bring the stew to a gentle simmer; cover tightly and cook for 2 or 3 hours, until meat is tender. If the stew begins to go dry, add a little water. You want it to be good and moist, but not soupy. Add the tomato paste, and season to taste with salt and pepper.

SERVES 6.

Sauerbraten

A German stew thickened with gingersnaps. The meat must be marinated a day or two before being cooked. It is excellent served in the traditional manner with noodles or boiled potatoes.

½ cup vinegar
1 cup water
1 medium onion, peeled and chopped
1 carrot, peeled and cut in chunks
1 stalk celery, scrubbed and sliced
3 bay leaves
6 whole cloves
2 tablespoons sugar
½ teaspoon dry mustard
¼ teaspoon black pepper
½ teaspoon salt
4-pound piece of beef, perhaps chuck or round
3 tablespoons vegetable oil
¼ cup raisins
6 gingersnaps

Two days before you plan to cook the stew, combine the vinegar, water, onion, carrot, celery, bay leaves, cloves, sugar, mustard, pepper, and salt in a nonmetal bowl. Add the beef. Cover the bowl and refrigerate it until you wish to cook the sauerbraten; turn the meat over occasionally to make sure that all of it is exposed to the marinade.

Remove the beef from the marinade and wipe it off with paper towels. Heat a heavy cooking pot, put in the oil, and brown the beef on both sides. Add the marinade to the pot, cover, and simmer for about 3 hours, or until the meat is tender. Add water from time to time if the stew dries out.

Add the raisins and crumble in enough gingersnaps to thicken the gravy; do this gradually, as the cookies thicken after they have been in the liquid a little while. Serve hot.

SERVES 8.

Sherried Beef Stew

Serve this Spanish-style beef with rice.

1½ pounds cubed stew beef
2 tablespoons olive oil
Pinch ground cumin
Dash ground cloves
¾ cup dry sherry
8 pimiento-stuffed olives
3 tablespoons raisins (optional)
Pepper to taste

Brown the beef on all sides in oil. Add the rest of the ingredients except for the pepper and simmer in a covered pot until tender, about 3 hours. Add water if needed; you want to end up with about ⅓ cup liquid in the pot. Season with pepper; meat cooked this way needs very little salt.

SERVES 2 OR 3.

Ragbag Stew
(Ropa Vieja)

The name of this traditional Cuban stew, ropa vieja, *means "old clothes," perhaps because the vegetables make it colorful. I have translated the name rather freely.*

2 slices bacon
1½ pounds cubed stew
  beef
1 carrot, peeled and
  sliced
1 turnip, peeled and cut
  up
2 onions, peeled and
  chopped
One 1-pound can Italian
  plum tomatoes with
  juice
1 clove garlic, peeled and
  minced
1 green pepper, seeded
  and chopped

2 tablespoons olive oil
1 bay leaf
4 whole cloves (optional)
¼ teaspoon salt, or to
  taste
⅛ teaspoon pepper
½ teaspoon hot paprika
2 ounces chopped
  pimientos or stuffed
  green olives
2 tablespoons fine dry
  bread crumbs
  (optional)

Fry the bacon in a heavy pot; add the beef and brown slightly in the bacon fat, breaking up the bacon slices with a spoon. Add the carrot, turnip, half the chopped onions, and the tomatoes; cover and simmer until the meat is very tender, about 3 hours. At this point, the stew can be cooled and put aside to finish later.

Fry the remaining onion, garlic, and green pepper in the olive oil until limp. Add these vegetables plus the bay leaf, cloves, salt, pepper, paprika, and pimientos or olives to the stew; simmer for a few minutes to reheat and blend the flavors. If the stew is very liquid, thicken it with bread crumbs.

SERVES 4.

Meat Pasty

This British dish is quite unfussy, and can be varied with other vegetables and meats. It is like pot pie without gravy and is especially good on a cold day. It would be authentically British to make individual pasties instead of one large pie, as I have done.

Pastry

> 1½ cups flour
> ½ teaspoon salt
> ¾ cup margarine or vegetable shortening
> About ⅓ cup water

Set out a shallow baking dish, about 7 by 12 inches.

Prepare the crust: Sift the flour and salt together into a bowl and cut in the margarine or vegetable shortening until the pieces are about the size of peas. Stir in just enough water so that the dough clings together, and knead it a few strokes on a floured surface.

Roll out half to two-thirds of the dough to a size large enough to cover the bottom and come partway up the sides of your baking dish. Line the baking dish with the pastry. Roll out the rest of the pastry to a size that will about cover the top of your baking dish, and set it aside. (It is easier to roll the dough out all at once, while your hands are still dry and floury.)

Filling

1 small turnip (about
  ¼ pound), peeled and
  diced,
or 2 carrots, peeled and
  cut into ¼-inch-thick
  rounds
2 medium onions, peeled
  and chopped

1 medium potato, peeled
  and diced
About ¾ teaspoon salt
Pepper to taste
1 pound lean ground
  beef

Strew the chopped vegetables over the pastry-lined baking dish, and sprinkle with salt and pepper to taste. Crumble the raw ground beef over the vegetables, and sprinkle with a little more salt and pepper. Cover with the top crust. It is not necessary to seal the top crust; just lay it loosely over the filling and cut a few slits in it to let steam escape.

Bake at 375° for 50 to 60 minutes. Serve hot with horseradish sauce (page 116) or ketchup, or at room temperature, without any sauce.

SERVES 4.

Meat Loaf

Meat loaf is usually made with milk, or with bread that was made with milk. You can easily make your own favorite recipe milk-free by using milk-free bread crumbs, or by using rolled oats instead of bread crumbs. Use water, tomato juice, or beef broth instead of milk. This is my favorite meat loaf. It's good hot, or at room temperature with tomato sauce, or sliced cold in a sandwich.

⅓ cup rolled oats
¼ teaspoon salt
⅛ teaspoon pepper
1 medium onion, peeled
   and chopped
2½ pounds lean ground
   beef, or a mixture of
   equal parts of beef,
   pork, and veal

¼ cup ketchup (optional)
3 slices uncooked bacon
   (optional)

Mix the rolled oats, salt, pepper, and onion together in a bowl. Add the ground beef and mix lightly, handling the ground meat gently (not squeezing or pounding) to avoid toughening it.

Put the meat mixture into a 5- by 9-inch loaf pan. If you like, you can spread ketchup over the meat loaf, then top it with bacon. Bake at 350° for about 2 hours. A meat thermometer stuck into the middle of the meat loaf should read 150° for an all-beef loaf, or 185° for one made with pork. If you let the meat loaf rest in the pan for 10 minutes or so before serving, it will slice more easily.

SERVES ABOUT 6.

Meatballs

Meatballs are good with rice or noodles, or with boiled or baked potatoes.

¼ cup rolled oats
1 small onion, peeled
    and grated
¼ teaspoon salt
Dash pepper
¼ teaspoon
    Worcestershire sauce
1 pound lean ground
    beef

2 tablespoons vegetable
    oil
5 or 6 sliced mushrooms
    (optional)
1 cup liquid: beef broth,
    or water plus
    ½ bouillon cube
1 tablespoon flour

Mix the rolled oats, onion, salt, pepper, and Worcestershire sauce in a bowl; gently mix in the ground beef. Form the mixture into meatballs about the size of large walnuts.

Brown the meatballs on both sides in the oil. Just before they finish browning, add the mushrooms if desired and sauté until the mushrooms are lightly browned. Add the liquid, cover the pan tightly, and simmer gently about 30 minutes. If you make larger meatballs, cook them longer. Mix the flour with 1 tablespoon cold water, and stir in a ladleful of the broth from the meatballs. Add all the flour mixture to the meatballs and simmer gently until it is cooked and thickened, about 2 minutes.

MAKES ABOUT 16 MEATBALLS; SERVES 3.

Filled Hamburgers

2½ pounds ground beef, or enough to make 6 good-
    sized hamburgers
½ cup Jalapeño Dip (page 23)
6 Hamburger Buns (page 219)

Form the meat into 12 thin patties about as big around as you usually make them, but only half as thick. Top 6 of the patties with 1 tablespoon each of the jalapeño dip; top these hamburgers with the remaining patties, and press the edges firmly together to seal.

Cook the hamburgers as you usually do. Serve them on rolls, with sliced tomato and a little extra jalapeño dip.

SERVES 6.

Sloppy Joes

1 medium onion, peeled and chopped
1 clove garlic, peeled and minced
1 green pepper, seeded and chopped
1 tablespoon vegetable oil
¾ pound lean ground beef
One 8-ounce can tomato sauce
½ teaspoon dried parsley
¼ teaspoon dried oregano
⅛ teaspoon dried basil
Dash cayenne pepper
Salt to taste
2 Hamburger Buns (page 219), split and toasted, or 2 large slices plain bread, toasted

Sauté the onion, garlic, and green pepper in the oil for a few minutes, stirring often, until they are limp and beginning to brown. Remove from the pan and set aside. Break up the ground beef in the pan with a spoon, and sauté for a few minutes until it has lost its pink color. Return the vegetables to the pan, add the tomato sauce and seasonings, and cook and stir for a few minutes to heat thoroughly and blend the flavors. Serve over the buns or toast.

SERVES 2.

Baked Ham

A cooked ham is an excellent resource to have on hand if you are going to be feeding a lot of people. It keeps beautifully and can be served hot or cold, with mustard or raisin sauce (page 113) if you like.

These directions are for the so-called semiboneless hams, but the timing is about right for most types of ham.

Set the ham fat side up in a pan deep enough to catch the drippings, and bake until a meat thermometer pushed deep into the meat but not near the bone reads 170°. Cut the rind off the ham before serving.

A ham half, weighing about 8 pounds, will take about 3½ hours to bake at 350°. A whole ham bakes in about 5 hours.

A HALF HAM WILL SERVE 8 TO 10 PEOPLE; A WHOLE HAM WILL SERVE A CROWD.

Roast Pork

Set a pork loin roast in a roasting pan and cook at 350° for about 3 hours, or until it reaches an internal temperature of 185° as measured by a meat thermometer placed so that the tip is near the center of the roast, but not near a bone. A large pork loin is longer but not much thicker than a small pork loin; weight does not have much to do with the length of time it takes to cook.

Serve hot, with mashed potatoes (page 182), gravy (page 109), and applesauce (page 292).

A 3½-POUND ROAST WILL SERVE 4; A 5- TO 6-POUND ROAST WILL SERVE 6.

Roast Pork with Prunes

A Scandinavian way with roast pork, easy and good. Serve with gravy and mashed potatoes.

> 8 cooked, pitted prunes
> ¼ cup brandy (optional)
> One 3- to 4-pound pork roast

Use either cooked prunes that you have pitted or moist-pack pitted prunes just as they come from the package. If you like, soak the prunes in brandy for several hours before you plan to cook the roast.

Using a long, thin, sharp knife, cut a slit in the roast between the meat and the bone, parallel to the backbone. Repeat at the other end of the roast. Using your fingers and something long and blunt such as a table knife or an iced tea spoon, stuff the prunes into the slits; the prunes should not be visible from the outside when you are finished. Cook as directed for roast pork.

SERVES 4.

Leftover Roast Pork

We're fond of fresh hot pork, but we almost prefer the leftovers when they're prepared this way.

> About 1½ cups leftover roast pork, cut into small
> chunks
> 1 cup pork gravy
> Freshly cooked rice to serve 2
> Cranberry sauce

Heat the meat in the gravy in a saucepan, adding water as necessary to keep it from sticking. Serve immediately over hot boiled rice, and pass the cranberry sauce at the table.

SERVES 2.

Spicy Pork Chops

3 medium-thick pork
chops
1 clove garlic, peeled and
minced
1/4 cup orange juice

1 teaspoon honey
1 teaspoon
Worcestershire sauce
Dash cayenne pepper

Brown the chops on one side in a heavy skillet; turn. Mix the remaining ingredients together and pour them over the chops. Lower the heat and simmer, covered, for about 15 minutes, until the pork is tender and the sauce is thick. Watch carefully at the last, as the sauce can burn quickly.

SERVES 2 TO 3.

Pork Stew with Apple Cider

You can do most of the preparation for this stew the day before serving. Cook it until just before adding the vegetables; refrigerate until needed. A good company dinner, especially if you've been out of the house all day.

4 pounds boneless pork,
cut in 1-inch cubes
1/2 cup flour
3/4 teaspoon salt
1/4 teaspoon pepper
1/3 cup vegetable oil
A pork bone or two for
flavor
3 leaves fresh sage, or 1/8
teaspoon dried sage

3 cups apple cider, plus
extra if needed
3 large carrots, skinned
and cut into chunks
1 bunch leeks, well
rinsed of all grit and
sliced
1 cup mushrooms,
cleaned and sliced

Coat the pork pieces with a mixture of the flour, salt, and pepper. Heat 2 tablespoons of the oil in a heavy stew pot and brown the pork cubes about 1 pound at a time, adding more oil as necessary with each batch. Add the pork bones, the sage, and the cider and simmer gently, covered, for about 3 hours, or until the meat is tender, adding extra cider occasionally only if necessary to prevent meat from sticking. Stew should be moist but not soupy.

About 30 minutes before you wish to serve the stew, add the carrots; 10 minutes later, add the leeks and the mushrooms. Let everything simmer 20 minutes. Season to taste with salt and pepper.

SERVES 6 TO 8.

Polish Stew

Really good imported paprika makes a big difference in this recipe and others calling for paprika.

2 or 3 onions, peeled and chopped
2 tablespoons vegetable oil
2 pounds pork or beef, in 1-inch cubes
1 teaspoon sharp Hungarian paprika

1 pound kielbasa or kosher salami, cut in chunks
1 to 1½ cups water or white wine
2 pounds sauerkraut, rinsed

Sauté the onions in the oil until limp. Remove them from the pan, add the meat and paprika, and brown the meat about 1 pound at a time. Return the onions to the pot with the kielbasa or salami and add the wine or water. Cover and simmer gently for about 2 hours, or until the meat is tender.

Rinse the sauerkraut under cold water and drain. Repeat. Add the sauerkraut to the pot, heat well, and serve. The stew will probably not need extra salt or pepper.

SERVES 4 TO 6.

Pork Chops and Sauerkraut

Easy to prepare, goes well with boiled potatoes.

3 pork chops
1 pound sauerkraut
1 apple, washed, cored, and sliced (optional)
2 teaspoons caraway seed (optional)

Brown the pork chops on one side, and turn them over. Meanwhile, rinse the sauerkraut under cold water and drain. Cover the chops with the sauerkraut and add the apple and/or the caraway seeds if you like. Turn the heat down, cover the pan, and simmer for about 45 minutes, until the pork is done.

SERVES 2 TO 3.

Quick Pork Stew

This is really quick, half an hour to prepare and cook.

1/4 cup vegetable oil
3 medium onions, peeled and sliced
1 pound ground pork
1 pound canned or frozen tomatoes, with juice

1/2 cup tomato sauce
1 teaspoon Worcestershire sauce
One 10-ounce package frozen corn kernels

Heat the oil in a skillet or heavy pot, and brown the onions. Remove the onions and brown the pork, breaking it up into small pieces with a spoon as you do so. If the pork has given up a lot of fat, drain it from the pan. Add the tomatoes, tomato sauce, Worcestershire sauce, and corn, and simmer, covered, for about 15 minutes to heat the stew thoroughly and blend the flavors. You won't necessarily need to add any salt.

SERVES 3 OR 4.

Stir-fry Dinner

This is an excellent quick supper, which takes longer to describe than to prepare. It can be ready to eat about half an hour after you walk in the door. Stir-frying is a good way of using a little of this and a dab of that, seasoning it any way you please. The following is a method with a list of possibilities. You wouldn't want to use all these ingredients for one dinner.

Although this recipe is included with recipes that use pork, shrimp, scallops, or any meat will work well. Of course you can leave out meat entirely and have a vegetarian stir-fry dinner.

Cook only enough to feed two people. If you try to stir-fry too much at once, the foods will steam in their own juices instead of frying. If you are feeding more than two, do as the Chinese do and prepare several different dishes. Serve with freshly made hot boiled rice.

About ¼ pound meat per person, cut in ¹⁄₁₆- to ⅛-inch strips

Garlic, peeled and minced

Fresh ginger, peeled and minced

Cornstarch

Cooking oil of your preference

A variety of raw vegetables sliced thin: onions, mushrooms, green pepper, zucchini, yellow crookneck or white patty pan squash, shredded carrots, fresh spinach leaves, fresh tomatoes. These do not need to be steamed.

Vegetables that cook much more quickly if they're steamed, so should be added last: broccoli florets, peeled slices of broccoli stem, eggplant cubes, snow peas, cauliflower florets

Water, beef broth, chicken broth, sherry

Chinese hot chili sauce or black bean sauce

Soy sauce

Sesame seeds, about 1 tablespoon per serving

Prepare and slice the meat and vegetables. It's easier to slice meat thinly if it's partially frozen. If you're using scallops or shrimp, leave them whole.

Heat a large frying pan, add a tablespoon of oil, and start to cook. You'll need only one pan for the stir-fry. Cook each item separately and then remove it from the pan, working more or less in the order above. I like to cook garlic and ginger with the meat and I nearly always use them, but leave them out if you don't like their taste.

The vegetables in the second list cook much more quickly if you steam them, which you do by adding a tablespoon or so of liquid (water, broth, or sherry) along with the vegetables and then covering the pan. Any of the vegetables should be cooked until just barely done, usually less than 5 minutes.

When every ingredient is cooked, put the chili sauce or black bean sauce and sesame seeds in the frying pan. Return the cooked meat and vegetables to the pan, add soy sauce if you wish, stir well and heat through. Serve immediately on the hot rice. There is usually no need to add salt, just pass a bottle of soy sauce.

Here is one combination we like:

½ pound pork, sliced into thin strips
1 medium onion, peeled and sliced
1 large clove garlic, peeled and minced
6 medium mushrooms, sliced

One 6-ounce package frozen snow peas
¼ cup vegetable oil
2 teaspoons Chinese hot chili sauce with garlic
1½ tablespoons sesame seeds

Roast Lamb

A half leg of lamb, weighing about 4 pounds, serves 4 to 6. If you wish, insert slivers of garlic into the meat before roasting as the French do. For a 4-pound roast, use 2 cloves of garlic. Peel them, cut them into slivers, and insert each sliver into a slit you have cut in the meat with a thin, sharp knife.

Put the meat into a heatproof dish, set in the oven, and roast at 350°, or until a meat thermometer inserted into the thickest part of the meat, but not near a bone, reads 140°. This will take about 1½ hours for the half leg of lamb, and only a little longer for the whole leg. Some cookbooks tell you to roast the lamb until the meat thermometer reads 170°, but I think this toughens the meat. Let the roast rest outside the oven in a warm place for 5 or 10 minutes before carving.

Serve with mint jelly, wine jelly, or gravy (page 109).

Herbed Lamb Chops

Rice pilaf (page 186) goes very well with this, and makes a quick meal.

1 teaspoon dried thyme
½ teaspoon dried marjoram
½ teaspoon dried oregano
2 shoulder lamb chops or 4 rib chops

Mix the herbs well and rub the mixture onto both sides of the chops. Rub the fat edge of the chops over a hot ungreased heavy iron skillet. Sear the chops on both sides until they are lightly browned on the outside but still pink near the bone. Serve immediately.

SERVES 2.

Marinated Lamb Chops

A good treatment for lamb chops, or for boneless lamb cut into cubes and threaded on skewers for marinating, to cook as shish kabob. Serve with rice or groats.

6 tablespoons vegetable oil

2 tablespoons lemon juice

1 clove garlic, peeled and minced

1 generous pinch dried thyme

1 generous pinch dried oregano

Dash cayenne pepper

2 thick shoulder lamb chops or 4 thick loin lamb chops

Mix the oil, lemon juice, garlic, herbs, and pepper in a shallow glass or ceramic bowl. Dip both sides of each chop in this marinade, cover the bowl, and leave the chops for about 2 hours at room temperature, or overnight in the refrigerator. Turn the meat occasionally to expose both sides to the marinade.

Broil the lamb until just done.

SERVES 2.

Satay

I was introduced to this famous dish many years ago by an Indonesian neighbor in a large apartment house in Philadelphia. One day I became alarmed by the smoke pouring out under her door. She explained that the smoke was from the satay she was cooking over the gas burner of her American stove, and very kindly gave me both some satay and the recipe. I hope you'll like this Far East version of shish kabob as much as we do, but I recommend you cook it outdoors over a grill! Serve with rice.

1 scallion, both white and green parts, minced

1 clove garlic, peeled and minced

1 slice fresh ginger about twice the thickness of a nickel, peeled and minced

1/4 teaspoon red pepper flakes

1 teaspoon soy sauce

2 teaspoons peanut butter

2 teaspoons lime juice

1 teaspoon brown sugar

1 tablespoon corn oil or sesame oil, if needed

3/4 pound lamb, in 3/4-inch cubes

Mix the scallion, garlic, ginger, pepper flakes, soy sauce, peanut butter, lime juice, and brown sugar in a bowl. If the mixture is stiff, stir in enough oil to loosen it. Add the meat cubes, stir to coat well with the sauce, and let set for an hour or two to marinate.

Thread the meat onto skewers and broil over high heat for about 10 minutes.

SERVES 2.

Poultry

Roast Chicken
Broiled Chicken Oregano
Sherry-Soy Broiled Chicken
Oven-fried Chicken
    Crusty Oven-fried Chicken
Fried Chicken
Chicken with Honey and Lime
Chicken with Bacon and
    Sherry
Chicken in Orange
Chicken Paprika
Barbecued Chicken
Arroz con Pollo
Chicken Curry
Chicken Cacciatore
Chicken with Sausage
Chicken Mushroom Pie
Chicken under Biscuit

Roast Turkey
Roast Turkey with Stuffing
Turkey and Dressing Casserole

Roast Duck
  Roast Goose

Roast Chicken

Very good with mashed potatoes (page 182) and gravy (page 109).

1 whole roasting chicken, about 3½ pounds
1 or 2 teaspoons lemon juice (optional)
¼ teaspoon dried thyme or rosemary (optional)

Rinse the chicken and remove the package of giblets and the neck. Pull off any fat that is easy to reach and discard it. If you like, sprinkle the inside of the chicken with lemon juice, and thyme or rosemary. Set the bird in an open metal pan and tuck the wing tips under the back. Tie the ends of the legs together with string.

Roast at 350° for about 1½ to 2 hours, until the skin is pleasantly browned and a leg moves freely when you wiggle it, and the juices run clear when you pierce the thigh with a skewer or fork.

SERVES 4.

NOTE: If, right after the meal, you simmer a leftover chicken carcass in about 2 cups of water for half an hour to an hour, then let it cool to room temperature, you can get a great deal of meat off the bones. The meat will remain moist, whereas roast chicken left on the carcass is apt to be dry. The liquid in which you simmered the chicken becomes chicken broth, which can be frozen for future use as a soup or a sauce base.

Broiled Chicken Oregano

Good for a small family or a large group. The recipe is written for 2 servings, but it can easily be expanded to serve a great many people.

½ chicken, cut up (see note)
2 tablespoons lemon juice
2 tablespoons olive oil
⅛ teaspoon dried oregano
Salt to taste

Put the chicken pieces in a nonmetal dish and sprinkle with the lemon juice, olive oil, oregano, and salt. Cover, and let set in the refrigerator between 2 hours and overnight. Turn the pieces several times, to expose all sides to the marinade.

Broil 45 minutes to 1 hour, until chicken parts are tender but not dry.

SERVES 2.

NOTE: Please feel free to interpret my directions for cut-up chicken very loosely and use any combination of parts you like. For this recipe you could use one each of a breast half, wing, back, thigh, and drumstick or you could use 2 breast halves, or 5 thighs. A 3- to 3½-pound chicken serves four; for two people 1½ to 1¾ pounds is about right for chicken with the bone in.

Sherry-Soy Broiled Chicken

This is good hot but even better cold, a fine dish to take to a picnic.

⅓ cup soy sauce
⅓ cup sherry
Dash cayenne pepper
1 clove garlic, peeled and minced
One 3½-pound chicken, cut up

Mix the soy sauce, sherry, cayenne, and garlic in a nonmetal bowl. Add the chicken pieces, turn to coat them well, cover the bowl, and let set to marinate in the refrigerator between 2 hours and overnight. Turn the chicken pieces several times while they marinate.

Broil the chicken pieces 45 to 60 minutes, until cooked through but still moist.

SERVES 4.

Oven-fried Chicken

Very easy.

¼ cup margarine
½ chicken cut into 3 or 4 pieces
Salt and pepper

Preheat the oven to 350°, and set a 9- by 9-inch baking pan containing the margarine in the oven until the margarine melts. Remove the excess fat from the chicken pieces and rub the chicken with salt and pepper. Dip the skin sides of the chicken pieces into the melted margarine and then set the pieces, skin side up, in the pan.

Bake about 1 hour. Every 15 minutes or so, turn the chicken pieces over, so that they will brown on both sides.

SERVES 2.

Crusty Oven-fried Chicken

Roll the chicken pieces in ⅓ cup finely crushed cracker crumbs mixed with a pinch of thyme, black pepper, and ⅛ teaspoon salt before you place them in the pan.

Fried Chicken

Old-style, home-style fried chicken without the traditional milk bath.

> One 3½-pound chicken, cut up
> ½ cup flour
> ½ teaspoon salt
> ¼ teaspoon pepper
> At least ½ cup fat (vegetable oil or lard)

Put the flour, salt, and pepper into a clean paper bag. Shake each piece of chicken in the bag to coat with flour, then put the chicken aside on a large plate.

Preheat the oven to 300°. Put an empty baking pan in the oven to receive the browned chicken.

Heat the fat medium-hot in a large, reasonably deep pan that has a cover. Start with the thicker pieces of meat, such as the breasts and drumsticks. Fry only one layer of chicken pieces at a time. Cover the pan immediately after putting in the chicken.

Peek occasionally, and as each piece browns turn it over and brown the other side. As each piece finishes browning, place it in the baking pan in the oven and replace it with another piece of chicken. Add more fat to the frying pan as necessary. Serve hot.

SERVES 4.

Chicken with Honey and Lime

Good with rice pilaf (page 186).

> 1 lime
> 2 tablespoons honey
> ¼ cup margarine
> Pinch of salt
> 1 whole chicken breast cut in half, or 4 chicken thighs

Preheat the oven to 350°. Wash the lime and, using a good sharp knife or a clean single-edged razor blade, cut off 4 thin slices. Squeeze the rest of the lime to get about 1 tablespoon juice. Mix the juice with the honey, the salt, and 2 tablespoons of the margarine; you may need to heat it gently to get the margarine to combine with the honey and juice.

Brown the chicken in the remaining 2 tablespoons of margarine in an ovenproof frying pan. Remove the chicken from the pan and drain off and discard the fat. Return the chicken to the skillet, drizzle with the honey-lime mixture, and top with the lime slices.

Put the chicken in the oven, and cook for about 30 minutes, basting once or twice with the pan juices.

SERVES 2.

Chicken with Bacon and Sherry

An unusual combination, this is delicious and quick to prepare. With rolls and a salad, it makes a good meal.

1 strip bacon	2 tablespoons water
1 medium onion, peeled and chopped	2 tablespoons sherry
3 half chicken breasts with the skin and bones removed	Salt and pepper

Cook the bacon in a heavy frying pan over medium heat. When the bacon is browned, add the chopped onion and sauté it in the bacon fat until it's limp and transparent. Remove the bacon and onion from the pan and set them aside.

Add the chicken to the skillet and brown on both sides. Return the bacon and onions to the pan, add the water, cover the pan, and simmer for about 10 to 15 minutes, until the chicken is cooked. Add a little more water if needed to keep the chicken and onions from sticking to the pan. Add the sherry, turn up the heat, and cook a minute or two until the liquid is nearly gone. Season with salt and pepper and serve immediately.

SERVES 3.

Chicken in Orange

A family favorite.

One 3- to 3½-pound chicken, cut up	2 teaspoons soy sauce
1 tablespoon vegetable oil	1 tablespoon brown sugar
¾ teaspoon ground ginger	3 ounces frozen orange juice concentrate
	3 tablespoons water

Brown the chicken lightly in the oil. Add the rest of the ingredients, bring to a boil, and simmer, tightly covered, until the chicken is tender, about 1 hour. Serve over rice, pouring the sauce from the pan over the portions.

SERVES 4.

Chicken Paprika

Sweet Hungarian paprika from a good spice shop is best for this dish.

1 medium onion, peeled and sliced	¼ cup water
1 clove garlic, peeled and minced	½ chicken, cut up
2 tablespoons olive oil	½ pound canned or fresh tomatoes
6 medium mushrooms, sliced (about 1½ cups)	¼ pound (½ cup) soft tofu (optional)
1 tablespoon Hungarian sweet paprika	Salt and pepper

Sauté the onion and garlic in olive oil until limp; add the mushrooms and sauté until they wilt and the onions start to brown. Stir in the paprika and cook for a minute or two. Stir in the water, add the chicken pieces, and coat the chicken with the mixture. Add the tomatoes, turn down the heat, cover the pot, and simmer slowly until the chicken is cooked, about 45 minutes.

If you use the tofu, put it into a blender or food processor along with several big spoonsful of the sauce from the cooking pan; blend or process until smooth, and stir into the juices in the pan. Let set a minute or two. Add a little salt and pepper if needed, and serve with rice or noodles.

SERVES 2.

Barbecued Chicken

Spicy. I cook this in a covered pan on top of the stove, but you might want to brush the sauce over the chicken pieces before grilling outdoors.

¼ cup lemon juice or
  vinegar
1 tablespoon
  Worcestershire sauce
3 tablespoons ketchup or
  tomato sauce
2 tablespoons brown
  sugar
1 tablespoon vegetable
  oil

¼ teaspoon cayenne
  pepper
½ teaspoon dry mustard
½ teaspoon salt
2 teaspoons chili powder
  or hot paprika
One 3- to 3½-pound
  chicken, cut up

If you like a mild barbecue sauce, start with half the amount of the spices; add more toward the end of the cooking time if you wish. Mix the lemon juice, Worcestershire sauce, ketchup, brown sugar, oil, cayenne, mustard, salt, and chili powder in a heavy pot. Add the chicken pieces and turn them to coat with the sauce. Bring to a boil and simmer, covered, for about 1½ hours, or until very tender. Check occasionally, and add water if the meat seems in danger of burning or drying out. Turn the chicken pieces at least once during cooking, so all of the meat gets exposed to the sauce. Adjust seasoning to taste.

SERVES 4.

Arroz con Pollo

Spanish for rice with chicken. Its many variations are favorites in Latin America.

2 cloves garlic, peeled
  and minced.
2 large onions, peeled
  and chopped
¼ cup olive oil
One 3- to 3½-pound
  chicken, cut up
One 28-ounce can
  Italian-style tomatoes
  with juice
1 bay leaf
⅛ teaspoon dried
  oregano

Dash cayenne pepper
¼ teaspoon salt
¾ cup raw rice
½ bunch fresh asparagus,
  cleaned, or one
  10-ounce package
  frozen asparagus or
  artichoke hearts
5 ounces shelled peas
  (about 1 cup)

Sauté the garlic and onions in olive oil in a large heavy pan. When they are limp and getting yellow, remove them from the pan; put in the chicken pieces and brown lightly. Return the onions and garlic to the pan, pour the tomatoes, bay leaf, oregano, cayenne, and salt over the chicken, cover the pan tightly, and simmer until tender, about 1 hour.

Stir in the rice. If there does not appear to be a generous 2 cups of liquid, add some water or chicken broth. After 10 minutes, add the asparagus; after another 5 minutes, add the peas. (Artichokes should be added at the same time as the peas.) Cook gently until the rice and vegetables are done, about 5 minutes more. Taste the dish, correct the seasoning if necessary, and serve. (It is easier to cook the rice separately, but the dish will be watery.)

SERVES 4.

Chicken Curry

The quality of any curry depends very much on your curry powder, which should be pungent and very fragrant. The good ones come from specialty spice shops or from Indian groceries. A curry is often served hot on boiled rice accompanied by small dishes of chutney, chopped peanuts, grated coconut, chopped hard-boiled eggs, and banana slices. Use one or all.

2 large onions, peeled
  and chopped
3 cloves garlic, peeled
  and minced
2 tablespoons olive oil
2 teaspoons curry
  powder
2 tablespoons flour

3 cups chicken broth
¼ cup chunky peanut
  butter
Meat from one 2½- to
  3-pound cooked
  chicken
½ teaspoon salt

Sauté the onion and garlic in the olive oil until they are golden. Add the curry powder and stir for a few seconds. Stir in the flour until all of it is moistened, then carefully add the 3 cups of chicken broth. Simmer, stirring often, for about 2 minutes to cook the flour thoroughly. Stir in the peanut butter and then the chicken meat; simmer for a few minutes, adding salt and more broth and curry powder if necessary.

SERVES 4.

Chicken Cacciatore

This dish reheats very well. Serve with freshly cooked spaghetti for a quick meal.

1 medium onion, peeled and chopped
1 clove garlic, peeled and minced
¼ cup olive oil
4 large mushrooms, chopped
One 4-pound chicken, cut up
1 pound Italian-style tomatoes with juice
1 bay leaf
¼ teaspoon dried oregano
¼ teaspoon dried basil
Good dash cayenne pepper
¼ cup dry white wine, or a light red wine such as zinfandel
½ teaspoon salt

Sauté the garlic and onion in the oil until they are limp and just beginning to brown. Add the mushrooms; cook and stir until they're limp. Remove the vegetables from the pan and brown the chicken pieces lightly in the hot fat, a few at a time.

Return the mushrooms, onions, and garlic to the pan, add the tomatoes, bay leaf, oregano, basil, cayenne, wine, and salt, and bring to a gentle simmer. Cook, covered, for about an hour; check from time to time and add more wine if necessary. Adjust the seasoning.

SERVES 6.

Chicken with Sausage

A real one-pot meal; start ¾ hour before dinnertime.

¼ pound Italian bulk
  sausage, or links cut
  into ½-inch rounds
About ¾ pound chicken,
  in 2 pieces
⅔ cup raw rice
1 medium tomato, cut
  up, or 8 ounces
  canned tomatoes with
  juice

1 beef bouillon cube
1½ cups water
½ pound fresh or frozen
  green peas, broccoli,
  or green beans

Brown the sausage in a heavy pot. Remove and reserve the sausage, and brown the chicken on both sides in the sausage fat. Cover the pot, reduce the heat to medium-low, and cook the chicken for 10 minutes. Drain off the fat, and discard it.

Add the rice, tomato, bouillon cube, sausage, and water to the chicken and bring to a gentle boil. Cover the pot and cook for 10 minutes. Stir broccoli into the dish, cover again, and simmer 10 minutes more, until the rice is done. (If instead of broccoli you choose to use peas or green beans, add them only 5 minutes before the rice is done.) You may want to add about ¼ cup extra water near the end of the cooking time, just enough to keep things from sticking to the pot.

SERVES 2.

Chicken Mushroom Pie

Classic, and simple; a favorite.

Crust

> ½ cup flour
> Salt
> ¼ cup margarine or vegetable shortening
> 1 tablespoon water

Preheat the oven to 400° and grease a 2-quart casserole.

Make the crust. Sift the ½ cup flour and a pinch of salt into a bowl and cut in the margarine or vegetable shortening until the particles are about the size of peas. Mix in the water, knead the crust for a few strokes, and then roll it out on a floured countertop to a size that will fit the top of your casserole. This amount will give you a circle about 9 inches in diameter.

Filling

> 1½ to 2 cups cooked
>   chicken meat
> Salt and pepper
> 2 tablespoons margarine
> 1½ to 2 cups sliced
>   mushrooms
>
> 1 tablespoon minced
>   onion
> 2 tablespoons flour
> 1 cup chicken broth

Prepare the filling: Arrange the chicken pieces on the bottom of the prepared casserole. Sprinkle with a little salt and pepper (if you aren't using a boullion cube or canned broth).

Melt the margarine in a frying pan and sauté the mushrooms and onion until tender. Take the pan off the heat, sprinkle the flour over the mushrooms and onion, and stir until all of it is moistened. Stir in the chicken broth and cook over medium heat, stirring constantly, until the sauce thickens and boils for about 2 minutes. Pour this hot mixture over the chicken in the casserole, and cover with the crust. Cut a few slits in the crust.

Bake for 30 minutes, or until the pie is bubbly and the crust browned. Serve hot.

SERVES 3.

Chicken under Biscuit

Another good use for cooked chicken—chicken pie with a biscuit crust.

Biscuit dough

2 cups flour	6 tablespoons margarine
2 teaspoons sugar	or vegetable
4 teaspoons baking	shortening
powder	¾ cup water
¼ teaspoon salt	

Preheat the oven to 425° and grease a 2-quart round casserole.

Start the biscuit dough: Sift the flour, sugar, baking powder, and salt into a bowl; cut in the margarine or the vegetable shortening until the pieces are the size of small peas. Set aside.

Chicken mixture

2 tablespoons margarine	1½ cups chicken broth
1 tablespoon minced	2 cups cooked chicken
onion	Salt, if needed
2 cups sliced mushrooms	Dash pepper
3 tablespoons flour	

Prepare the chicken mixture: Melt 2 tablespoons margarine in a skillet; lightly sauté the onion, then add the mushrooms and cook until they are limp. Remove the pan from the heat. Stir in 3 tablespoons flour until all of it is moistened, then stir in the chicken broth; return the pan to medium heat and cook, stirring constantly, until the sauce thickens and boils for 2 minutes.

Add the chicken, season to taste with salt and pepper (if you use canned chicken broth or a bouillon cube you probably will not need to add salt), and bring just to a boil. Pour this mixture into the prepared casserole.

Stir the ¾ cup water into the biscuit dough, and quickly roll the dough out to a circle that will fit the top of the casserole. Top the chicken with this circle of biscuit dough and cut a few slits in it. Bake for about 20 to 25 minutes, or until the top is browned.

SERVES 4.

NOTE: If you have leftover chicken gravy, dilute 1 cup gravy with ½ cup chicken broth or water and substitute it for the chicken broth and flour in the recipe.

Roast Turkey

Don't buy a self-basting turkey without first reading the label carefully; these birds have often been treated with milk products. If your supermarket doesn't carry fresh turkeys, you may be able to order one at a butcher shop or farm stand.

There are tables that tell you how long to cook birds of various weights, but I have never found them much help. An unstuffed 16-pound turkey takes 3 hours; allow about half an hour less for a smaller bird of, say, 9 pounds, or allow about 4 hours for a very large bird (about 25 pounds). A cooked turkey can wait very well if you set it in a warm place and loosely replace the aluminum foil cover under which you baked the bird.

Allow about 1 pound of turkey per person. If you like lots of leftovers (we do), allow 2 pounds.

Remove the neck and giblets, and any extra fat in the body cavity. Rinse the turkey well, and set it in a large baking pan. Tuck the wing tips under the back, and tie the legs together with white cotton household string. Grease one side of a piece of heavy-duty aluminum foil big enough to cover the top of the turkey, and lay it gently over the bird.

Roast at 350° until the turkey is nicely browned and a leg moves pretty freely when you wiggle it. Remove the foil during the last half hour or so of roasting so the bird will brown.

Roast Turkey with Stuffing

As in Thanksgiving turkey. The description is long in case this is the first time you've prepared one. It usually takes me about 45 minutes.

The procedure for a stuffed turkey is very similar to that for roasting a plain turkey, but it takes longer to cook. At 325°, an 11-pound turkey will cook in about 4½ hours; a 16-pound bird in about 6 hours; and a 23-pound bird in about 7 hours. I find that set cooking times for stuffed turkey are just ball-park figures, especially for larger birds. A slight variation of 10 or 15 degrees in oven temperature can mean a half hour less or more of cooking time. The best way to deal with this is to have the rest of the meal all ready to be cooked about 1 hour before you think the turkey will be done. Then you can finish cooking the meal whenever the turkey comes from the oven. The turkey is done when a leg moves freely when you wiggle it, and when the juice runs clear (not cloudy) from a small cut. A roasted turkey is all the better for sitting on a platter in a warm place, covered with its aluminum foil tent, for half an hour before being carved.

The amounts given here will amply stuff a 21-pound bird.

1 turkey, not self-basting
1 pound milk-free white
　bread, slightly dry
3/4 teaspoon minced fresh
　sage or a good-sized
　pinch of dried sage
Pepper
1 tablespoon cold
　margarine, cut into
　small chunks

1 small onion, peeled
　and chopped
1 stalk celery, scrubbed
　and chopped
1/4 cup boiling water

Have ready: a large roasting pan, a piece of aluminum foil big enough to cover the turkey, some margarine to grease it with, 4 or 5 metal skewers, several feet of strong clean white cotton string, a very large mixing bowl or a dishpan, and wire cutters to cut the wire that holds the turkey's feet close to the body.

Grease the foil on one side. Tear the bread into 1- to 1½-inch pieces, putting them into the dishpan or large bowl as you do so. Sprinkle the sage, pepper, and margarine over the bread and then mix with your hands. (Salt is usually unnecessary.) Mix in the onion and celery. Drizzle the boiling water over the stuffing, then toss it lightly to mix. You want the stuffing to be a bit dry and a bit bland when you put it into the bird; the flavors—sage, onion, celery, pepper—will intensify as it bakes and it will absorb moisture.

The next part is easier if you have a helper, especially if the turkey is a big one. If the turkey is bound with a wire band, cut the wire at its midpoint between the bird's ankles, and carefully pull out both halves. The far ends of the wire are hooked, so you will need to twist the wire to get it out. Remove the neck and giblets from the body cavity and the neck pouch and set them aside.

Rinse the inside of the bird, drain it, and stand the turkey up on its neck end in a corner of the sink. Fill the body cavity lightly with the stuffing; shake the bird lightly to settle the stuffing but don't pack it in or squeeze it. Tuck the tail up to fill part of the opening. Using a long skewer, pick up and pierce the skin at one side of the opening, then the other side. Repeat this process with other skewers until you think there are enough to close the opening—a large bird will usually take several skewers.

Using a piece of string about 2 feet long, make a figure 8 around both ends of a skewer, drawing the skin at both ends of each skewer closer together as you do this. Repeat this with the next skewer. When you have used up all of the skewer ends, and crisscrossed the opening several times, tie off the ends of the string; a bowknot works well.

Turn the turkey tail side down and put more stuffing into the neck cavity to give the bird a nice rounded shape. Use another skewer to secure the flap of neck skin to the back.

Put the turkey in the roasting pan and tuck the wing tips under the back of the neck. With another piece of string, tie a figure 8 around the ankles, drawing them gently together as you do this, and tie the ends of the string together (another bowknot).

Cover the turkey loosely with the foil, greased side down, and set the whole thing on a low shelf in a 325° oven.

If you have extra stuffing, put it in a greased casserole, moisten it well with water or broth, cover, and bake 1 hour. When the turkey has roasted for about two-thirds of the estimated time, remove the foil cover so that the bird will brown attractively.

For giblet gravy, simmer the neck and giblets in 2 cups of water for an hour. You can remove the liver and the heart after about 20 minutes, as they cook much quicker than the neck and gizzard. When the giblets are cooked and cool, cut off the tough parts and discard them, then cut the meat into small pieces. Use the broth for the turkey gravy. You can either add the giblets to the cooked gravy or pass them separately, if there is a difference of opinion in the family about giblet gravy.

NOTE: Remove stuffing from the turkey before storing the turkey in the refrigerator. Refrigerate the stuffing separately.

Turkey and Dressing Casserole

One of the many good uses for leftover turkey. Serve it with cranberry sauce and a vegetable and dessert that did not appear at The Meal. Plain turkey sandwiches and turkey soup are other ideas.

1/2 cup turkey gravy, thinned with about 1/4 cup water
1 cup turkey stuffing
1 cup turkey meat

Reheat the gravy in a saucepan and grease a shallow casserole. Preheat the oven to 350°.

Break up the stuffing and strew it over the bottom of the casserole. Spread the turkey meat over the stuffing, pour the hot gravy over the meat, and bake until well heated, about 30 minutes.

SERVES 2.

Roast Duck

One 5- to 6-pound duck

Pull off any loose fat, then put some cut-up fruit in the body cavity to flavor the meat as it roasts. Use 2 oranges, or 1 lemon and 1 apple, or some other combination. (You cannot eat the fruit; it will be too greasy.)

Pierce the skin at both sides of the opening into the body cavity with a skewer, then loop a piece of clean white string around both ends of the skewer. Gently bring the 2 pieces of skin together by tightening the string, and tie off the ends.

Place the duck on a roasting rack to keep it up out of the fat as it cooks. Set this rack in an ovenproof pan and tuck the tips of the wings underneath the upper back.

Roast the duck at 350° for about 2½ hours, or until the skin is brown and a leg moves freely when you wiggle it.

If you're going to make duck gravy (page 109) from the pan drippings, pour off and discard about half of the fat first. You can serve currant jelly sauce (page 113) instead of or in addition to the gravy.

SERVES 2.

Roast Goose

Follow the preceding directions for roasting duck, but roast for the first hour at 400°, then turn the heat down to 350°. The total cooking time for an 8-pound goose is about 2 hours; for a 10-pound goose, it's about 3 hours.

NOTE: You might want to save some duck or goose fat to use in making pie crust. This fat should be about half of the shortening you use for the pie crust; if you use it all by itself the pie crust will be delicious, tender, and nearly impossible to handle.

Gravy and Other Sauces

Gravy
Hot Egg Sauce
Mushroom Sauce
Tomato Sauce with
    Mushrooms and Red Wine
Fresh Tomato Sauce
    Sauce Andalouse
Raisin Sauce
Currant Jelly Sauce
Cranberry Sauce
Mayonnaise
Blender Mayonnaise
Horseradish Sauce
Summer Sauce
Hot Mustard

Gravy

Once you've made a few batches of gravy, you will know what it looks like and won't need to bother with measuring. It is an easy process and quite quick to do, but since many people have trouble with gravy, here are detailed instructions.

Drippings from roast meat or fowl
Twice as much flour as drippings
8 or 9 times as much water as drippings
Salt and pepper to taste

You should have on hand a flat-bottomed coil whisk.

Remove the roast from the cooking pan to a platter. Measure the drippings, then return them to the pan. A typical beef roast yields 1/3 cup of drippings, so for this you would use 2/3 cup of flour. If there isn't enough fat, add some margarine, but usually the fat given off by a roast will make the right amount of gravy for that piece of meat. Stir the flour in well, until all of it is moistened with the fat, then set the pan over medium heat. Cook and stir for a minute or two to brown the flour.

Remove the pan from the heat. Add the water, about 1 cup at a time, stirring with the whisk all the while. This is the stage at which gravy forms lumps if you aren't careful. For 1/3 cup drippings and 2/3 cup flour, use 3 cups of water. Whisk in enough water to make the gravy the consistency you like. Cook over medium heat, stirring constantly for several minutes, until the gravy is thickened. Try to get all the browned bits from the bottom of the pan into the gravy, as they add flavor. Season to taste with salt and pepper, and serve hot with the roast.

Hot Egg Sauce

Dresses up cold meat or meat loaf.

2 tablespoons margarine
3 tablespoons flour
1 cup chicken broth
2 tablespoons white
   wine
2 tablespoons fresh
   parsley, or 1 teaspoon
   dried parsley

Dash Tabasco sauce
Pinch of dried savory
1 teaspoon lemon juice
1 hard-boiled egg,
   chopped

This is closely related to gravy and is made in much the same way. Melt the margarine in a small, heavy saucepan. Remove it from the heat and stir in the flour, then the chicken broth and wine. Stir and simmer over moderate heat for 2 or 3 minutes, until thickened. If the sauce forms lumps, remove it from the heat and beat briskly with a whisk until smooth. Add the remaining ingredients. Serve hot.

MAKES ABOUT 1¼ CUPS SAUCE.

Mushroom Sauce

Serve hot on meat or fish.

2 tablespoons margarine
5 large mushrooms, wiped clean and sliced, or one
   4-ounce can mushrooms, drained
2 tablespoons flour
1 cup beef or chicken stock
2 tablespoons sherry (optional)

Melt the margarine in a small frying pan. If you are using fresh mushrooms, sauté them in the margarine until just cooked. Remove the pan from the heat and stir in the flour until it is thoroughly moistened. Add the stock, stirring until it is well mixed and there are no lumps. Return the pan to the heat and cook, stirring, until the mixture has boiled gently for 2 minutes. If you are using sherry or canned mushrooms, stir them in now. When the sauce is thoroughly hot and has just begun to simmer again, it is ready. Serve hot.

MAKES ABOUT 1½ CUPS SAUCE.

Tomato Sauce with Mushrooms and Red Wine

For hot meats.

1 clove garlic, peeled and minced
6 mushrooms, wiped clean and sliced
2 tablespoons olive oil
One 6-ounce can tomato paste

¾ cup red wine
¼ teaspoon dried basil
⅛ teaspoon salt
Dash cayenne pepper
Dash black pepper

Sauté the garlic and the mushrooms in the olive oil until the mushrooms are limp. Add the remaining ingredients to the pan, bring the sauce just to a boil, season to taste, and serve.

MAKES ABOUT 1½ CUPS OF SAUCE.

Fresh Tomato Sauce

Good with meat, pasta, or other main dishes. Make extra in summer, and freeze it for winter use.

2 tablespoons olive oil
1 clove garlic, peeled and minced
1 medium onion, peeled and chopped
1½ pounds (6 cups) tomatoes, preferably plum tomatoes, washed and cut into chunks

1 tablespoon chopped fresh basil, or
½ teaspoon dried basil
½ teaspoon salt
⅛ teaspoon pepper

Heat a heavy saucepan and add the oil, then the garlic and onion. Sauté over medium heat until the onion is wilted and transparent. Add the rest of the ingredients and simmer slowly, uncovered, until the sauce is as thick as you like it. Stir occasionally. The simmering should take about 30 minutes. Serve hot or chilled.

MAKES ABOUT 3 CUPS SAUCE.

Sauce Andalouse

For cold meat or fish.

Mix equal quantities of fresh tomato sauce and mayonnaise with just a little cayenne pepper. Serve cold.

Raisin Sauce

Good with ham.

½ cup raisins	Dash of ground cloves
1¼ cups water	Pinch of salt
6 tablespoons brown	3 tablespoons vinegar
sugar, tightly packed	1 tablespoon margarine
1 tablespoon cornstarch	

Simmer the raisins and water in a small saucepan for about 5 minutes to plump up the raisins.

Stir the sugar, cornstarch, cloves, salt, and vinegar together until there are no clumps of cornstarch; stir this into the simmering raisins and cook for a minute or more, until the sauce is clear and thick. Stir in the margarine. Serve hot or warm.

MAKES ABOUT 2 CUPS OF SAUCE.

Currant Jelly Sauce

For roast duck or goose or any game; a quick version of Cumberland sauce. This sauce is strong-flavored, and a little goes a long way.

½ cup currant jelly	Pinch of ground ginger
¼ cup frozen orange	Pinch of ground cloves
juice concentrate	Pinch of ground allspice
2 tablespoons brown	1 teaspoon cornstarch
sugar, packed firm	1 teaspoon
3 tablespoons white	Worcestershire sauce,
wine or vermouth	or a dash of Tabasco
2 tablespoons margarine	sauce
Dash of salt	

Mix all of the ingredients in a small saucepan and bring slowly to a boil, stirring occasionally. Simmer for a few minutes. Serve warm.

MAKES ABOUT 1 CUP OF SAUCE.

Cranberry Sauce

Freshly made cranberry sauce is entirely different from the canned product, and is very easy to make. Please try it.

4 cups fresh cranberries (about 1 pound)
2 cups sugar
2 cups water

Rinse and pick over the cranberries, then put them into a medium-large saucepan with the sugar and water. Bring to a boil, and simmer uncovered until the skins pop, 5 or 10 minutes. Let cool and then store in a covered nonmetal container, in the refrigerator.

1 POUND OF CRANBERRIES YIELDS 1 QUART SAUCE.

NOTE: Cranberries nowadays come in 12-ounce bags, so for a 12-ounce bag of berries you would use 1½ cups of sugar and 1½ cups of water. You can vary the amounts of sugar and water to suit yourself; you may prefer a thicker sauce, or a less sweet one. The sauce will thicken as it cools.

Mayonnaise

Mayonnaise is one of the basic sauces of French cooking. You can vary it easily. For instance, you can add a good curry powder and make curry mayonnaise. With the addition of puréed spinach, parsley, and tarragon you get elegant green mayonnaise.

Mayonnaise has the reputation of being tricky to make, but should work reliably for you if it's treated gently. Mayonnaise will "break" if too much oil is added, if the oil is added too quickly, if the mayonnaise gets too cold, or if its temperature is changed too quickly. If the mayonnaise does curdle, beat another room-temperature egg yolk in a bowl and, beating continuously as you did at first, pour the mayonnaise into it in a very thin stream.

Be sure to store mayonnaise chilled and use it within a day or two, since homemade mayonnaise lacks the preservatives added to the commercial product.

1 egg yolk (see warning on page 4)
2/3 cup olive oil or good-quality vegetable oil
Pinch of dry mustard
Pinch of salt

Dash of pepper
2 teaspoons lemon juice or vinegar
1 1/2 teaspoons water (optional)

All of the ingredients should be at room temperature when you begin. Mayonnaise must be beaten continuously while it's being made. Use a whisk, or an electric beater, or a blender.

Beat the egg yolk until light, then beat in about 1 tablespoon of oil and the mustard, salt, pepper, and lemon juice or vinegar. Pour the remaining oil into a small pitcher to make slow pouring easy. Beat the remaining oil in very slowly, drop by drop in the beginning, until about 1/3 of the oil has been incorporated into the egg yolk. Continuing to beat hard, pour in the rest of the oil in a very thin, slow stream. Adjust the seasoning and continue to beat for another minute or two.

MAKES 3/4 CUP MAYONNAISE.

Blender Mayonnaise

1 egg, at room temperature (see warning on page 4)
1/8 teaspoon salt
Pinch of pepper,

preferably white,
or 1/8 teaspoon dry mustard
1 1/3 cups vegetable oil
1 1/2 tablespoons vinegar or lemon juice

Process the egg, the salt, pepper or mustard, about 2 table-spoons of oil, and 1 tablespoonful of the vinegar or lemon juice in a blender until light. While the blender is running, pour in the remaining oil in a very thin stream and continue processing until the mayonnaise is light and smooth. You may have to stop the blender occasionally and scrape down the sides. Taste the mayonnaise and add more seasoning and more vinegar or lemon juice as needed. Process about a minute longer.

MAKES ABOUT 1¼ CUPS MAYONNAISE.

Horseradish Sauce

Serve cold, with meat dishes.

½ pound soft tofu, rinsed
2 tablespoons mayonnaise
2 to 4 teaspoons grated horseradish
1 teaspoon Worcestershire sauce
¼ teaspoon salt

Beat all the ingredients together in a blender or a food processor with the steel blade until the sauce is smooth and creamy. Vary the amount of horseradish to taste.

MAKES ABOUT 1¼ CUPS OF SAUCE.

Summer Sauce

This is basically a tossed salad with mayonnaise, using very little lettuce. The sauce is especially good when made with fresh-picked tomatoes and served out-doors over hamburgers on a hot summer day.

1 large ripe tomato,
   chopped into small
   pieces
2 large lettuce leaves,
   torn in small pieces
Small amounts of
   cucumber, radish, and
   green pepper, chopped
   fine

1 tablespoon finely
   chopped onion
1½ tablespoons
   mayonnaise
1 tablespoon Oil and
   Vinegar Dressing
   (page 206)

Mix the vegetables with the mayonnaise and the oil and vinegar dressing, and serve as a relish.

SERVES 3.

Hot Mustard

Very hot, very easy to prepare. Good on ham or cold roast beef.

1 tablespoon dry mustard
About 1½ teaspoons water

In a very small serving dish stir just enough water into the mustard to make a thin paste. Serve immediately or store, covered, in the refrigerator.

MAKES ABOUT 2 TEASPOONS MUSTARD.

Dried Beans

Boston Baked Beans
Baked Mixed Beans
Nontraditional Baked Beans
Beans with Ham
Beans with Lamb
Black Beans with Rice
Jedra
Chili con Carne

About Dried Beans . . .

The following recipes are written for dried beans instead of canned, partly for uniformity, partly because so many more kinds of beans are available in dried form. If your supermarket doesn't have a wide choice of beans, a health food store is almost certain to.

Eating cooked dried beans causes intestinal gas in most people; however, it has recently been discovered that the factor that causes the gas leaches out into the water in which beans are soaked before cooking. If you discard the soaking water and cook the beans in a fresh batch of water, you shouldn't have trouble with gas. Lentils and split peas don't seem to give the trouble that the rest of the tribe do.

The old way to prepare dried beans for cooking is to soak them overnight in plenty of cold water. A newer way is to cover the beans with a good deal of water, bring them to a boil and boil for 3 minutes. Turn off the heat and let the beans set for one hour. Whichever method you've used, you then drain the beans and cook them in fresh water according to your recipe.

Cooking time varies for different kinds of beans. Lentils cook in about 20 minutes and need no presoaking; navy beans need soaking, and take 1 to 2 hours to cook, or sometimes more. Cooking time also may vary from batch to batch of the same kind of beans.

You should always pick through dried beans before soaking to remove grains of wheat, small stones, or clumps of dirt.

Boston Baked Beans

Real, old-style New England baked beans. Some people use maple syrup in place of the molasses and brown sugar. There are several opinions on the proper bean to use for this dish, but I like navy beans. Boston baked bread (page 249) and coleslaw (pages 194–95) round out the meal. Fruit pie is a good choice for dessert, as are baked apples (page 298), which can share the oven for the last hour of cooking.

1 pound (about 2¼ cups)
dried navy or pea
beans

¼ cup molasses

1 tablespoon brown
sugar

½ teaspoon dry mustard

1 teaspoon salt

1 small onion, peeled
and left whole
(optional)

¼ pound salt pork, cut
into ½-inch cubes, or
¼ pound bacon, cut
into 1-inch strips

Boiling water

Pick over the beans and rinse them in several changes of water. Add 3 quarts water to the beans, and soak overnight, or boil them for 3 minutes and let soak in the same water for an hour or two. Drain the beans, cover with 2 quarts fresh water, and boil until the skins curl when you pick up a few beans in a spoon and blow on them (an old Yankee test). This usually takes half an hour to an hour of cooking.

Drain the beans and put them into a 3-quart nonmetal casserole with a close-fitting lid. Mix the molasses, brown sugar, salt, and dry mustard into the beans and add salt if desired, remembering that bacon and salt pork are salty. Bury the onion in the middle of the beans, then push the pieces of salt pork or bacon in around it. Add enough boiling water to cover the beans, cover the casserole, and bake 5 to 7 hours at 275°. Look at the beans occasionally, and add more boiling water if they aren't covered with liquid.

About half an hour before serving, remove the cover. Don't add any more water so that the top layer of beans will dry out and become crisp.

MAKES 2 QUARTS; SERVES 6 TO 8.

Baked Mixed Beans

A good variation on Boston baked beans. Corn bread (page 247) or Boston baked bread (page 249) go well with this.

½ cup dried lima beans
½ cup dried kidney beans
½ cup dried pinto beans
½ cup dried navy beans
¼ cup molasses
2 tablespoons honey
1½ teaspoons dry mustard
1½ teaspoons ground ginger
1½ teaspoons salt
1 small onion, peeled and minced
3 strips bacon, cut into squares
Boiling water

Pick over the beans, rinse them in several changes of water, and soak them overnight in 2 quarts of water. Drain them, cover with 2 quarts fresh water, and boil until tender but not mushy, about 1 hour. Blow on a spoonful of beans; if the skins split and curl, the beans are done.

Mix together the molasses, honey, mustard, ginger, and salt. Drain the beans, mix them with the onion, and put them into a 3-quart casserole. Poke the pieces of bacon in among the beans. Pour the molasses mixture over the top, then pour enough boiling water over the beans to cover them. Cover the casserole with a lid.

Bake in a very slow oven (225°) for about 5 hours. Check the beans from time to time to see that they are still covered with liquid, and add more boiling water if not. To give the beans a crusted top, remove the cover half an hour before they're done.

SERVES 4 TO 6.

Nontraditional Baked Beans

A nonsweet variation on baked beans, with rum added. This has more meat than baked beans usually do.

1 pound (2¼ cups) dried pea beans
½ pound ham, cut in chunks (1½ cups)
3 slices bacon, cut in squares
2 onions, peeled and chopped
1 clove garlic, peeled and minced
6 tablespoons rum
1 teaspoon dry mustard
½ teaspoon salt
½ teaspoon dried savory
¼ teaspoon black pepper
Boiling water

Pick over and rinse the beans. Cover them with 3 quarts water and either soak them overnight or boil them for 3 minutes and then let them soak for a couple of hours.

Drain the beans, cover them with 2 quarts fresh water, and boil for about 1 hour or until just tender.

Drain the beans again and mix with the ham, bacon, onion, and garlic; put them into a 3-quart casserole. Mix ¼ cup of the rum with the seasonings, pour it over the beans, and add boiling water to just cover the beans. Cover the casserole and bake at 350° for 1 hour. Add boiling water as necessary from time to time to keep the beans just barely covered. After the beans have cooked for an hour, remove the cover, add the remaining 2 tablespoons of rum, and continue cooking for an additional half hour to brown the top.

SERVES 4 TO 6.

Beans with Ham

A traditional favorite in central Illinois, this is usually served with corn bread (page 247) or cornmeal muffins (pages 265–66).

1 meaty ham bone
1 pound (2¼ cups) dried navy or pea beans
Salt and black pepper to taste
Pinch of cayenne pepper
¼ teaspoon dried savory (optional)

The night before you plan to serve this dish, cut the fat off the ham bone. Put the bone and 2 quarts of water into a large pot, bring to a boil, and simmer gently for 2 or 3 hours.

Meanwhile, pick over the beans and rinse them well. Cover with 3 quarts water, and leave to soak overnight.

When the ham bone has cooked for 2 or 3 hours, long enough so that the meat comes easily off the bone, turn off the heat and let the ham cool in the stock overnight. In the morning, skim the fat from the broth and chill the ham and bone in the broth until you are ready to continue cooking.

About 1½ hours before you wish to serve supper, drain the beans and add them to the ham broth; bring to a boil and simmer gently until the beans are cooked. They should be tender but whole, and there should be plenty of broth. Remove the ham bone and break up the meat and return it to the broth. Season to taste with salt, black pepper, cayenne pepper, and savory. Serve hot, in soup bowls.

SERVES 4 TO 6.

Beans with Lamb

A hearty stew that is good with a green salad and French bread.

½ pound (1¼ cups) navy
  beans
1 strip bacon
1½ pounds bony lamb
1 bay leaf
1 small onion, peeled
  and chopped
1 clove garlic, peeled and
  minced
1 small potato, peeled
  and cubed

1 pound tomatoes, fresh,
  frozen, or canned
¼ teaspoon dried basil
¼ teaspoon dried thyme
¼ teaspoon dried parsley
Dash cayenne pepper
Salt and black pepper to
  taste

Sort and rinse the beans; cover them with about 2 inches of water, bring to a boil, and simmer for 3 minutes. Turn off the heat and leave the beans to soak for an hour or two.

Meanwhile, fry the bacon in another pot. Brown the lamb in the bacon fat, then cover with 2 cups of water, bring to a boil, and simmer for half an hour.

Drain the beans and add them to the lamb along with the bay leaf, onion, garlic, and 1 cup of water. Cook for about 1 hour, or until the beans are almost done. At this point you can let the stew cool, to be finished later.

Add the potato cubes, tomatoes, herbs, cayenne, salt, and black pepper and simmer for about 20 minutes, or until the potato cubes are tender. Serve hot.

SERVES 4.

Black Beans with Rice

This is a delicious Cuban dish. Drain the beans before adding water and rice, so that there will be just enough water to cook the rice but leave no extra liquid.

1 pound (2¼ cups) black
  beans
1½ cups rice
1 bay leaf
4 whole cloves
2 medium onions, peeled
  and chopped fine
3 cloves garlic, peeled
  and minced
1 green pepper, washed,
  seeded, and cut into
  small pieces

½ cup olive oil
½ pound ham, cut in
  small pieces (about 1½
  cups)
About 2 teaspoons salt
Black pepper
Dash cayenne pepper

Pick over and rinse the beans. Soak them overnight in 3 quarts water; or boil the beans in the water for 3 minutes and let them set for an hour or two.

About an hour and a half before you plan to eat, drain the beans and cover them with 2 quarts water. Boil for 40 minutes, or until the beans are tender but not quite cooked. Drain the beans; add the rice, 1 quart water, the bay leaf and cloves, and half of the onion, garlic, and green pepper. Cook gently until the rice is done, about 20 minutes. Check occasionally to make sure that there is enough water in the pot.

Meanwhile, heat the olive oil in a frying pan and add the ham and the remaining onion, garlic, and green pepper. Sauté, stirring occasionally, until the ham and vegetables are beginning to brown. When the rice is cooked, stir in the fried mixture with all of the olive oil, and season to taste with salt, black pepper, and cayenne pepper. Serve hot or at room temperature.

SERVES 8 TO 10.

Jedra

Sometimes called Esau's dish, this is one of my favorite basic bean dishes. It cooks quite quickly, and with pita bread and a salad it makes a satisfying meal.

1 cup lentils
½ cup raw rice
¼ cup olive oil
2 or 3 onions, peeled
   and sliced

¾ teaspoon salt
Pepper

Pick over the lentils and rinse them in 2 or 3 changes of water. Put the lentils and 3 cups of water in a heavy saucepan and bring to a boil. Simmer, covered, for 20 minutes. Add the rice and continue to cook for another 20 minutes, or until both rice and lentils are tender. Add a little water if the mixture threatens to dry out and stick to the pan.

Meanwhile, heat the olive oil in a frying pan and add the sliced onions; cook, stirring, until the onions are limp and beginning to brown. When the lentil–rice mixture is cooked, stir in the onions and the salt and pepper. Adjust seasoning to your taste, and serve hot or at room temperature.

SERVES 3.

Chili con Carne

Chili recipes vary widely; this version is medium-hot. Chili reheats well.

1 pound (2¼ cups) dried
   red kidney beans
2½ pounds ground beef
3 tablespoons olive oil
2 large onions, peeled
   and chopped
4 cloves garlic, peeled
   and minced
3 to 4 cups tomato purée

1 tablespoon vinegar or
   lemon juice
2 tablespoons hot chili
   powder
One 6-ounce can tomato
   paste
1 teaspoon salt
½ cup beer, red wine, or
   water

Pick over and rinse the beans. Cover them with 3 quarts water, bring to a boil, and boil for 3 minutes; remove from the heat and let set for an hour or two. Drain the beans and cover them with fresh water, then simmer until done, anywhere from 20 minutes to an hour or more. Set aside.

Meanwhile, in a heavy pot, cook the ground beef, a pound at a time, until it loses its pink color; remove and set aside.

Add the olive oil to the pan and sauté the onions and garlic until the onions just begin to brown. Return the beef to the pan along with the tomato purée, vinegar, chili powder, tomato paste, and salt. Use the ½ cup of liquid (beer, wine, or water) to rinse out the cans of tomato purée and tomato paste and then add it to the meat. Bring the contents of the pot to a gentle boil and simmer, covered, for 20 minutes to 1 hour. Stir occasionally, and add a little more liquid if it seems to be getting too thick.

The seasoning of chili is a very personal matter; some like it mild, some like it hot. Also, chili powder is not a pure spice, but a mixture of spices. Two tablespoons of hot chili powder in this dish is about right for my taste.

When you are ready to serve the chili, heat the beans to a boil, drain them, add to the hot chili, and mix well. Adjust the seasoning and serve.

SERVES 6 TO 8.

Pasta and Pizza

Pasta with Pine Nuts
Clam Sauce for Pasta
Spaghetti Sauce with Meat
Pasta Salad
Pasta with Tomatoes

Pizza

Pasta

To cook pasta, bring plenty of salted water to a vigorous boil in a large pot. You need 3 or 4 quarts of water for a half pound of pasta, 5 or 6 quarts for a pound. Add the pasta, watching the pot carefully while you bring it to a boil again; it's apt to boil over suddenly. Stir the pasta sometimes as it cooks, so that the pieces swim about freely and do not stick together. Start timing after it reaches the boil. Very thin pastas, such as linguini and angel hair, cook in a couple of minutes. Thick pastas like macaroni take longer, about 15 minutes. Occasionally remove a piece of pasta from the boiling water and taste it; properly cooked pasta will be firm, not mushy. Drain the pasta, sauce it, and serve immediately.

The best dried pastas are Italian, made from 100 percent semolina flour. Fresh pastas, often available in the freezer case of a good market or delicatessen, cook in about half the time it takes for dried pasta.

If pasta is to be your main dish, allow about 4 ounces (1/4 pound) of uncooked pasta per person. If it is to replace rice or potatoes as a side dish, allow about 2 ounces of uncooked pasta for each person.

Pasta with Pine Nuts

This side dish is quick and simple.

2 tablespoons olive oil
2 tablespoons margarine
1/2 pound freshly cooked
    hot vermicelli or
    linguini
Salt and pepper to taste

1/4 cup pine nuts, or tiny
    new peas, cooked
    briefly
Grated Romano cheese
    (optional)

Toss the oil and margarine with the hot pasta; add salt and pepper to taste. Stir in the pine nuts or peas and top with cheese if desired. Serve immediately.

SERVES 4.

Clam Sauce for Pasta

Easy and very good.

About 2 dozen raw
  clams in the shell, to
  give about ¾ to 1 cup
  meat, or one 7-ounce
  can minced clams
1 clove garlic, peeled and
  minced
4 large mushrooms,
  sliced

3 tablespoons olive oil
Dash of freshly ground
  pepper
2 or 3 tablespoons
  grated Romano cheese,
  optional

Scrub the clams and set them in a large pan containing about 1 inch of cold water. Cover the pot and cook over medium heat just until the clams open, about 20 minutes. Discard any that didn't open. Save the broth to use in fish soup. Remove the clams from their shells, chop, and set aside. If using canned clams, drain them, rinse with cold water, and drain again. Cook your pasta now.

Sauté the garlic and mushrooms in the olive oil until they begin to color. Add the chopped clams and the pepper; serve immediately on hot, drained pasta. Top with grated Romano cheese.

MAKES ENOUGH SAUCE FOR ½ POUND OF FETTUCCINE OR OTHER PASTA; SERVES 2.

Spaghetti Sauce
with Meat

2 cloves garlic, peeled
and minced
3 medium-large onions,
peeled and chopped
6 tablespoons olive oil
1 pound lean ground
beef
1 carrot, skinned and
sliced thin
1 stalk celery, scrubbed
and sliced thin

½ pound mushrooms,
sliced
2 pounds chopped
tomatoes, either fresh
or canned
One 6-ounce can tomato
paste
¾ cup dry red wine
1 teaspoon dried basil
About ½ teaspoon salt
Cayenne pepper to taste

In a large saucepan brown the garlic and onions lightly in
¼ cup of the olive oil. Remove the onions and garlic from the pan
and reserve. Brown the ground beef until it is no longer pink,
breaking it up with the edge of a spoon. Remove the beef from the
pan and drain off excess fat. Add the remaining 2 tablespoons of
olive oil to the pan, lower the heat, and sauté the carrot, celery,
and mushrooms until limp.

Return the onions, garlic, and ground beef to the pan and add
the tomatoes, tomato paste, wine, basil, salt, and cayenne. Cover
the pot and simmer slowly for 1 or 2 hours, stirring occasionally.

To thicken the sauce, remove the cover and let it reduce; add
water or wine to thin it. The sauce freezes well.

MAKES ABOUT 2 QUARTS OF SAUCE, OR ENOUGH FOR 2 POUNDS OF
SPAGHETTI; SERVES 8.

Pasta Salad

A basic salad to which all sorts of things can be added. Try substituting chopped pimientos and pickled artichoke hearts for the jalapeño sauce, eggs, and peanuts. This multiplies easily for a crowd.

½ pound pasta such as
  bows or small elbow
  macaroni
2 tablespoons olive oil
1 tablespoon vinegar or
  lemon juice
1 tablespoon finely
  chopped onion

2 teaspoons jalapeño
  sauce
2 hard-boiled eggs,
  peeled and chopped
6 tablespoons peanuts,
  chopped
Salt and pepper

Cook the pasta al dente and drain thoroughly. Toss it with the oil, vinegar, onion, and jalapeño sauce. Cover the salad and refrigerate it until ready to use, or just let it cool for a minute or two before proceeding. (Cooked pasta tossed with oil keeps well in the refrigerator in a large plastic bag.) Add the chopped hard-boiled eggs and the peanuts, adjust the seasoning, toss, and serve.

SERVES 4.

Pasta with Tomatoes

Especially good in August, when tomatoes from your garden or a roadside stand are at their peak.

1 cup, or ¼ pound,
uncooked pasta, such
as elbow macaroni or
small shells
2 tablespoons olive oil
Salt and pepper to taste
3 leaves fresh basil,
minced, or a generous
pinch dried basil

1 clove garlic, peeled and
minced
2 tablespoons pine nuts
2 tomatoes, cut in
chunks (about 2 cups)

Cook the pasta in about 6 cups boiling salted water until firm but not mushy. Drain well and toss with the olive oil, salt, and pepper. Let set a few minutes to cool, then toss with the rest of the ingredients and serve.

SERVES 4.

Pizza

In Italy pizza is often made without any cheese at all. Pizza dough can wait very well if you want to make it up ahead of time. It will continue to rise, so you should knead it down about every hour and a half.

Pizza dough

1 cup warm water
1 package active dry
yeast
1 teaspoon sugar
1 teaspoon salt

2 tablespoons any
vegetable oil or olive
oil
About 3 cups flour

Put the water in a warmed mixing bowl and sprinkle the yeast over it; add the sugar and salt. Let set about 5 minutes, then add the oil and most of the flour and knead until very smooth, about 5 minutes. Add more flour as necessary to get a good elastic dough. (You can let the dough rest a while at this point.)

Scrape the flour off the countertop, divide the dough in two, and roll out each piece into a circle about 12 inches in diameter. (The countertop should be reasonably free of flour, so that you can roll the dough out very thin.) Put each circle of dough on a lightly greased baking sheet and let rise for about 20 minutes. Preheat the oven to 425°.

Tomato sauce

One 6-ounce can tomato
  paste
$\frac{1}{2}$ cup hot water
$\frac{1}{2}$ teaspoon dried
  oregano
$\frac{1}{2}$ teaspoon dried basil
$\frac{1}{2}$ teaspoon salt
Dash cayenne pepper

Mix the tomato paste, water, oregano, basil, salt, and cayenne together and spread half of it on each pizza, being careful not to spread it right to the edge of the dough.

Strew the top with any or all of the following:

Pizza toppings

Ground beef, bulk sausage, Italian sausage, sliced
  salami, sliced pepperoni, cooked tiny shrimp,
  olives, chopped onion, chopped green pepper,
  cooked or canned mushrooms, sliced olives,
  anchovies
$\frac{1}{2}$ pound sliced or grated kasseri cheese
2 tablespoons olive oil
1 teaspoon oregano
$\frac{1}{4}$ cup grated Romano cheese

If using raw meat such as ground beef or sausage, cook it first in a frying pan until it is no longer pink. Drain off the fat. Fresh mushrooms should also be sautéed before use. Cool the meat or mushrooms slightly before placing them on the pizza. Onion and green pepper don't need to be precooked.

Finish by sprinkling with the following:

Final topping

>   2 tablespoons Romano cheese (optional)
>   1 tablespoon olive oil
>   ½ teaspoon dried oregano
>   Hot red pepper flakes (optional)

Bake for about 15 minutes, or until done. Serve immediately.
MAKES TWO 12-INCH PIZZAS.

Eggs, Granola, and Sandwiches

Boiled Eggs
Scrambled Eggs
   Scrambled Eggs with Bacon
Omelet
Frittata

Granola

Western Sandwich
Toasted Cheese Sandwiches
Grilled Kasseri Sandwich
Melt Sandwich
Mushrooms on Toast

See also:

Boiled Eggs

Put eggs into a panful of cold tap water, about 2 cups for 1 or 2 eggs, about 4 cups for 4 to 6 eggs. Cover the pan and bring the water to a gentle boil. Time the eggs when the water just starts to boil; boiling for about 2 minutes gives a very soft-boiled egg, 7 minutes gives an egg in which the white is solid and the yolk is still a bit soft, and 10 minutes gives a hard-boiled egg. Please see caution concerning raw and lightly cooked eggs on page 4. Remove the eggs from the water immediately with a slotted spoon. Plunge hard-boiled eggs into cold water right away to make it easier to peel off the shells. (Very fresh eggs may be difficult to peel no matter what you do.) Eggs that have been around too long are apt to crack during boiling; if you think you'll have trouble with this, prick a small hole in the pointed end of each egg with a darning needle. Starting the raw eggs in cold water and bringing it slowly to a boil will help keep the eggs from cracking.

Grandmother's description of a tough hard-boiled person may help you remember how long to cook eggs—"He's as hard as a 10-minute egg."

Scrambled Eggs

Scrambled eggs are usually prepared with milk or cream, but they are just as good or better when you use water instead.

Allow 2 eggs, 2 teaspoons of water, salt and pepper,
and about 2 teaspoons of margarine per person.

Melt the margarine in a pan set over moderate heat. Mix the eggs and water in a bowl and pour them into the pan. Cook over medium heat, stirring constantly with a fork, until the eggs are the consistency you like. Serve immediately with a little salt and a grating of pepper. (Eggs scrambled in a cast-iron skillet taste just fine, but look slightly gray.)

Scrambled Eggs with Bacon

A quick, light main dish.

Add 1 strip of bacon for every 2 eggs, and omit the margarine. Sauté the bacon until crisp; remove the bacon from the pan and crumble it. Add the bacon bits to the eggs and water, and scramble the eggs in the bacon fat.

Omelet

Opinions vary widely on how to make omelets. Some add cream to the eggs, some add milk, some use water, and some use no liquid at all. The following is a plain, everyday, more or less French omelet. It makes a quick and inexpensive lunch or supper.

> 2 eggs
> 2 teaspoons water
> Pinch of salt
> 2 teaspoons margarine for the pan

Optional fillings

> 2 mushrooms, sliced and sautéed lightly in margarine
> 1/4 cup diced cooked chicken
> 2 tablespoons jelly

Although a special omelet pan with curving sides is not necessary, a fairly heavy nonstick or well-seasoned pan is—otherwise, the omelet will stick. The pan size is important; if it's too small, the omelet will be too thick to cook through. If it is too big, the omelet may be overcooked before you can rescue it. A 6-inch pan is about right for a 2-egg omelet, an 8-inch pan would be better for a 3-egg omelet. Small omelets are easier to deal with. It is better to make two 2-egg omelets than one 4-egg omelet.

Heat the pan medium-hot. Meanwhile briefly mix the eggs,

water, and salt in a small bowl with a fork; you don't want a frothy mixture.

Add the margarine to the pan, and when it foams and begins to brown, pour in the eggs all at once. Cook only a couple of minutes, until the bottom is set and the top not quite cooked. Lift up the edges from time to time with a spatula, to check progress. It's okay if some of the uncooked egg runs down around the edge when you do this. If you wish to fill the omelet lay the filling ingredient on half of the omelet now. Fold the other half of the omelet over the filling, and serve immediately.

SERVES 1.

Frittata

This Italian omelet makes a good quick meal. You can substitute other vegetables for the zucchini and mushrooms.

2 large mushrooms, cleaned and sliced thin	3 eggs
	Pinch of salt
3 tablespoons olive oil	Dash of pepper
2 inches of a medium-sized zucchini cut into small cubes or thin slices	2 tablespoons grated Romano cheese (optional)

Heat a large heavy frying pan, about 9 inches in diameter. Sauté the mushrooms in the oil until lightly browned. Remove them from the pan and reserve; sauté the zucchini over medium heat, covered, for several minutes, stirring occasionally, until it also is lightly browned. Turn the heat to medium-low and return the mushrooms to the pan. Remove the pan from the heat while you prepare the eggs.

Break the eggs into a small bowl, add the salt and pepper, and beat with a fork until the eggs are reasonably well blended. Pour the egg mixture over the vegetables in the pan; quickly spread the vegetables out to distribute them evenly. Return the pan to the heat and cook until the frittata holds together pretty well, about 4 minutes. Loosen the frittata from the pan, then turn it over as you would a pancake. Cook for about a minute longer, until the frittata is done.

Sprinkle with the cheese if you use it, fold the frittata in half, and serve immediately.

SERVES 2.

Granola

Homemade granola is much less sweet than the store-bought product. Eat this as is or pour fruit juice over it.

4 cups rolled oats	1/2 cup sesame seed
3/4 cup unsweetened coconut, shredded or flaked	1/2 teaspoon salt
	1/2 cup honey
	1/2 cup vegetable oil
1 cup chopped nuts— almonds, peanuts, or whatever you like	1 cup raisins or other dried fruit cut into raisin-sized pieces
1/2 cup wheat germ	(optional)

Preheat the oven to 300°. Mix the dry ingredients in a large bowl. Heat the honey and oil in a saucepan until they combine, then stir into the oatmeal mixture. Spread the granola out in a 11- by 18-inch baking pan and bake for about 30 minutes.

Twice during the baking period, remove the pan briefly from the oven and stir the contents. Watch carefully near the end of the specified time, as the cereal goes from nicely toasted to burned very quickly. Remove the granola from the oven, stir once more, and cool in the pan to room temperature.

Stir in the dried fruit if you use it, and store the granola in a closely covered container.

MAKES ABOUT 2 QUARTS OF CEREAL.

Western Sandwich

1 egg
½ teaspoon minced
    onion
1 tablespoon minced
    green pepper
About 1 tablespoon
    cooked meat such as
    ham, pepperoni, or
    salami, cut into small
    pieces

Salt and pepper
1 tablespoon margarine
    or vegetable oil
2 slices bread

Mix the egg, onion, green pepper, meat, and some salt and pepper in a small bowl. Heat a small frying pan and add the oil or margarine; tilt the pan to grease it all over. Pour the egg mixture into the pan and cook without stirring just until set, then turn the western over and cook the other side. Serve immediately on bread with a spicy sauce, like A-1 sauce, if desired.

MAKES 1 SANDWICH.

Toasted Cheese Sandwiches

Plain-Jane, all-American toasted cheese sandwiches. The secret is in choosing your cheese wisely; it should melt well, and must be either milk-free or made from 100 percent sheep's milk.

Slices of bread, spread with margarine on one side
Sliced sheep's milk kasseri cheese (if you can have
    sheep's milk products), or sliced Soya Kaas
    mozzarella-style soy cheese
Sliced lunchmeat, or strips of cooked bacon (optional)

Heat a skillet to medium-hot and place a slice of bread, margarined side down, in the skillet. Top with the cheese, and the meat if you use it. (Soya Kaas is very bland, and will taste better if you use something flavorful such as pepperoni with it.) Top the sandwich with the second slice of bread, margarined side up.

Toast until the bottom slice is pleasantly browned, then turn the sandwich over and cook until the sandwich is hot and the cheese melted.

SERVE AT ONCE.

Grilled Kasseri Sandwich

The sophisticated old-world cousin of a toasted open-faced cheese sandwich. Greek kasseri cheese is made from sheep's milk; avoid domestic kasseri, which is usually made with cow's milk. With fresh fruit, this makes a wonderful lunch.

Sliced French bread or halves of pita bread
Sliced kasseri cheese made from 100 percent sheep's
 milk
Minced garlic
Olive oil

Top the bread with the kasseri, sprinkle some minced garlic over the cheese, and then drizzle a little olive oil over all. Broil just until the cheese is melted. Serve immediately.

Melt Sandwich

With a bowl of soup, this makes a good snack or light meal. Make sure that the cheese is free of lactose or of cow's milk.

4 mushrooms, cleaned
  and sliced
1 tablespoon margarine
1 slice bread
¼ cup fresh sprouts
Sliced olives (optional)

2 slices tomato, or about
  4 slices dill pickle
1 slice sheep's milk
  kasseri cheese or 1
  slice Soya Kaas soy
  cheese

Sauté the mushrooms in the margarine. Spread the bread with a little additional margarine, and pile on the mushrooms and all the other ingredients in the order listed. (You might want to sprinkle the sprouts or tomato with a little salt.) Broil until the cheese is nicely melted, just a couple of minutes. Serve immediately.
MAKES 1 OPEN-FACED SANDWICH.

Mushrooms on Toast

This is a popular luncheon dish near Kennett Square, the heart of the Pennsylvania mushroom-growing country.

12 ounces mushrooms,
  cleaned and sliced
3 tablespoons margarine
2½ tablespoons flour
1 cup beef broth, or 1
  cup water plus 1 beef
  bouillon cube

1 tablespoon sherry
  (optional)
Salt and pepper if needed
4 pieces toast

Sauté the mushrooms in the margarine in a skillet until they give up their moisture. Remove the pan from the heat and stir in

149

the flour until it is thoroughly moistened. Stir in the broth or water and crumble the bouillon cube (if used) into the pan.

Return the pan to the heat and cook, stirring constantly, until the mixture has simmered gently for 2 minutes or so—until the sauce is thick and smooth. Stir in the sherry, season to taste with salt and pepper, and serve immediately on toast.

SERVES 2.

Pancakes and Waffles

Pancakes
   Apple Pancakes
   Blueberry Pancakes
   Cornmeal Pancakes
Whole Wheat Pancakes
   Apple Whole Wheat
   Pancakes
Yeast-raised Pancakes

Waffles
Yeast-raised Waffles
French Toast

About Making Pancakes . . .

Pancakes are easy to make, and are a good choice if people will be showing up for breakfast at different times—the batter will keep well for several hours in the refrigerator, and you can cook up fresh hot pancakes for each new arrival. It's nice to bake pancakes in an electric frying pan at the table, so that the cook can socialize.

Pancake batter should be beaten only briefly; overbeating will make the pancakes tough. Lumpy pancake batter is okay.

If you cannot eat eggs, substitute 2 tablespoons of water for 1 egg in the recipes for pancakes.

A setting of 375° is about right for cooking pancakes on most electric frying pans. Use medium-high heat if you cook on top of the stove. An old way of testing to see whether a skillet is hot enough is to flip a few drops of water onto it; if the drops bounce and dance before disappearing from your dry ungreased frying pan, it is ready.

Cook pancakes in the hot frying pan until the tops are bubbly and the bottoms browned. Turn the pancakes over to cook the other side. Four minutes per side is usually enough.

Pancakes

If you like, put 1 or 2 tablespoons of cornmeal into the cup before you measure the flour. This gives a good texture, though it isn't necessary.

1 cup flour	2½ tablespoons
3 tablespoons sugar	margarine
2¼ teaspoons baking	¾ cup water
powder	1 egg or 2 tablespoons
¼ teaspoon salt	water

Sift the flour, sugar, baking powder, and salt together into a mixing bowl.

Heat a frying pan and melt the margarine in it. Tip the pan from side to side to grease it well all over. Pour out the melted margarine into a small bowl, add the water and egg, and mix well. Stir liquid into the flour mixture until it's thoroughly moistened. It is okay if the batter is still lumpy. Cook the pancakes according to directions on page 153. Serve hot with margarine and honey, brown sugar, or maple syrup.

MAKES 6 PANCAKES; SERVES 3.

Apple Pancakes

Add half a small apple that has been peeled, cored, and coarsely grated (⅓ cup). Mix the grated apple into the sifted dry ingredients before you add the liquid mixture.

Blueberry Pancakes

Stir about ½ cup fresh or frozen blueberries into the batter just before you add the liquids. Small blueberries, if you can get them, are much better than big ones.

Cornmeal Pancakes

Substitute cornmeal for half the flour.

Whole Wheat Pancakes

⅓ cup white flour
2 tablespoons sugar
1½ teaspoons baking powder
¼ teaspoon salt
⅓ cup whole wheat flour

2 teaspoons wheat germ or bran
1½ tablespoons margarine
½ cup water
1 egg or 2 tablespoons water

Heat a frying pan and melt the margarine in it. Tip the pan from side to side as you do this, so that the margarine will grease the pan all over.

Sift the white flour, sugar, baking powder, and salt together into a bowl. Stir in the whole wheat flour and the wheat germ or bran.

In a small bowl mix together the water, egg, and melted margarine from the skillet, then stir this mixture into the dry ingredients and continue stirring just until the flour is all moistened. The batter can be a little lumpy; if you beat too much the pancakes will be tough.

Cook the pancakes and serve them hot with margarine and brown sugar, honey, or maple sugar.

MAKES 4 PANCAKES; SERVES 2.

Apple Whole Wheat Pancakes

Add ½ small apple that has been peeled, cored, and grated (about 3 tablespoons grated apple). Toss the grated apple with the dry ingredients just before adding the liquids.

Yeast-raised Pancakes

These are adapted from a family recipe that was written down about 1880. They are easy to make, unusual, and good, but must be started the night before you plan to cook them. They are then quick to cook in the morning. Please refer to the section on dealing with yeast (pages 215–17). If you prefer, you can use all white flour instead of white and whole wheat.

¾ cup warm water
1¼ teaspoons
   (½ package) active dry
   yeast
2 tablespoons sugar
¼ teaspoon salt
½ cup whole wheat
   flour

½ cup white flour
1 egg or 2 tablespoons
   warm water
2 tablespoons margarine,
   melted

Put the water into a medium-sized mixing bowl and sprinkle the yeast over it; add the sugar and the salt and stir well. Add the flour, then beat briefly by hand until the batter is smooth. Cover the bowl with aluminum foil or plastic wrap and refrigerate it overnight or longer.

When you are ready for the pancakes, beat the egg and the melted margarine into the batter. Cook the pancakes according to directions on page 153.

MAKES 6 PANCAKES; SERVES 2 OR 3 PEOPLE.

How to Use a Waffle Iron

If you have a new, unused waffle iron, brush both of the cooking surfaces thoroughly with melted margarine; do not use oil! Plan to cook one waffle more than you plan to eat, as you will almost certainly have to throw the first one away. (When the waffle iron is well seasoned after several uses, you won't have to allow for this throw-away waffle.)

Preheat an electric waffle iron until the light goes out (about 5 minutes), then add enough batter to not quite cover the bottom plate of the waffle iron. Close the waffle iron and cook the waffle until the light goes out again; this should take about 5 minutes.

For a modern waffle iron with a temperature control, you may need to experiment to find the right temperature. On a scale of 1 to 5, 3½ is apt to be right. Undercooked waffles will stick to the grids. As for overcooked waffles, you'll know them when you see them.

When you have finished cooking waffles, unplug the waffle iron and leave it standing open until cool.

There is no need to wash a waffle iron after use; it will only remove the seasoned surface you have just created, and make the next batch of waffles stick.

Waffles

The basic waffle. Beating the egg white separately makes these lighter than most. Serve waffles hot with margarine and honey, maple syrup, or brown sugar.

2½ tablespoons (⅓ stick) margarine, melted	1½ teaspoons baking powder
½ cup plus 1 tablespoon flour	¼ teaspoon salt
1 tablespoon sugar	1 egg, separated
	½ cup water

Preheat the waffle iron, and melt the margarine in a small pan. Sift the flour, sugar, baking powder, and salt together into a bowl. In a small bowl beat the egg white until stiff.

Add the egg yolk, water, and melted margarine to the sifted dry ingredients and stir together just until smooth. Fold in the beaten egg white, pour onto the waffle iron, and cook according to directions for your waffle maker.

MAKES ONE 10-INCH SQUARE WAFFLE; SERVES 2.

Yeast-raised Waffles

Make the batter the night before you want to cook these. They are not as light as baking powder waffles, but they taste pleasantly of yeast. See page 215 for advice on yeast.

1 teaspoon active dry yeast	¾ cup flour
¾ cup warm water	3 tablespoons margarine, melted
2 teaspoons sugar	1 egg
⅛ teaspoon salt	

157

Dissolve the yeast in the water; add the sugar and salt, then the flour, and beat until smooth. Cover well, and refrigerate overnight.

In the morning, melt the margarine and heat the waffle iron. Add the egg and the melted margarine to the batter and beat with a rotary eggbeater until smooth. To get a lighter waffle, set the bowl into a large bowl full of very warm water for a few minutes to warm the batter. Bake according to directions for your waffle maker.

MAKES ONE 10-INCH SQUARE WAFFLE; SERVES 2.

French Toast

Very easy to make, and a good one for overage bread.

1 egg	Pinch of salt
¼ cup water	4 slices bread
2 teaspoons sugar	Margarine for sautéeing

Put the egg, water, sugar, and salt into a shallow dish; mix them together with a fork. Dip both sides of each slice of bread briefly into the mixture, and sauté the slices in a little margarine until lightly browned. Turn once during cooking. Serve immediately with margarine and honey, maple syrup, or brown sugar.

MAKES 4 PIECES OF FRENCH TOAST; SERVES 2.

Vegetables

Artichokes
Jerusalem Artichokes
Asparagus
Green Beans
  Wax Beans
Lima Beans
Beets
  Harvard Beets
Broccoli
  Chinese-style Broccoli
Brussels Sprouts
Cabbage
Carrots
Cauliflower
Celery
Chayotes
  Stuffed Chayotes
Corn on the Cob
Eggplant

Greens: Spinach, Kale,
   Collards, Mustard
   Greens, Beet Greens,
   Swiss Chard
Kohlrabi
Mushrooms
Parsnips
Peas
Sugar Snap Peas
   (Edible-pod Peas)
Peppers (Bell Peppers)
Spaghetti Squash
Summer Squash
   Hot Zucchini Salad
Baked Winter Squash
   Steamed Winter
   Squash
   Winter Squash with
   Potatoes
Tomatoes
   Stewed Tomatoes
Turnips or Rutabagas

Vegetables are best when young, tender, and as fresh as you can get them. It makes a big difference to the cooking time how old the vegetable was when picked, and exactly how big the pieces are, so the cooking times given can only be approximate.

Artichokes

The edible parts of an artichoke are the innermost fleshy part, called the heart, and the bases of the leaves. You eat the leaves one at a time by dipping them into the sauce and pulling off the soft pulp with your teeth. When you get to the center of the artichoke, cut out and discard the fuzzy choke, then cut the heart into bite-sized portions.

2 artichokes	2 tablespoons olive oil
2 cloves garlic, peeled and sliced	¼ cup margarine, melted
	Pinch of salt
2 tablespoons, plus 2 teaspoons, lemon juice	

Rinse the artichokes well, pull off any old or damaged bottom leaves, and cut off all but ¼ inch of the stem. (If you are serving artichokes to guests, you may want to cut off the spiny tips of the leaves with a scissors.) Arrange the artichokes in a pot large enough to hold them upright. Put 1 to 2 inches water in the pot and add the garlic, 2 tablespoons of the lemon juice, and olive oil. Bring to a boil and simmer, covered, for half an hour or longer—until it is easy to pull off one of the leaves.

Melt the margarine, add the remaining 2 teaspoons lemon juice and a pinch of salt, and serve in small bowls alongside the hot artichokes. Or serve at room temperature with little dishes of oil and vinegar dressing.

SERVES 2.

Jerusalem Artichokes

Jerusalem artichokes are not true artichokes; they resemble little potatoes, but have a sweeter flavor. Cook and serve as you would potatoes.

Peel the artichokes, then cut them into 1/4-inch slices and simmer just until tender, about 5 minutes. Drain, and serve with margarine, salt, pepper, and a few drops of lemon juice (optional).

1/2 POUND SERVES 2.

Asparagus

Asparagus stalks should be crisp; store with the cut ends in water until just before cooking. Since the lower ends of asparagus spears are apt to be tough, begin by snapping each spear in two, as near the lower end as it will break. Remove the scales with a knife or vegetable parer, and rinse the asparagus well.

You can stand the spears upright in a narrow pot into which you have put a little water. Simmer until the asparagus is tender but not limp, about 10 minutes. Or cook the asparagus laid flat in a pan with a little water.

Serve hot with salt, a little margarine, and a few drops of lemon juice, or cold with a little oil and vinegar dressing.

ALLOW 5 OR 6 SPEARS, OR MORE, OF FRESH ASPARAGUS FOR EACH PERSON.

Green Beans

Rinse the beans well and cut off the stem and blossom ends. If they are large, cut the beans into 1-inch lengths; otherwise leave them whole. Put them in a pan with about 1 inch of water, bring to a boil, and simmer just until they are tender, 5 to 10 minutes. Young tender beans cook more quickly than older beans. Drain, and serve with salt and a little margarine.

Or, you can sauté 1 clove of garlic, peeled and minced, in some olive oil and toss the beans in it. Whole green beans are good chilled and served with oil and vinegar dressing. A few thin slices of red onion add pizzazz. For ½ pound beans use 3 tablespoons olive oil, 1 tablespoon vinegar, ⅛ teaspoon salt, a dash of cayenne pepper, and 2 thin slices of red onion.

½ POUND GREEN BEANS SERVES 2.

Wax Beans

These are just like green beans, but pale yellow in color. Cook and serve them as you would their green cousins. Green beans and wax beans look pretty cooked and served together, either hot or in a salad.

Lima Beans

Very young lima beans have much better flavor than older ones.

To open a pod, grasp the stem end in one hand and the blossom end in the other and twist hard. Shell and rinse the beans, then simmer them gently in a covered pan for about 10 minutes, until just done. Salt the hot beans and serve them with a little margarine.

Allow about 1 pound of limas for 2 people if the beans are still in the pod; if the beans have already been shelled, allow about 6 ounces, or 1 cup, for 2 people.

Beets

Cut off the root ends and all but about 1 inch of the stems; scrub the beets well, and put them in a pot with enough water to cover. Bring to a boil and simmer, covered, for 30 or 40 minutes, or until the largest beet is tender when you attempt to pierce it with a fork.

Drain the beets and add some cold water to the pot to cool them. I recommend wearing rubber gloves to peel hot beets. Impale the beet through the stem end with a long fork; using a small knife, slip the skin off and then slice the beet if desired. Set the peeled beet in a warm place while you finish peeling the rest of the beets. Serve the beets hot with a little margarine and some salt.

½ POUND BEETS SERVES 2.

Harvard Beets

This is an old-fashioned way of preparing beets in a thickened sweet and sour sauce.

¼ cup sugar	⅛ teaspoon salt
1 teaspoon cornstarch	1 tablespoon margarine
¼ cup vinegar	1 pound cooked beets
¼ cup water	

Mix the first 6 ingredients together in a saucepan, bring to a boil, and simmer gently, stirring constantly, for about 1 minute, or until thick and clear. Pour this sauce over the hot beets, and serve immediately.

SERVES 6.

Broccoli

Broccoli should be dark green. If the head looks yellow, it is too old; don't buy it.

Rinse the broccoli very thoroughly, and cut off the blossoms with about 2 inches of stem. Cut the blossoms into bite-sized pieces. Peel the remaining stems and cut them into slices ¼ inch thick. Put all of the pieces into a pan with about ½ inch of water, bring to a boil, and simmer about 5 minutes.

Serve hot with a little margarine and salt, or cold with an oil and vinegar dressing. Or sprinkle the cooked broccoli with a little crumbled feta or Roquefort cheese, and keep it hot for a while to melt the cheese.

½ POUND BROCCOLI SERVES 2.

Chinese-style Broccoli

1 pound broccoli
1 or 2 tablespoons oil
1 clove garlic, peeled and sliced
2 nickel-sized slices fresh ginger, peeled and minced

2 tablespoons water
Salt to taste

Prepare the broccoli: Rinse it and cut off the florets with about 2 inches of stem. Cut these broccoli tops into bite-sized pieces. Peel the remaining stems and cut them crosswise into ¼-inch slices.

Pour the oil into your pan and heat it until it shimmers. Add the sliced garlic and minced ginger to the oil and brown them lightly. Add the broccoli, stir to coat it with oil, add the 2 tablespoons water, and cover.

Cook over low heat for a few minutes, just until the broccoli turns very bright green but is still crisp. Sprinkle with salt, stir again, and serve.

SERVES 4.

Brussels Sprouts

Rinse these tiny members of the cabbage family well, and cut off the stems and the tough outer leaves. Cook in 1 inch of boiling water for about 5 minutes, until they are just done. Any cabbage, including brussels sprouts, gets unpleasantly strong-flavored if it is too old or if it is overcooked. Drain, and serve with a little margarine, salt, and grated Romano cheese if desired.

½ POUND BRUSSELS SPROUTS SERVES 2.

Cabbage

Look for a fresh, young cabbage. Savoy cabbage is tender, has a nice flavor, and is too little known; it looks like a wrinkled head of ordinary cabbage. Treat it as you would ordinary cabbage. Remove and discard the tough outer leaves, then cut as much cabbage as you plan to use into pieces approximately 1½ inches square. Melt 1 or 2 tablespoons of margarine in your pan, add the cabbage and a few tablespoons of water, and cook very briefly just until done; this will take only a couple of minutes. You may not need to drain the cabbage, since so little water was used. Serve with salt and perhaps a little cheese.

½ POUND OF CABBAGE SERVES 2.

Here is another good way to cook cabbage. Cut 1 or 2 strips of bacon into several pieces and cook them in a saucepan until they start to brown. Add ¾ pound cut-up cabbage and a couple of tablespoons of water. Cover the pan and cook over moderate heat just until the cabbage is done, about 3 or 4 minutes. Add a little pepper, and salt if needed, and serve.

SERVES 3.

Carrots

Peel the carrots with a vegetable peeler, and cut off the stem and root ends. Slice the carrots into rounds or thin lengthwise strips about half the thickness you would use for carrot sticks. Boil in approximately 1 inch of water or beef broth for about 5 or 10 minutes, or until tender. Drain, salt, and serve with a little margarine.

If you are fortunate enough to find or grow baby carrots, cut off the tip and stem ends but do not peel them. Scrub well with a stiff brush and simmer until barely tender—about 5 minutes.

4 MEDIUM CARROTS (ABOUT ½ POUND) SERVES 2.

Cauliflower

Rinse the cauliflower well, and separate the florets into bite-sized pieces. Cook in about 1 inch of water or chicken broth for approximately 5 minutes. Drain, salt, and add a little margarine and perhaps a sprinkling of lemon juice. You can also top with grated Romano cheese.

The average head of cauliflower serves 5. Allow about ¼ pound of cauliflower for each person.

Celery

Celery makes a tasty and unusual cooked vegetable.

Scrub the stalks, cut off the leaves, and slice the stalks crosswise as you would for salad, about ¼ to ½ inch thick. Cook the slices in a little water for about 5 minutes, until they begin to look transparent and are tender but still crisp. Drain the celery, salt it, and serve with margarine.

Allow about 1 to 1½ large stalks per person.

Chayotes

This lovely, mild tropical vegetable has been appearing lately in most supermarkets. It resembles a hard, pale green pear with prickly skin.

Peel a chayote, cut it in quarters, and cut out the soft seed. Slice the flesh about ¼ inch thick, and simmer it in a little water until tender, about 10 minutes. Drain, salt, and serve with margarine.

ONE CHAYOTE SERVES 2.

Stuffed Chayotes

Mother lived in the tropics for many years, and this is her way of preparing stuffed chayotes.

1 chayote
Soft bread crumbs, about
   ⅓ as much as there is
   chayote pulp
1 teaspoon minced onion
Salt and pepper
Grated Romano or
   kasseri cheese
   (optional)

1 tablespoon fine dry
   bread crumbs
1 tablespoon melted
   margarine

Scrub the chayote, cut it in half but don't peel it, and scoop out the seed. Boil the halves until the flesh is tender and you can scoop it out of the shells, about 10 minutes.

Remove the chayote pulp with a spoon, being careful not to break the shells, and mash it. Squeeze out some of the water. Add the soft bread crumbs, minced onion, salt, pepper, and perhaps some Romano cheese or kasseri. Pile the mixture into the chayote shells, top with fine dry bread crumbs, and drizzle melted margarine over the top.

Broil briefly to brown the tops of the chayotes.

SERVES 2.

Corn on the Cob

Corn should be very fresh; a few hours old is the best, certainly no more than a day old. Some families pick the corn from their garden only when the water is already boiling in the pot.

Strip the husk and the silk from the corn, and break off the stem end; if the tip is undeveloped, break it off too.

Unless you have a very large pot and plan to serve a crowd, 6 ears is about as many as can be cooked at one time. If you have more than this, put the next batch of corn into the boiling water as soon as you remove the first one.

Bring 3 or 4 quarts of water (don't salt it) to the boil in a large pot. Put in up to 6 ears of corn. When the water begins to boil again, start timing. The corn should boil for 3 to 5 minutes. Remove the corn from the water with tongs, and serve immediately with margarine and salt. Cut leftover cooked corn off the cob and freeze for winter soups.

People vary in the amount of corn they like; it's a good idea to ask. Usually 2 ears per person is about right.

Eggplant

Eggplant absorbs a great deal of fat when fried, so I usually bake or broil it. First peel your eggplant and cut it crosswise into slices about ½ inch thick. Brush the slices well with oil. Broil them for about 3 minutes on each side, or bake at 350° for about 40 minutes. The slices should be tender and light brown. Sprinkle with salt and serve immediately.

A LARGE EGGPLANT, WEIGHING ABOUT 1 TO 1½ POUNDS, WILL SERVE 4.

Greens: Spinach, Kale, Collards, Mustard Greens, Beet Greens, Swiss Chard

Rinse your greens very thoroughly: Fill a dishpan with cold water, swirl the fresh greens around in it, remove the greens to a colander and let them drain briefly. Repeat this rinsing twice more, with fresh batches of water. Snap off the stems. Put the greens into a saucepan with about 3 or 4 tablespoons of water, salt lightly, cover the saucepan, and cook just until the greens are wilted, only a couple of minutes. Drain, season with pepper and margarine, and serve. Sprinkle a little vinegar over the greens at the table if desired.

¾ POUND GREENS SERVES 2.

Kohlrabi

A delicately flavored vegetable.

Cut off the stems and the woody root ends, then peel the bulbs with a vegetable peeler. Slice about ¼ inch thin. Simmer in salted water or chicken broth until done, about 5 minutes. Serve hot seasoned with salt and pepper or grated Romano cheese.

½ POUND OF KOHLRABI SERVES 2.

Mushrooms

Wipe the mushrooms with a damp cloth (if you rinse them, they will absorb too much water), cut the damaged ends off the stems, and slice. (If they are very small, keep them whole.) Sauté them until golden in a little margarine. Salt lightly and serve immediately.

MUSHROOMS SHRINK WHEN COOKED; ¾ CUP (ABOUT 2 OUNCES) SERVES 1.

Parsnips

Cut off the stem and root ends. Peel the parsnips with a vegetable peeler and cut into ¼-inch slices. Put in a saucepan with about ½ inch water and ¼ teaspoon sugar and cook for 5 minutes, or until tender but not mushy. Serve hot with salt, pepper, and margarine.

½ POUND PARSNIPS SERVES 2.

Peas

Buy only freshly picked young peas, since old peas are tough and take a long time to cook. Shell the peas by pressing hard on the blossom end of each pod to split it open, then remove the peas. Rinse the peas, bring them to a boil in about ½ inch of water, and simmer just until tender, less than 5 minutes. Serve hot with salt and a little margarine.

1 POUND PEAS IN THE POD SERVES 2.

Sugar Snap Peas (Edible-pod Peas)

These resemble snow peas, but the pods are a little fatter. They are excellent raw in salads, or they can be cooked. Whichever way you serve them, the peas should be prepared by rinsing them and then removing the strings. To do this, snap off the stem end of each pod and pull off the string that will come with it from the inside curve. Cut off the blossom end if it doesn't come with the string.

To cook the peas, simmer them gently in about ½ inch of water, for 5 minutes or less, until the pods begin to brighten in color. They should still be crisp. Drain the peas, salt them, and add a little margarine.

½ POUND SERVES 2.

Peppers (Bell Peppers)

Sweet peppers make a wonderfully colorful, versatile addition to meals. Red, yellow, and green varieties are regularly available.

2 medium-sized peppers
1 strip bacon
1 small onion, peeled and chopped

171

Scrub the peppers, discard the seedy core, and cut the green outer part into pieces about 1 inch in diameter.

Sauté the bacon in a saucepan until it begins to brown. Leaving the bacon in the pan, sauté the onion until limp. Add the green pepper, turn the heat to low, cover the pot, and cook just until the pepper is tender, about 5 minutes. Season to taste with salt if needed (the bacon may have added enough) and pepper.

SERVES 2.

Spaghetti Squash

A delicately flavored winter squash.

Scrub the squash and boil in enough water to almost cover it until the flesh feels soft when pierced with a skewer, about 45 minutes for a 2-pound squash.

Cut the hot squash open, remove the seeds, lift off the skin, and put the flesh in a serving dish. Scrape the flesh with a fork to separate it into spaghettilike strands. Toss it with salt, pepper, and margarine. Serve hot.

½ POUND SERVES 1.

Summer Squash

Zucchini, yellow crookneck, and white pattypan are all summer squash. About 8 inches is a good length for crookneck or zucchini squash; pattypan squash should weight ¼ pound or less apiece. These squashes give up quite a lot of water as they cook.

Scrub the squash, cut off the stem and blossom ends, and slice crosswise about ¼ inch thick. Melt 1 or 2 tablespoons margarine in your saucepan, add the squash slices, and cook over medium heat, covered, for about 10 minutes, until the squash is just tender.

Stir from time to time. Season to taste with salt and pepper, and serve.

Or steam: Cut the washed squash in chunks about ½ inch thick, place in a steamer basket, and cook over boiling water about 15 minutes, until tender but still crisp. Season with a little curry powder if you like.

¾ POUND SERVES 2.

Hot Zucchini Salad

¾ pound zucchini
3 tablespoons olive oil
1 tablespoon minced onion

1 tablespoon vinegar
Pinch dry mustard
Pinch salt

Scrub and slice the zucchini about ¼ inch thick. Sauté the slices in the olive oil for about 15 minutes, until they just begin to brown. Add the onion, vinegar, mustard, and salt and heat through. Serve immediately.

SERVES 2.

Baked Winter Squash

This method of cooking acorn or buttercup squash is less complicated than the usual one of filling the halves with brown sugar and margarine before baking, and squash has much better flavor when cooked this way. Avoid very large squash, as they may be mealy.

Scrub the squash and prick holes in the top with a fork or skewer. Place in a baking pan and bake at 400° for about 1¼ hours, or until the squash is no longer firm and feels soft when pricked with a skewer.

Cut the squash in two, remove the seeds with a spoon, and serve with margarine, salt, and pepper.

ONE MEDIUM-SIZED ACORN SQUASH SERVES 2.

Steamed Winter Squash

Wash, quarter, and remove the seeds from the acorn, butternut, or hubbard squash; steam the quarters in a vegetable steamer until tender, about 20 minutes. Scoop the flesh out of the shell and serve with margarine, salt, and pepper; or chill the squash to be reheated later on.

For faster cooking, cut off the squash rind, remove the seeds, and cut the squash into slices about ⅛ inch thick before steaming. Squash prepared in this way will cook in about 10 minutes.

ONE AVERAGE-SIZED BUTTERNUT SQUASH OF ABOUT 2½ POUNDS SERVES 4.

Winter Squash with Potatoes

Cut some cooked squash into medium-sized chunks, and set them aside while you boil a few potatoes, also cut into chunks. When the potatoes are nearly done, add the squash and finish cooking. This is a good use for a small amount of leftover cooked potatoes or winter squash.

Tomatoes

Usually we eat summer tomatoes raw, sliced, and sprinkled with a little salt.

If you wish to peel tomatoes, impale each one on a long-handled fork and immerse it in boiling water for a few seconds, until you can slip the skin off easily but not so long that you cook the tomato.

I often freeze summer tomatoes for winter use. They become soft when thawed, which makes them useless for salads, but they are fine for stewed tomatoes or in soups or stews. To freeze the tomatoes, rinse them, peel or not as you wish (I don't), cut them into chunks, and seal in plastic freezer bags.

Stewed Tomatoes

> 4 tomatoes
> 1 green pepper, seeded and coarsely chopped
> 2 stalks celery, coarsely chopped
> 1 medium onion, peeled and sliced
> Salt and pepper

Cut the tomatoes into coarse chunks and put them in a saucepan. Add the pepper, celery, onion, and 2 tablespoons water. Simmer gently until soft, perhaps 10 minutes, season with salt and pepper, and serve.

SERVES 4.

Turnips or Rutabagas

Turnips are small, white, and delicate in flavor; rutabagas are large and yellow.

As with cabbage, turnips and rutabagas will be unpleasantly strong-flavored if they are overcooked, or if they are too old. Peel the vegetables and slice them about ¼ inch thick, or cut them into ½-inch dice. Steam them, or simmer in about 1 inch of water, until tender; about 10 minutes. Add ½ teaspoon sugar to the water, to improve the flavor. Season to taste with salt and pepper, add margarine, and serve.

Allow about ¼ pound per person.

Grains, Rice, and Potatoes

Bulgur
   Baked Bulgur
   Bulgur Pilaf
Couscous
Kasha

Baked Potatoes
Boiled Potatoes
Mashed Potatoes
Oven-roasted
   Potatoes
Potatoes with Garlic
   and Olive Oil
Potato Pancakes
Sweet Potatoes
   Candied Sweet
   Potatoes

Rice
Rice Pilaf
Wild Rice

Bulgur

This is cracked wheat that has been precooked so that the grains will be separate and not mushy. It cooks very quickly; serve it in place of rice or potatoes.

⅔ cup bulgur
1⅓ cups water or broth
⅛ teaspoon salt, if you cook
    the bulgur in water

Stir the bulgur, water and salt together in a saucepan; cover, and bring to a gentle boil. Simmer for 5 minutes. You should lift the lid and stir the bulgur once or twice during cooking. Remove the covered pan to a warm place and let it set for another 5 minutes. Serve hot.

SERVES 2.

Baked Bulgur

A good dish for company. It is a bit unusual and requires very little attention from the cook.

2 cups bulgur
2 tablespoons margarine
3 cups boiling water, or beef broth or chicken broth
Salt to taste

Melt the margarine in a skillet, add the bulgur, and toast for about 5 minutes, or until it smells nutty; stir often. Put the bulgur into a greased casserole, add the water or broth and salt, and cover the casserole. Bake at 350° for 30 minutes.

SERVES 6.

Bulgur Pilaf

You can make pilaf with bulgur just as you do with rice.

½ onion, peeled and
 chopped
2 tablespoons margarine
 or olive oil
About 6 mushrooms,
 sliced

⅔ cup bulgur
1⅓ cups beef or chicken
 broth
Salt to taste

Sauté the onion in the margarine or olive oil until limp. Add the mushrooms and sauté until they too are limp. Stir in the bulgur. Add the broth and, if it isn't salty, add a little salt.

Cover the pot, bring it to a gentle boil, and simmer for about 5 minutes. Remove the pot to a warm place and let it set, covered, for another 5 minutes. Serve immediately.

SERVES 2.

Couscous

Here is a quicker and easier way to prepare this North African wheat dish than the authentic Moroccan method. Serve it in place of rice. You can prepare couscous in the dish you plan to serve it in if the dish is reasonably heatproof.

⅔ cup couscous
Pinch of salt
1 cup boiling water
Pepper (optional)
1 teaspoon olive oil or margarine (optional)

Warm the dish by rinsing it with some boiling water, drain, and place the couscous in the dish. Stir in the salt and the boiling water. Let set for about 5 minutes, stir once or twice, and it's ready to serve. Stir in some pepper and olive oil or a little margarine, if you like.

SERVES 2.

Kasha

This is a general term for coarsely ground grain, meant to be cooked with water or broth and served in place of rice or potatoes. The kind usually sold in health-food stores is buckwheat groats.

> ½ cup toasted buckwheat groats
> 1½ cups water or broth
> ¼ teaspoon salt, if the broth wasn't salted

Put all the ingredients in a saucepan and simmer, covered, for about 5 minutes. Stir once or twice. Leave the lid on the pan and let it set for a few minutes in a warm place before serving.
SERVES 2.

Baked Potatoes

Scrub the potatoes with a brush, and bake them at 400° for 1 hour. Very big potatoes may take a little longer, very small ones may not take quite so long. Baked potatoes are done when they give if you squeeze them (use a potholder to protect your fingers) or when a skewer goes into them very easily. Serve with salt and margarine.

Baking nails, which are aluminum nails sold in housewares departments, will cut the baking time to about 45 minutes if one is inserted into each raw potato.

Use 1 medium or large potato per person.

Boiled Potatoes

Scrub the potatoes well, put them into cold water, and bring to a boil. Boil the potatoes just until they are tender, about 30 minutes for medium-sized potatoes. Very small potatoes may cook in as little as 10 minutes.

If you scrub the potatoes and slice them about ½ inch thick before boiling, they will cook in about 10 minutes, a decided advantage on a busy evening.

Choose small or medium potatoes for boiling; allow 1 or more potatoes per person, depending on the size of the potatoes.

Mashed Potatoes

It was a pleasant surprise to find that our family prefers mashed potatoes prepared with water instead of the usual milk, as milk masks the good potato flavor. Save any leftover mashed potatoes to add to biscuit or yeast doughs. (See pages 272, 220, and 235, for example.)

Peel and slice the potatoes. Put just enough water in the pot to cover the potatoes, add a little salt, and boil until the slices are tender when pierced with a fork, about 10 minutes. Drain the potatoes and save the water. Using a potato masher or an electric mixer, mash the potatoes. Add a little of the cooking water you drained earlier, just enough to moisten the potatoes, and keep on mashing until the lumps are gone and the potatoes fluffy. Add salt and pepper, and perhaps some margarine, to taste.

Serve the potatoes at once, or let them set in a very warm place, such as the turned-off oven in which you recently cooked a roast, for half an hour or so to make them fluffier.

If you're preparing just a small amount of mashed potatoes, it's easier to rice them. You do this by using the back of a tablespoon to press the cooked potatoes through a strong wire sieve. Add enough of the cooking water to the riced potatoes to make them as moist as you wish.

Allow about 1 medium potato per person.

Oven-roasted Potatoes

Potatoes browned in the oven with a roast of meat.

Peel the potatoes, or scrub them well, and cut into large chunks of about 2 inches. Boil until tender, about 15 minutes. About 45 minutes before the roast meat is done, remove it from the oven. Twirl each potato chunk in the pan drippings to coat it with fat. Arrange the potatoes around the meat in the pan, and roast all together until the meat is done. Turn the potatoes over once so they will brown on both sides.

Potatoes with Garlic and Olive Oil

This recipe originates in the Third World, where food is scarce and it is important to preserve nutrients when cooking. Boiling the potatoes with the skins left on keeps vitamins and minerals from leaching out into the cooking water.

2 medium-sized potatoes	1 teaspoon lemon juice
1/4 teaspoon salt	2 cloves garlic, peeled
A good-sized pinch of	and minced
pepper	2 tablespoons olive oil

Scrub the potatoes and boil them gently in water just until done, perhaps 30 minutes. Cool them a little, peel them and then mash the flesh or put it through a ricer. Moisten the potatoes with some of the cooking water. Season to taste with salt and pepper, and add lemon juice if desired.

Sauté the garlic in the olive oil. When the garlic is golden and fragrant, spoon this hot sauce decoratively over the potatoes. Serve warm or at room temperature.

SERVES 2.

Potato Pancakes

One of those cooperative recipes that do not need exact measurements; a handful of this plus a dash of that works well. Good as a side dish, either plain or with ketchup.

1 medium potato, to give 1 cup grated raw potato	⅛ teaspoon salt
	Dash of pepper
	1 egg
1 tablespoon grated onion	About 1 tablespoon margarine or bacon fat to grease your skillet
1 tablespoon flour	

Mix potato, onion, flour, salt, and pepper in a bowl; add the egg and mix well.

Drop the mixture by tablespoonsful onto a moderately hot, well-greased skillet; flatten each pancake with the back of your spoon. Sauté until brown on both sides and cooked completely in the middle, about 10 minutes. If the outsides are getting too brown before the centers are cooked, cover the skillet for a while.

MAKES 4 TO 6 PANCAKES, TO SERVE 2 OR 3 PEOPLE.

Sweet Potatoes

Sweet potatoes can be baked, boiled, or mashed according to the methods given for ordinary potatoes. Very large sweet potatoes need a longer baking time, say 1½ hours. In addition, you can make:

Candied Sweet Potatoes

2 medium-large sweet
potatoes, or about 1
pound canned sweet
potatoes
2 tablespoons margarine

⅓ cup brown sugar,
packed
1 tablespoon orange or
pineapple juice
⅛ teaspoon salt

Scrub and boil raw potatoes whole until tender, about 45 minutes. Cool the potatoes until you can handle them easily, then peel them and cut them into chunks. If you use canned potatoes, just open the can and drain off the liquid.

Melt the margarine in a heavy saucepan or skillet. Remove the pan from the heat and stir in the brown sugar, juice, and salt. Set the pan back on the burner, turn the heat to low, and stir the mixture until smooth and bubbly. Add the potatoes; stir carefully to coat the potatoes with the sugar mixture, and leave over low heat for about 10 minutes, stirring occasionally, to get thoroughly hot.

SERVES 3 OR 4.

Rice

⅔ cup rice—not precooked
or treated
1½ cups water
⅛ teaspoon salt

The basic method for cooking rice is to use 2 measures of water, plus a tablespoon or 2 of extra water "for the pot," for each measure of rice. You can substitute chicken or beef broth for the water (or add a bouillon cube for each 1 or 2 cups of water, and omit the salt). Put all the ingredients into a saucepan, cover, and bring to a

boil. Reduce the heat to a simmer, cook the rice until done, about 20 minutes for white (polished) rice, or 40 minutes for brown rice.
SERVES 2.

Rice Pilaf

This dressed-up rice is amenable to whatever vegetables or seasonings you want to add to the recipe; here is my version.

½ onion, peeled and chopped
2 tablespoons margarine or olive oil
6 mushrooms, wiped clean and sliced

⅔ cup rice
1½ cups beef broth or chicken broth
Salt, if needed

Sauté the onion just until limp in the margarine or olive oil; add the mushrooms and sauté until they too are limp. Add the rice, and stir to coat it with the fat. Add the broth and salt. Cover the pot, bring it to a boil, reduce heat, and simmer for about 20 minutes, or until the rice is tender.
SERVES 2.

Wild Rice

Until very recently wild rice, actually a grain not a rice, was scarce and extremely expensive. It makes a most elegant dish, is simple to prepare, and goes very well with duck or game.

½ cup wild rice
1 cup water
⅛ teaspoon salt

Put the wild rice, water, and salt into a saucepan. Cover, bring to a boil, reduce heat, and simmer for about 40 minutes. Serve plain, or with a little margarine. If any is left over, chill it and use it in salad.

SERVES 2.

Salads and Salad Dressings

Tossed Salad
  Wintertime Green Salad
  Simplified Chef's Salad
Spinach Salad
Tomato-Cucumber Salad
Cucumber Salad
Coleslaw
Carrot Salad
Celery Salad
Cauliflower Salad
Potato Salad
Chick-pea Salad
Apple Salad
Peanut Butter Apple,
  a Walking Salad
Egg Salad
Supper Salad with Tuna
Summer Salad Plate

Fish Salad
Shrimp Salad
  Crab Salad
Lobster Salad
Tossed Salad with Shrimp or
  Lobster
Salmon-Cabbage Salad
Chicken Salad
  Chicken Salad with Bacon
  and Olives

See also:
  Pasta Salad (page 136)
  Pasta with Tomatoes
  (page 137)

Oil and Vinegar Dressing
  Roquefort Dressing
Best Salad Dressing
Russian Dressing
  Thousand Island Dressing

A salad can be a simple tossed green salad, a sweet fruit salad that can double as a dessert, a hearty potato salad, or a main dish salad such as a chef's salad. Use only very fresh ingredients.

To get a salad ready ahead of time, prepare the ingredients (cook, cut or tear into pieces) and refrigerate them without the dressing. Finish the salad by adding the dressing just before you serve it; it will only take a minute and the salad will taste fresh. Chunks of salad too big to eat without being cut up are embarrassing; make sure the pieces are bite-sized.

Asparagus spears, whole green beans, or broccoli florets are all good additions to a salad plate if they are just blanched until crisp-tender in a little salted water and then chilled. Serve lightly coated with an oil and vinegar dressing or toss mixed cooked vegetables with a small amount of minced onion and just enough mayonnaise to moisten.

You can put almost anything you like in a salad; the following recipes are suggestions for combinations we have liked. If you usually use bottled salad dressing, you will be surprised at how easy and inexpensive it is to make your own.

Tossed Salad

One of the charms of tossed salad is that it's rarely the same twice. This recipe is just a suggestion; use what you have on hand. Popular ingredients for a tossed salad could include lightly cooked vegetables, sliced red onion, thinly sliced mushrooms, celery, cucumber, nuts, crumbled crisp bacon, grated Romano cheese, and sprouts. Use several kinds of lettuce if you can get them. If you can't find good tomatoes, use thinly sliced dill pickle.

Lettuce for 3 people
8 cherry tomatoes,
  halved
1 radish, scrubbed and
  sliced thin
1 scallion, washed and
  sliced thin
1 inch of a small
  cucumber or zucchini,
  scrubbed and sliced
  thin

¼ green pepper, sliced
2 tablespoons Roquefort
  cheese, crumbled
  (optional)
Oil and Vinegar
  Dressing (page 206) or
  Best Salad Dressing
  (page 207)

Cherry tomatoes seem to have a longer season than regular tomatoes. Slice cherry tomatoes in half before adding to the salad so that you will be less apt to squirt tomato at your neighbor while eating.

Put all the ingredients except the dressing into a bowl, sprinkle with the dressing of your choice, toss, and serve.

SERVES 3.

Wintertime Green Salad

Add 3 scallions, 3 radishes, and 3 tablespoons imported feta cheese (see pages 17–18).

Simplified Chef's Salad

A true chef's salad is made with strips of roast beef or ham or chicken. Since I seldom have two or three of these on hand at the same time, I make this simplified version that makes a fine meal in late summer. Serve with freshly baked hot bread (pages 218–26) or biscuits (page 271), blueberry cake (page 247), and iced tea.

Mix into a green salad one or two choices of 1 cup cold cooked meat sliced into thin strips, ¾ pound cooked, shelled shrimp, a medium-sized can of tunafish, 3 tablespoons crumbled imported feta cheese (see pages 17–18).

SERVES 3.

Spinach Salad

2 cups loosely packed
  fresh spinach, well
  washed
1 hard-boiled egg, sliced
1 radish, scrubbed and
  sliced
2 medium-large
  mushrooms, wiped
  clean and sliced

1 scallion, washed and
  sliced thin
1 tablespoon olive oil
Dash of salt
Pinch of pepper
1 teaspoon lemon juice
1 slice crumbled crisp
  bacon, or 1 tablespoon
  hulled sunflower seeds

Spinach is sometimes sandy so rinse spinach leaves in several changes of water, and drain well. Tear the spinach into bite-sized pieces and put them in a salad bowl along with the egg, radish, mushroom, and scallion.

Sprinkle the olive oil, salt, and pepper over the salad and toss it. Sprinkle the lemon juice over the salad and toss again just before serving. Top with the bacon or sunflower seeds.

SERVES 2 OR 3.

Tomato-Cucumber Salad

A decorative, easy summer salad.

Pour oil and vinegar dressing (page 206) seasoned with fresh basil over a ring of very fresh tomato slices topped with a ring of cucumber slices. You can make this on a large plate from which people serve themselves, or you can prepare individual salads on small plates.

Cucumber Salad

This old-fashioned dish is more a relish. It makes a cool, refreshing addition to a summer meal and it looks pretty in a glass dish.

> 1 cucumber, scrubbed and sliced $1/16$ inch
>   thin
> 4 teaspoons vinegar
> $1/4$ teaspoon salt
> Dash of freshly ground black pepper

Mix all of the ingredients together and chill about 1 hour before serving.

SERVES 2 OR 3.

Coleslaw

$3/4$ pound cabbage
1 small carrot, peeled
$1/2$ green pepper, washed
1 scallion
3 tablespoons vegetable
  oil

1 tablespoon vinegar
$1/4$ teaspoon salt
Dash of pepper

By hand: Grate the cabbage and the carrot. Slice the green pepper and the white part of the scallion thin. Toss all of the ingredients in a bowl and either serve immediately or chill about an hour.

With a food processor: Using a thin slicing disk, slice the green pepper and the scallion. Leave them in the bowl, and change to a medium or coarse shredding disk. Cut the cabbage into wedges that fit the feed tube, and grate the cabbage and the carrot into the food processor bowl. Remove all of the vegetables to a serving dish; add the remaining ingredients, mix well, and chill or serve immediately.

SERVES 4.

Carrot Salad

A good, fast winter salad.

> 2 or 3 carrots, peeled and coarsely grated
> 1/4 teaspoon grated onion
> 2 tablespoons Oil and Vinegar Dressing
>   (page 206)

Mix everything together and serve.

SERVES 2.

Celery Salad

Another quickie; good and crunchy.

> 3 stalks celery
> 2 tablespoons Oil and Vinegar Dressing
>   (page 206)

Scrub the celery stalks well with a brush, and cut off the bottom ends and the leaves. Slice thin, toss with the oil and vinegar dressing, and serve cold.

SERVES 2.

Cauliflower Salad

This is an unusual combination, and a very good one.

1½ cups thinly sliced
  cauliflower
¾ cup thinly sliced
  mushrooms
1 carrot, skinned and
  coarsely grated (about
  ¼ cup)

1 scallion, thinly sliced
Salt and pepper to taste
2 tablespoons vegetable
  oil
2 teaspoons white wine
  vinegar

Mix everything together well and chill briefly before serving.
SERVES 3.

Potato Salad

This makes a good hot-weather meal when served with frankfurters or Polish sausage. To get a head start on the salad, cut up the potatoes and toss them with the oil and vinegar dressing. Cover the mixture and refrigerate it until just before serving time. Then proceed with the rest of the recipe.

1¼ pounds potatoes,
  preferably new
  potatoes, boiled and
  cooled
2 tablespoons
  mayonnaise
2 tablespoons Oil and
  Vinegar Dressing
  (page 206)
¼ teaspoon salt
Pepper to taste

1 radish, scrubbed and
  sliced thin
¼ green pepper, washed
  and sliced
¼ cucumber or small
  zucchini, scrubbed and
  sliced thin
Lettuce, as desired
A good pinch marjoram
1 tomato, cut in wedges
1 hard-boiled egg,
  chopped

Peel the potatoes and cut them into ½-inch cubes. Add the mayonnaise, oil and vinegar dressing, salt, and pepper, and mix thoroughly. Stir in the radish, green pepper, and cucumber or zucchini; add more salt and pepper if needed.

Line a bowl with lettuce leaves, pile the potato salad into it, and sprinkle with marjoram. (Or tear the lettuce leaves into small pieces and mix them into the salad.) Garnish with the tomato wedges and the hard-boiled egg.

SERVES 3.

Chick-pea Salad

In this good bean salad the bland chick-peas and the strong-flavored anchovies and garlic balance each other.

1 cup (½ pound)
    uncooked chick-peas,
    or two 1-pound cans
    chick-peas
⅓ cup olive oil
⅓ cup vinegar
One 2-ounce can flat
    fillets of anchovy,
    drained and cut into
    small pieces

4 thin slices peeled red
    onion
1 clove garlic, peeled and
    minced
½ teaspoon dried
    marjoram
½ teaspoon salt
Dash cayenne pepper

If you use uncooked chick-peas, pick them over and rinse them. Cover with about 5 cups of water, bring to a boil, and boil for 3 minutes. Remove the pot from the heat and let stand for an hour or more. Drain the chick-peas, cover with plenty of fresh water, bring to a boil, and boil gently for about 2 hours or until the peas are tender but not mushy. Let the chick-peas cool for a while in the water or, if you are in a hurry, drain them and rinse with several changes of cool water. In any case, drain the chick-peas well before going on.

If you use canned chick-peas, drain them and rinse well. Taste the salad before adding salt; you may not need any.

Add all of the remaining ingredients to the chick-peas and re-frigerate the salad in a covered nonmetal serving dish for several hours or overnight. Serve either chilled or at room temperature.
MAKES ABOUT 3 CUPS OF SALAD; SERVES 4 TO 6.

Apple Salad

1 medium apple
Sprinkle of salt
2 teaspoons mayonnaise
1 tablespoon raisins or chopped nuts

Scrub the apple. Core it and cut it into chunks. Leave the apple skin on. Sprinkle a very little salt over the apples, mix in the may-onnaise and raisins or nuts, and serve.
SERVES 2.

Peanut Butter Apple, a Walking Salad

This portable salad is perfect for a brown-bag lunch.

Wash the apple, quarter it, and cut out the core. Spread about ¾ teaspoon peanut butter on each quarter. For travel, just reassemble the quarters into the apple shape and wrap in waxed paper.

Egg Salad

Radish slices make this light supper salad colorful if you serve it on a plate, but in a sandwich they are messy to eat, so it is wiser to leave them out.

4 hard-boiled eggs
1 tablespoon mayonnaise
1 tablespoon Oil and
  Vinegar Dressing
  (page 206)
1 teaspoon minced onion
  (optional)

2 teaspoons pickle relish
  (optional)
2 radishes, scrubbed and
  sliced thin (optional)
Salt and pepper

Shell the eggs and use a fork to mash them in a small bowl. If you are going to serve the salad on plates, the pieces can be pretty large; if you are going to use it as sandwich filling, you should mash the egg pieces pretty small. Add the remaining ingredients and mix well.

SERVES 2 AS A SALAD, OR MAKES ENOUGH FILLING FOR 4 SAND-WICHES.

Supper Salad
with Tuna

Another good, quick supper for a hot evening. Serve with muffins (page 261) or breakfast buns (page 275).

1 medium potato, boiled
  and cooled
One 7-ounce can tuna
Lettuce for 2 people
1 tablespoon minced
  onion
2 radishes, scrubbed and
  sliced thin

1 medium tomato,
  chopped
2 ounces pitted ripe
  olives
Salt and pepper
3 tablespoons
  mayonnaise

Peel the potato and chop it into ½-inch dice. Drain the tuna, flake it, and add to the potato. Tear the lettuce into bite-sized pieces. Toss lightly with all the remaining ingredients and serve.

SERVES 2.

Summer Salad Plate

This is a composed salad that makes a very good light summer meal. Serve with hot bread, perhaps corn bread (page 247).

4 lettuce leaves
2 eggs, hard-boiled or deviled
4 ounces canned tuna or salmon
¼ cup feta (see pages 17–18) or Roquefort cheese (optional)
1 tomato, cut up
4 radishes, scrubbed
4 scallions, washed and trimmed

6 olives
½ cup cold cooked vegetables such as beans or beets
2 tablespoons mayonnaise
Oil and Vinegar Dressing (page 206)

Line each plate with lettuce leaves and decoratively arrange everything but the mayonnaise and the salad dressing on them. Put a dollop of mayonnaise on each plate, and pass the bottle of oil and vinegar dressing at the table for each person to drizzle over his or her own salad.

SERVES 2.

Fish Salad

When we have fish for dinner, I usually cook more than necessary so we can have this the next day. Try making it with fresh salmon.

3/4 pound cooked fish (about 2 cups) or
  two 7-ounce cans tuna, drained
2 large scallions, minced
2 tablespoons mayonnaise or tartar sauce
Salt and pepper
Lettuce leaves

Flake the fish with a fork and mix it with the scallions and mayonnaise or tartar sauce. Add more mayonnaise if desired. Season to taste with salt and pepper. Serve on lettuce leaves.
SERVES 2.

Shrimp Salad

The ultimate; almost pure shrimp.

1/2 pound shelled, cooked
  shrimp
1 scallion, minced
1 tablespoon mayonnaise
  or Oil and Vinegar
  Dressing (page 206)

Salt (optional)
Lettuce leaves
1 tomato, cut into
  wedges

Mix the shrimp with the scallion and salad dressing. Serve on lettuce leaves, and garnish with tomato wedges.
SERVES 2.

Crab Salad

More economical than the preceding recipe.

12 ounces crabmeat,
  flaked
2 stalks celery, sliced
  thin
½ dill pickle, chopped
  fine

2 tablespoons Oil and
  Vinegar Dressing
  (page 206)
1 tablespoon mayonnaise
Dash cayenne pepper
Salt and black pepper

Mix all together well, and serve cold, on lettuce leaves.
SERVES 4.

Lobster Salad

Cooked lobster legs are a colorful decoration for the salad bowl. Lobster, crab, and shrimp can be used either together or in place of each other in these salads.

1½ pounds cooked
  lobster meat
3 tablespoons
  mayonnaise
1 tablespoon vegetable
  oil
1½ teaspoons lemon
  juice

3 tablespoons roasted
  sunflower seeds
1 ounce stuffed green
  olives
Salt and pepper

Mix well together and season to taste. Serve cold, on lettuce leaves.
SERVES 6.

Tossed Salad with Shrimp or Lobster

A quick, cool, light hot-weather supper; serve with rolls and iced tea.

Lettuce enough for 2 people, torn into bite-sized pieces
1 ripe tomato, washed and cut up
1/4 green pepper, washed, seeded, and sliced thin
2 radishes, scrubbed and sliced thin

1/2 pound small shrimp or lobster meat, cooked and peeled
1 teaspoon minced onion
2 tablespoons Oil and Vinegar Dressing (page 206) or Best Salad Dressing (page 207)

Mix all ingredients together in the order given, and serve.
SERVES 2.

Salmon-Cabbage Salad

Unusual and good. This is a favorite at potluck dinners, for which I usually double or triple the recipe. With a hot bread, this is a whole meal for two.

One 8-ounce can salmon
2 cups coarsely grated cabbage
2 hard-boiled eggs, peeled and chopped
1/4 cup mayonnaise
1 tablespoon corn relish or sweet pickle relish
1 tablespoon olive oil or other good salad oil

1 tablespoon ketchup
1 teaspoon vinegar
1 teaspoon minced onion
1 teaspoon sugar
1/4 teaspoon salt
1/2 teaspoon Worcestershire sauce
1/8 teaspoon dry mustard
Dash of black pepper

Drain the salmon, remove the bones and skin, and flake the flesh. Put the cabbage, salmon, and eggs into a serving bowl. Mix the remaining ingredients together in another bowl, then toss them with the salmon mixture. Add extra mayonnaise if needed to moisten the salad.

SERVES 2.

Chicken Salad

In hot weather, chicken salad makes a good one-dish meal. Add a hot bread and some white wine.

1 cup cooked chicken, in
    bite-sized pieces
1 tablespoon mayonnaise
1 tablespoon oil
1 teaspoon white wine
    vinegar or lemon juice
1 teaspoon minced onion
Pinch of marjoram
    (optional)

Salt and black pepper to
    taste
3 large lettuce leaves,
    torn in bite-sized
    pieces
1 radish, scrubbed and
    sliced thin (optional)
1 tomato, washed and
    cut up

Mix the chicken, mayonnaise, oil, vinegar or lemon juice, and seasonings well together. Add the remaining ingredients, toss lightly, and serve.

SERVES 2.

Chicken Salad with Bacon and Olives

A richer chicken salad.

Omit the marjoram, lettuce, and radish from the preceding salad and add:

½ green pepper, washed, seeded, and cut in pieces

2 strips bacon, fried crisp and crumbled

1 ounce (about ⅓ cup) pitted black olives

1 additional tablespoon mayonnaise

Dash of cayenne pepper

1 hard-boiled egg, peeled and sliced

Reserve the tomato and the egg to use as garnish. Mix the remaining ingredients together in a bowl. Arrange the egg slices and the tomato wedges or slices decoratively around the salad, and serve it.

SERVES 2.

Salad Dressings

The classic way to dress a green salad is to mix the dressing on the salad. Toss the prepared salad with oil. Measure the oil first, as you will want to use ⅓ this amount of vinegar or lemon juice. The oil-coated greens can wait a few minutes while you finish the salad. Just before serving, sprinkle salt and pepper over the salad, then the vinegar or lemon juice. If you use 3 tablespoons of oil, use about ¼ teaspoon of salt, a pinch of pepper, and 1 tablespoon of vinegar or lemon juice.

Vary oil and vinegar dressings by using a choice of oils such as olive oil, a good vegetable oil like corn oil, or one of the more exotic oils, hazelnut or walnut oil; use cider vinegar, wine vinegar, one of the specialty flavored vinegars, or lemon juice. Flavor the dressing with herbs and a little grated Romano cheese if you can have it.

A sprinkling of salt and pepper on your salad greens can substitute for dressing—it's amazing how this treatment can perk up the flavor of an otherwise undressed salad.

Toss the salad gently so that all of it is lightly coated with dressing, and serve immediately.

Oil and Vinegar Dressing

Easy and economical to make, convenient to keep on hand.

¾ cup oil
¼ cup vinegar or lemon
  juice
½ teaspoon salt
⅛ teaspoon black pepper
Pinch dry mustard
  (optional)
½ teaspoon grated onion
  or dry onion flakes
  (optional)

Herbs as desired—
  thyme, oregano,
  marjoram, or others
  (use very small
  amounts)

Place all ingredients in a clean bottle, cover, and store in the refrigerator. Shake well before using.

Roquefort Dressing

Add 1 tablespoon mayonnaise and 1 tablespoon crumbled Roquefort cheese to 3 tablespoons of the oil and vinegar dressing.

As always, if your problem is allergy to cows' milk, make sure the Roquefort cheese is made from 100 percent sheep's milk (see page 18). If you are lactose-intolerant and sensitive to small amounts of lactose, skip this recipe.

MAKES ⅓ CUP DRESSING; SERVES 2 OR 3.

Best Salad Dressing

This excellent salad dressing should be kept cold, and used within a day or so. You don't really taste the anchovies, they just add depth.

1 medium-small onion,
  peeled and chopped
7 anchovy fillets, drained
  and cut up
1 large clove garlic,
  peeled and cut up
1⅓ cups vegetable oil
3 tablespoons white
  wine vinegar

¾ teaspoon salt
¼ teaspoon pepper
¼ teaspoon dry mustard
2 tablespoons water
2 eggs (see warning on
  page 4)

Place all the ingredients except the eggs in a blender or a food processor fitted with a steel blade. Blend until smooth, about 1 minute. Add the eggs and process a few seconds longer.

MAKES ABOUT 2 CUPS SALAD DRESSING.

Russian Dressing

⅓ cup ketchup
⅓ cup mayonnaise
1 teaspoon
  Worcestershire sauce
¾ teaspoon horseradish,
  or a dash or two of
  cayenne pepper

1½ teaspoons minced or
  grated onion

Mix together well.

MAKES ABOUT ⅔ CUP; SERVES 6.

Thousand Island Dressing

To the preceding recipe add:

> 1 hard–boiled egg, peeled and chopped
> 1 tablespoon pickle relish

Some Friendly Advice
on Baking

If you haven't done a lot of baking you will find it easier to start with some of the simpler things: Muffins, gingerbread, crumb cake, or easy apple cake would be good choices. Save biscuits, pies, and the fancier cakes for a time when you have more experience.

Either the white or the yolk of an egg counts as ½ egg; for most baked goods you can use either half. If you're worried about cholesterol, egg yolks have a great deal and egg whites have none. Given a choice, I use the yolk and freeze the white. When there are several egg whites in the freezer you can use them to make boiled icing or an egg white cake. Extra egg yolks can be used in scrambled eggs or baked goods. Count 2 egg yolks or 2 egg whites as equal to 1 whole egg, but don't use *only* egg yolks or egg whites unless the recipe so specifies.

Cookie sheets and other baking pans should be greased with solid fat, such as margarine. Greasing a pan with cooking oil will make the cake or cookies stick tightly, instead of releasing easily, after baking.

Always use *stick* margarine when a recipe calls for margarine. Unless specified, do not pre-sift flour.

Baking times given in this book are as accurate as I can make them and I always use an oven thermometer; however, most ovens are slightly off temperature, so your baked goods may cook more quickly or more slowly than the recipes indicate. An apple pie will bake in a longer or shorter time than indicated depending on the variety of apple used. You should learn to judge doneness and not depend entirely on time and temperature. Baking a cake or a loaf of bread until it is done is more important than baking it for a certain number of minutes. Baked goods are done when a skewer stuck into the center comes out clean—with no wet dough clinging to it.

If you wish to change the size of one of the recipes for baked goods given here, the following list of common pan sizes may help. It is easy enough to make one and a half times the recipe for a 2-layer cake to produce a 3-layer cake of the same diameter, but if you want to make one and a half times the recipe for a 9-inch square cake, you need to know the areas of your pans. Since $1\frac{1}{2} \times 81$ square inches = 121.5 square inches, a 9- by 13-inch pan, at 117 square inches, will do nicely. You can safely change the width and length of your cake, but changing its thickness may mean a baking failure.

    8-inch round = 50 square inches
    9-inch round = 64 square inches
    8-inch square = 64 square inches
    9-inch square = 81 square inches
    5- by 9-inch = 45 square inches
    9- by 13-inch = 117 square inches
    10.5- by 15.5-inch = 163 square inches

Baking Equipment

This book is written for someone who knows how to cook, but may not have done much baking. Because of your milk intolerance you must avoid most commercial baked goods, but by following the recipes in this book you can have muffins, pancakes, and cookies again.

I believe that most people who think they can't bake just have the wrong equipment. If you have good basic equipment and follow your recipe carefully, you should get good results.

Ovens are frequently off calibration; that is, the temperature you see on the dial is not necessarily the temperature you get. To get a temperature of 350° you may have to set the dial to 325°, or to 400°. If you are in doubt, buy an oven thermometer or have a serviceman check your oven. A too-hot oven will burn your cake; a too-slow oven will give you a coarse, pale cake that takes a long time to bake.

Accurate measuring is essential for success in baking.

A good 1-cup measuring cup is very important. The inexpensive aluminum kind, with the lines embossed into the metal *and* running all of the way around the cup, is best. It's hard to see just how much you have in a transparent glass or plastic cup, as the amount will seem different when viewed from different angles. It's convenient to have a set of uncalibrated cups in the ¼, ⅓, ½, and 1 cup sizes for measuring dry ingredients; sometimes you can find good plastic measuring cups.

You need a set of measuring spoons. Once again, the inexpensive aluminum ones are best. Try to find a set with "U.S.ST'D." on the largest spoon.

You should have a 5-cup or bigger rotary sifter to mix and aerate dry ingredients. Trying to sift 2 cups of flour and 1 cup of sugar together in a 1-cup sifter is frustrating. Avoid sifters with a handle that you must squeeze repeatedly; they are slow and tiring to use. The best sifter has a handle that turns around and around. A good-sized metal sieve about 8 inches in diameter makes an efficient sifter. Hold it over a bowl or a piece of waxed paper, put the dry ingredients into it and give the sieve a series of rapid shakes against your free hand.

A pastry blender, the sort that has a set of U-shaped blades attached to a wooden or plastic handle at the top of the U, is needed for any recipe in which you cut shortening into dry ingredients.

A set of glass or pottery mixing bowls is good to have in the 6-inch, 7½-inch, and 9-inch sizes. In a pinch you can use cooking pots, or casseroles, or anything else that comes to hand.

You need a few sturdy wooden or metal mixing spoons.

A hand-held, nonelectric rotary beater is useful for beating eggs and egg whites, but it isn't strong enough to handle mixing batter or creaming margarine.

You should probably have a rolling pin. The kind with a wooden body that goes around while the two handles (which you are gripping) stay still is the best, but any reasonable-sized cylindrical object like a wine bottle can be used.

A metal spatula with a flexible blade is useful for handling rolled doughs such as biscuits or pie crust, and for removing cookies from cookie sheets.

Cookie cutters are fun to collect and use but not necessary. Two of my favorites are an old tunafish can and an old tomato-paste can, labels removed, cans washed, and holes punched in the closed end of each. You can also use drinking glasses.

The most basic set of baking pans would consist of one each: cookie sheet, 9-inch pie pan, 8-inch square pan, 9-inch square pan, 9- by 13-inch oblong pan, 5- by 9-inch loaf pan, and muffin tin for 2½- to 3-inch muffins. Shiny metal pans are best, except that a nonstick coating on muffin pans makes removing popovers and cupcakes easy. If you use either black pans or glass pans for baking, lower the oven temperature by 25 degrees. You should also have a 2½-quart deep casserole, preferably in ovenproof glass or pottery.

Breads and Rolls

Casserole Bread
  Herb Bread
White Bread
    Hamburger Buns
    Hot Dog Rolls
Potato Bread
Egg Bread
Egg Bread Braid
Whole Wheat Bread
Health Bread
Anadama Bread
Oatmeal Bread
Best Raisin Bread
English Muffins

Basic Sweet Roll Dough
Refrigerator Roll Dough
Honey Whole Wheat Rolls

Cornmeal Dinner Rolls
   Pan Rolls
   Crescent Rolls
Onion Rolls
Hot Cross Buns
Bath Buns
Swedish Tea Ring
   Cinnamon Rolls
   Rum Buns
Lemon Rolls
   Orange Rolls
Yeast-raised Apple Cake
Stollen

How to Work with Yeast-raised Dough

Yeast is a mass of tiny living plants, which start to grow when you give them moisture (water), food (sugar), and warmth. They can be killed by too much heat; they do best at body temperature, or luke-warm. You can test this temperature by putting a finger into the water in which you plan to dissolve your yeast. If it feels neither cold nor hot it is right. I use ordinary dried yeast granules sold in glass jars or in individual packets. One packet equals 1 tablespoon. You can also use yeast cakes; one cake equals 1 tablespoon. There is a new fast-rising yeast on the market that grows best at high temperatures but I do not use it in any of the following recipes.

After you have made the dough, the growth of the yeast (and the rising of the bread) will be sped up or slowed down by the temperature of the room. Yeast doughs rise quickly on a warm summer day, more slowly on a cool winter day, very slowly in the refrigerator. If you put the dough into a warm oven to rise, you risk killing the yeast.

If you are unsure of the freshness of your yeast, "proof" it. To do this, sprinkle the yeast over lukewarm water, then sprinkle sugar over it. Let it set 2 minutes; if the mixture doesn't bubble and foam by the end of this time the yeast is dead, and dough made with it will not rise. Start over again with a different batch of yeast. If your yeast is in good shape, as it usually is, you can proceed with the recipe.

Warm the mixing bowl by filling it with hot tap water and then draining. Be sure the bowl is big enough; my 4-quart bowl, 10 inches across the top and 5 inches high, is just about large enough for a recipe that uses 2 cups of liquid—which makes 2 loaves of bread, or 4 dozen rolls. Rising dough can spill out of a too-small bowl in a most amazing way; even with a large bowl, I usually know the dough has risen enough when it starts to peek out from under the inverted bowl. If you make several loaves of bread at once, you might want to buy a bread-mixing pail with a crank, which is useful for the first stages of mixing; it will hold more

215

dough than a bowl will. If you do like to make several loaves of bread at a time, most of these recipes can easily be doubled or tripled.

I make yeast doughs entirely by hand, as I find it not at all difficult and my mixer isn't strong enough to handle most yeast doughs. If you use an automatic mixer for bread dough, reduce the times given for mixing and beating.

You can to some extent control the texture of your bread by the amount of flour you add and by the length of time you knead the dough. Less flour, kneaded for a short time, gives a coarser, softer, more cakelike dough. More flour—as much as you can easily knead in—and a longer kneading time of 10 minutes or so will give a stiffer, more fine-grained, drier loaf. In addition, flours vary in how much water they will absorb. The time and temperature of baking also play a part. For all of these reasons, the amount of flour specified in each recipe for a kneaded or rolled-out dough used for biscuits, breads, rolls, pie crust, and rolled cookies can be only approximate, not exact.

Many books would have you cover rising dough with a wet towel; however, I find this messy and inconvenient, as the dough often sticks to the towel and must be scraped off. I prefer to round the dough up into a ball on the countertop, and set a bowl upside down over the dough.

If you are unsure whether a yeast dough has risen enough, poke it with a floury finger. If a deep imprint remains, the dough can be considered to have doubled in volume.

Before being shaped, dough should be thoroughly kneaded to get rid of air bubbles, which would expand during the final rising and baking to make big holes in the bread.

If you are making loaves of bread for a small family, you might like to shape the dough this old-fashioned way: After the final rising and kneading, divide the dough for each loaf into two balls. Put these balls side by side in the greased bread pan, let rise, and bake as usual. When the bread is done, you can easily break each loaf in two; use one half-loaf now, freeze the other half for later.

If you don't have a loaf pan, you can bake two loaves side by side in a 9-inch square pan.

A recipe that makes one 9- by 5-inch loaf of bread will give you two 7½- by 4-inch loaves. You bake the small loaves at the same temperature you use for the large loaf, but for about ¾ of the time.

Any of the plainer recipes for bread (whole wheat bread, white bread, and so on) will also make good dinner rolls. A recipe calling for 1 cup of water, to make one 9- by 5-inch loaf of bread, will make about 2 dozen dinner rolls.

A metal spatula with a long flexible blade is a big help with yeast dough; you use it to free the dough from the countertop, to cut and shape the dough, and to help in cleaning up afterward. Cleaning up is easiest if your hands are thoroughly dry when you start. First, scrape the countertop with the spatula; next, wipe it down with some wet paper towel; the last step is to go over the counter with a damp sponge or dishcloth. Use cool water for the cleanup as flour turns gluey with hot water.

Bread is supposed to be done when it sounds hollow when you rap it with your knuckles. I have never been able to hear this, so I test bread for doneness by sticking a skewer into the middle of the loaf. When the skewer comes out clean, the bread is done. If damp dough clings to the skewer, bake for a while longer.

If you like your bread to have a crisp crust, turn it out onto wire cooling racks as soon as it comes from the oven. If you like a softened top crust, don't use a wire rack. Turn the loaf out of the pan and then put it back (it won't go all the way) lightly upside down in the pan to cool. If you let the bread cool in the pan without turning it out, it will have a crisp top crust but a soggy bottom one.

Use a serrated knife to cut bread.

If you cannot eat eggs, you can leave them out of most of the recipes for yeast-risen breads and rolls and reduce the amount of flour by ¾ cup for each egg omitted (see page 438).

Casserole Bread

The quickest of the yeast loaves, this is coarse, with a good flavor. Kneading is not necessary. It is best served freshly baked and warm.

1 cup warm water
1 package active dry
  yeast
1 tablespoon sugar
½ teaspoon salt
1 tablespoon oil

1 cup white flour
¼ cup cornmeal
  (optional)
¾ cup whole wheat
  flour

If you cannot eat cornmeal, substitute an extra ¼ cup of white flour.

Pour the warm water into a warmed mixing bowl, sprinkle the yeast over the water, then sprinkle the sugar and salt over that. Let set briefly to proof the yeast. Add the oil and the white flour; beat briefly with a spoon until the mixture is smooth. Add the cornmeal and the whole wheat flour and mix well.

Let stand, covered, in a warm place until doubled, about 30 minutes. Stir once or twice, and put into a greased 2-quart round casserole. Let rise until double again, about 30 minutes.

Bake in a preheated 375° oven for 45 minutes or until done.

MAKES ONE 8-INCH ROUND LOAF.

Herb Bread

Substitute white flour for the whole wheat flour in the preceding recipe. When you add the oil, also add ½ teaspoon dried herbs of your choice. Dried dill weed and dried thyme are one good combination.

White Bread

Plain, old-fashioned bread. This does not keep as well as other breads, and should be used within a day or two.

1 cup warm water	¾ teaspoon salt
1 package active dry yeast	2 tablespoons oil
1 tablespoon sugar	About 2½ cups flour

Pour the warm water into a warmed mixing bowl, sprinkle the yeast over the water, then sprinkle the sugar and the salt over the yeast. Let set a minute or two to proof the yeast. Add the oil, and stir in as much of the flour as you easily can—about 2 cups.

Work in enough of the rest of the flour to give you a dough that is easy to handle. Turn it out onto a floured countertop and knead until the dough is smooth and elastic, about 5 minutes. Round the dough up into a ball, cover it with the upturned mixing bowl, and let set in a warm place to rise until double in bulk, about 45 minutes.

Knead the dough until it is smooth and the bubbles are gone. Shape the dough into a loaf, put it into a greased 9- by 5-inch bread pan, and let rise again until doubled, about 45 minutes.

Bake in a preheated 350° oven for about 45 minutes, until done. MAKES 1 LOAF.

Hamburger Buns

Follow the recipe for white bread. After the dough has risen, divide it into 8 equal parts and use your hands to form each piece into a ball.

Set the balls of dough slightly apart on a greased baking sheet and let rise until doubled in bulk, about 45 minutes.

Bake in a preheated 350° oven for about 20 minutes, until done. If you want the buns to have soft crusts, when you remove them from the oven let them cool on the baking sheet for only a minute or two. Store the hot buns in some covered container such as a clean casserole or soup kettle.

MAKES 8 HAMBURGER BUNS.

Hot Dog Rolls

Follow the recipe for white bread. After the dough has risen, divide it into 8 equal parts and use your hands to form each piece into a 7-inch-long roll.

Place the rolls side by side in a greased 7- by 11-inch baking pan and let rise until doubled in bulk, about 45 minutes.

Bake in a preheated 350° oven for about 20 minutes, until done. If you want the rolls to have soft crusts, turn them upside down on the baking pan as soon as you remove them from the oven. When they are cool store them in a plastic bag or a clean casserole with a tight-fitting lid.

MAKES 8 HOT DOG ROLLS.

Potato Bread

Very much like plain bread but softer, and it keeps better. If you bake bread in the afternoon, you can have it freshly made for dinner.

1½ cups mashed potato	1 teaspoon salt
½ cup margarine	½ cup sugar
1½ cups warm water	1 egg (for ½ recipe, use
2 packages active dry	1 egg yolk)
yeast	About 7 cups flour

If you are using freshly cooked potatoes, put the potatoes through a ricer, or mash them well; add enough potato water to bring them to the consistency you would serve at a meal. Cut the cold margarine into chunks, stir into the hot potatoes, and let set a bit to melt the margarine and cool the potatoes to lukewarm.

If you are using leftover mashed potatoes, melt the margarine and stir in the potatoes; this will warm up the potatoes so they don't cool the dough and make it rise slowly. If you don't have 1½ cups potato, use 1 cup and reduce the amount of flour; your loaves will be a little smaller.

Pour the warm water into a warmed mixing bowl. (If you still have some of the water in which the potatoes cooked, use it.) Sprinkle the yeast over the water. Add the salt and sugar, and let set a bit to proof. Stir the potato mixture into the yeast, along with the egg and about 2 cups of flour.

Gradually stir in about 3 cups more flour. Turn the dough out onto a well-floured countertop and knead for about 5 minutes, working in as much flour as you need to have a soft dough that does not cling too badly to your hands and the countertop. Round the dough up into a ball and cover with the inverted bowl. Let rise for about 1 hour, or until doubled in bulk.

Knead the dough well, to get rid of air bubbles; you may want to use more flour at this time. Shape as desired (see yield below). Set the dough to rise in greased pans for about ½ hour, or until nearly doubled in bulk.

Preheat the oven to 350°, and bake. The big loaves take about 1 hour, the small loaves take about 40 minutes, and the rolls (if you've arranged them in 9-inch round pans) take about 25 minutes.

MAKES TWO 9- BY 5-INCH LOAVES OF BREAD, FOUR 7½- BY 4-INCH LOAVES OF BREAD, OR 4 DOZEN ROLLS.

Egg Bread

2 tablespoons margarine
1 cup warm water
1 package active dry
    yeast

2 tablespoons sugar
¾ teaspoon salt
1 egg
About 3½ cups flour

Melt the margarine. Pour the warm water into a warmed mixing bowl; sprinkle the yeast over the water, then the sugar and salt, and let set for a couple of minutes to proof the yeast. Add the egg and the margarine and mix well. Beat in flour, ½ cup at a time, until the mixture is reasonably smooth and sticky. Stir in as much additional flour as necessary to make a soft but not sticky dough. Turn it out onto a floured countertop and knead until smooth; 5 minutes should be plenty. Add more flour as necessary. Gather the dough into a ball, leave it on the counter, turn the mixing bowl upside down over it, and leave to rise until doubled in bulk, about 45 minutes.

Knead the dough down and then let it rise again until almost double, about 30 minutes.

Knead thoroughly to get all the bubbles out of the dough, then shape it into a loaf and put it into a greased 9- by 5-inch loaf pan. Cover with a clean damp cloth or paper towel and let rise until nearly double, about 30 minutes.

Bake in an oven preheated to 425° for 25 to 30 minutes.

MAKES 1 LOAF.

Egg Bread Braid

A fancy-looking bread, but easy to shape.

¼ cup margarine	¾ teaspoon salt
½ cup warm water	1 egg
1 package active dry yeast	¼ cup semolina flour (optional)
3 tablespoons sugar	About 2½ cups flour

Melt the margarine. Pour the warm water into a warmed mixing bowl and sprinkle the yeast over the water; add the sugar and the salt, and wait a bit to make sure the yeast is lively. Add the egg, margarine, semolina, and 1 cup of flour; beat until the batter is stringy. Add the rest of the flour gradually, using only as much as is necessary for a dough that is easy to knead.

Knead until smooth, about 5 minutes. Cover with the inverted mixing bowl and let rise until double, about 1 hour.

Knead the dough down and divide into 3 or 4 equal parts. Form the pieces of dough into ropes, each about 15 inches long, then lay them side by side on a greased cookie sheet and braid them together. Pinch the ends of the ropes together at both ends to keep them in place. Let rise until double, about 1 hour.

Bake in an oven preheated to 375° for about 20 minutes.

MAKES 1 LOAF.

Whole Wheat Bread

A good, light whole wheat bread.

½ cup margarine
2 cups warm water
2 packages active dry
   yeast
1 teaspoon salt
¼ cup sugar

¼ cup molasses (see
   note)
2 eggs
¼ cup wheat germ
4 cups whole wheat
   flour
4 to 4½ cups white flour

NOTE: Or use ½ cup honey in place of the sugar and molasses.

Melt the margarine and let it cool a little. Put the warm water into a warmed mixing bowl; sprinkle the yeast over the water, then the salt and the sugar, and let set a bit until the yeast makes the mixture bubbly. Stir in the molasses, eggs, and wheat germ. Beat in the whole wheat flour and the margarine.

Stir in about 3 cups of white flour, then turn the dough out onto a floured countertop and knead in as much of the remaining flour as it takes to make an elastic dough. Knead for 5 to 10 minutes, then cover with the upside-down bowl and let rise until doubled, about 1½ hours. Knead the dough down, and shape into 2 loaves. Place each in a greased 9- by 5-inch bread pan and let rise again until double, about 1 hour.

Bake in an oven preheated to 350° for 45 minutes, or until done.

MAKES 2 LOAVES.

Health Bread

This rather dense bread has a nice flavor, and when sliced thin it makes good toast or sandwiches.

1¾ cups rye flour
¼ cup vegetable oil
⅓ cup molasses or
  honey
1 teaspoon salt
1 cup boiling water
¼ cup warm water

1 package active dry
  yeast
¼ cup wheat germ
2 tablespoons bran flakes
1 cup white flour
About 1½ cups whole
  wheat flour

Put the rye flour, oil, molasses or honey, and salt into a large mixing bowl; pour the boiling water over the mixture, stir well, and let stand until it is at body temperature.

Using a spoon, form a hollow in the center of the rye flour mixture and pour the warm water into it; sprinkle the yeast over the water. When the yeast is dissolved and bubbly, add the wheat germ and the bran flakes and mix all very well together. Add the white flour and mix it in.

Knead in as much whole wheat flour as it takes to make a non-sticky, kneadable, fairly stiff dough. Knead for 5 to 10 minutes. Form the dough into a ball, cover it with the inverted mixing bowl, and let rise for about 1½ hours, or until it gives when you poke it with a finger. The bread will be a little better if, at this point, you knead it down and let it rise again for another 1½ hours. However, if you are pressed for time, it is perfectly okay to proceed to the next step and knead the dough down, then form it into a loaf and place it in a greased 9- by 5-inch bread pan. Cover with a damp towel and let rise again until it gives when you touch it, in another 1½ hours or so.

Bake for about 45 minutes in an oven preheated to 350°.
MAKES 1 LOAF.

Anadama Bread

Anadama is an old New England name for this cornmeal-molasses bread.

3/4 cup cornmeal
2 tablespoons margarine
1 1/2 teaspoons salt
2 tablespoons sugar
1 3/4 cups boiling water

1/2 cup molasses
1/2 cup warm water
2 packages active dry
yeast
5 1/2 to 6 cups flour

Put the cornmeal, margarine, salt, and sugar into a large mixing bowl. Stir in the boiling water, and let cool to lukewarm, about half an hour.

Mix in the molasses, then pour the warm water over the batter and sprinkle the yeast over all. Let set a few minutes to proof the yeast. Stir in 2 cups of the flour and beat it a bit by hand to mix well. Gradually add 3 more cups of flour, and turn out onto a well-floured countertop. Knead for about 5 minutes to form a smooth, elastic dough. (You will need to add about 1/2 to 1 cup flour as you knead, to keep the dough from being too sticky.) Form the dough into a ball, cover with the upside-down mixing bowl, and let rise until double, 1 to 1 1/2 hours.

Knead the dough down, shape it into 2 loaves, and set them in 2 greased 9- by 5-inch bread pans. Let rise until double, about 1 hour. Bake in an oven preheated to 350° for about 40 minutes.

MAKES 2 LOAVES.

Oatmeal Bread

Good when cooled, wonderful (although difficult to slice) when freshly baked.

2 cups regular rolled oats
2 tablespoons margarine
2 teaspoons salt
3 tablespoons brown
    sugar, packed firm
2 cups boiling water
1½ cups warm water

2 packages active dry
    yeast
⅔ cup molasses or
    honey
About 7 or 8 cups of
    flour

Put the oats, margarine, salt, and brown sugar into a large mixing bowl, then stir in the boiling water and let set until the mixture is lukewarm, about 45 minutes.

Pour the warm water over the top of the dough, and sprinkle the yeast over the water; let set a minute or two to proof the yeast. Stir in the molasses or honey, then stir in about 4 cups of flour.

Mix in as much of the rest of the flour as it takes to make a soft dough that just barely escapes being sticky, and knead for 2 or 3 minutes. This is best as a rather soft, moist bread; therefore, don't work in as much flour, or knead as long, as you would for another bread. Form the dough into a ball on the counter, cover with the inverted mixing bowl, and let rise until double, about 1 hour.

Knead the dough down, shape into 3 loaves, and set each to rise in a greased 5- by 9-inch bread pan. Let rise until nearly double, about 45 minutes to 1 hour.

Bake in an oven preheated to 350° for about 50 minutes.
MAKES 3 LOAVES.

Best Raisin Bread

Good fresh, this makes wonderful toast.

¼ cup margarine, melted	1 cup lukewarm water
About ½ cup leftover mashed potatoes	1 package active dry yeast
½ teaspoon ground cinnamon	⅓ cup sugar
	1 teaspoon salt
¼ teaspoon ground nutmeg	About 3½ cups flour
	1 cup raisins

Melt the margarine and mix it into the mashed potatoes to warm them up. You do not need to be terribly exact about the amount of mashed potato, any amount between ¼ cup and ½ cup is fine. If you use less potato, you will use slightly less flour, and get a slightly smaller loaf. Stir the spices into the potato mixture.

Warm a large mixing bowl. Put the warm water in it, sprinkle the yeast over the water, and then add the sugar and the salt. Let the mixture set for a few minutes to proof the yeast. Add 1½ cups flour to the yeast mixture and beat a little until it is stringy. Add the potato mixture and the raisins; mix well. Add as much flour as it takes to make a dough that can be kneaded. Turn the dough out onto a floured board and knead about 5 minutes, until the dough is elastic and smooth. A potato dough will stay soft and a little sticky; you will probably have to keep adding small quantities of flour as you work. Gather the dough into a ball on the counter, cover with the inverted mixing bowl, and let rise until double, about 1 hour.

Knead for a bit until the bubbles are gone, then shape dough into a loaf and put it into a greased 5- by 9-inch loaf pan. Cover with a damp towel and let rise until almost double, about 45 minutes.

Bake in a preheated 400° oven for about 40 minutes, or until done.

MAKES 1 LOAF.

English Muffins

2 tablespoons margarine
1 cup warm water
1 package active dry
 yeast
2 tablespoons sugar
½ teaspoon salt

2½ cups flour
Extra flour to roll out
 dough
2 tablespoons cornmeal
 (optional)

The idea is to make as soft and moist a dough as possible, so add as little flour as necessary and beat the dough well at first instead of kneading it later.

Melt the margarine. Put the warm water into a warmed mixing bowl, sprinkle the yeast over the water, and then sprinkle the sugar and salt over the yeast. When the yeast is bubbly, add the margarine and 1½ cups of flour; beat the mixture well, until it is smooth. Stir in another cup of flour, cover the mixing bowl with a damp kitchen towel, and let the dough rise until almost double, about 30 minutes.

When the dough has risen, stir it down. Add just enough flour to enable you to knead the dough for a few strokes, and then roll it out about ½ inch thick. Cut out the dough with a floured 2¾-inch cutter (I use a clean drinking glass), and set the muffins to rise on a baking sheet that may either be greased or sprinkled with cornmeal. The muffins may look small, but they will grow to the usual English muffin size during rising and cooking. Let rise until almost double, about 30 minutes.

Preheat an electric frying pan to 325°. Grease the pan lightly, and cook the muffins on it for about 25 to 30 minutes, or until a skewer inserted into the center of a muffin comes out clean. It helps if you cover the pan during cooking.

The muffins can be baked instead, but they are not as good. Bake them at 325° on a lightly greased cookie sheet for about 20 to 25 minutes, turning them over after they've been in the oven for about 10 minutes.

MAKES ABOUT 9 MUFFINS IF YOU USE A 2¾-INCH ROUND CUTTER.

Basic Sweet Roll Dough

Use this recipe to make everything from pan rolls to Swedish tea ring (page 238–39)

½ cup margarine	1½ teaspoons salt
2 cups warm water	3 eggs (for half recipe,
2 packages active dry	use 1 whole egg)
yeast	7 cups flour, plus about
¾ cup sugar	1½ cups extra flour

Melt the margarine. Pour the warm water into a large warmed mixing bowl. Sprinkle the yeast over the water, then the sugar and the salt. Let set for a minute or two to proof the yeast. Add the eggs and half of the flour and stir well; add the margarine and mix again. Stir in the rest of the flour, turn the dough out onto a well-floured countertop and knead in as much of the extra flour as it takes to give a smooth, elastic, medium-soft dough that is not sticky. The kneading should take about 5 minutes.

Form the dough into a ball on the counter, cover with the upside-down mixing bowl, and let rise until double, about 1 to 1½ hours. Knead down, shape, and bake into pan rolls (pages 232–33) or crescent rolls (page 233) or into one of the sweet rolls on pages 238 to 241.

MAKES ABOUT 4 DOZEN ROLLS.

Refrigerator Roll Dough

A good basic roll dough, not quite so rich as the preceding recipe. Convenient, because you can store the dough in the refrigerator for several days. Pull off as much as you need and bake as directed.

2 cups warm water	¼ cup vegetable oil
2 packages active dry yeast	1 egg
1½ teaspoons salt	About 7 cups flour of which 3 cups may be
⅓ cup sugar	whole wheat flour

Use a very large mixing bowl; it should be big enough to allow the dough to triple in volume.

Put the warm water into the warmed bowl and sprinkle the yeast over it. Add the salt and sugar and let rest a minute or two to proof the yeast; add the oil and egg and stir well. Add 3 cups of flour and beat briefly. Add the rest of the flour gradually, using only as much as necessary to get a dough that is elastic and not sticky; you will have to knead in the last cup or two of flour. Knead until smooth and elastic, about 3 to 5 minutes.

Put the dough back into the bowl. Grease one side of a piece of aluminum foil and cover the bowl with the foil, greased side down. Refrigerate until needed, up to 4 days. About 2 hours before you want to bake, remove as much dough from the refrigerator as you need. Shape the dough as desired, let rise until double—about 1½ hours—and bake.

You don't need to refrigerate this dough before use. After kneading the dough, let it rise until double at room temperature; this will take about an hour.

Shape and bake the rolls into pan rolls (page 232) or crescent rolls (page 233), or onion rolls (page 234), or into one of the sweet rolls on pages 238 to 241.

MAKES ABOUT 4 DOZEN ROLLS.

Honey Whole Wheat Rolls

Good dinner rolls.

¼ cup margarine	2 tablespoons wheat
1 cup warm water	germ
1 package active dry	2 cups whole wheat
yeast	flour
¾ teaspoon salt	About 2 cups white
¼ cup honey	flour

Set the margarine to melt while you mix the dough. When it has melted, let it cool for a minute or two before using.

Put the warm water in a large warmed mixing bowl. Sprinkle the yeast over the water, then add the salt and the honey. Let set a few minutes to proof. Stir in the wheat germ, the whole wheat flour, and the melted margarine.

Stir in as much of the white flour as it takes to get a dough that can be kneaded. Flour your countertop, turn the dough out onto it, and knead for about 5 minutes, or until the dough feels elastic. Round the dough up into a ball on the countertop and turn the mixing bowl upside down over it; let set for about 1 hour, until it has risen to double its previous bulk.

Knead the dough for a bit to get all of the bubbles out, then shape it and bake into pan rolls (page 232) or crescent rolls (page 233) or into one of the sweet rolls on pages 238 to 241.

MAKES ABOUT 2 DOZEN ROLLS.

Cornmeal Dinner Rolls

This unusual basic dough makes handsome rolls with good flavor.

1 cup yellow cornmeal, preferably stone-ground	2 packages active dry yeast
¼ cup margarine	1 teaspoon salt
1 cup boiling water	½ cup sugar
1 cup lukewarm water	1 egg
	5 cups of flour

Put the cornmeal and the margarine in a large mixing bowl, stir in the boiling water, and let set until lukewarm, about half an hour.

Pour the lukewarm water over the cornmeal mixture, and sprinkle the yeast over the water; let set a minute or two to soften. Sprinkle the salt and sugar over the yeast, and let set for a minute or two to proof. Add the egg and 2 cups of flour; beat well.

Add about 2½ more cups of flour, turn the dough out onto a well-floured countertop, and knead in as much of the remaining cup of flour as it takes to make a smooth, elastic dough. Form the dough into a ball on the counter, turn the mixing bowl upside down over it, and let set until doubled in bulk, about 1 to 1½ hours.

Shape into pan rolls (below) or crescent rolls (page 233) and bake at 350° for 30 minutes. Or make into one of the sweet rolls on pages 238 to 241.

HALF OF THE DOUGH MAKES 32 ROLLS; THE OTHER HALF WILL YIELD TWO 7½-INCH BY 3½-INCH LOAVES.

Pan Rolls

Use a full recipe of white bread dough (page 219), or a full recipe of honey whole wheat rolls (page 231), or a half recipe of one of the other roll doughs. Using your hands and working on a floured countertop, roll half of the dough into a long rope. Cut this rope in half, then each half into halves again, until you have 32 pieces of dough. Shape each piece into a ball and divide the balls evenly between 2 well-greased 8-inch round cake pans. (If you prefer, set the rolls slightly apart on a greased baking sheet.) Let rise until double, about 1 hour.

Preheat the oven to 350°, then bake the rolls for about 20 or 25 minutes if they are in the cake pans, a bit less time if they are on a baking sheet.

MAKES 32 ROLLS.

Crescent Rolls

Use a full recipe of white bread dough (page 219), or of honey whole wheat rolls (page 231), or a half recipe of one of the other roll doughs. Set out a cookie sheet, and grease it lightly.

Divide the dough into 4 parts and roll each part out into a circle about 10 inches in diameter. Spread the top of each circle with softened margarine about as thickly as you would spread it on toast. Using a dull table knife or spatula, cut each circle into 6 pie-shaped wedges. Starting at the wide end and finishing at the point, roll each piece of dough up, bend the ends toward each other to form a crescent, and place on the prepared cookie sheet. Tuck the point of the triangle underneath the roll. Let the rolls rise until double, about 1 to 1½ hours.

Bake in an oven preheated to 375° about 15 minutes.

MAKES 24 ROLLS.

Onion Rolls

These transform a plain soup-and-bread meal into something special. Or make a hit by taking them to a potluck supper. Best served warm, but also good at room temperature.

2 large onions (about ¾ pound), peeled and chopped
¼ cup olive oil or margarine
⅛ teaspoon salt
Dash pepper
½ recipe Refrigerator Roll Dough (page 230) or full recipe White Bread (page 219)

2 teaspoons Worcestershire sauce
2 tablespoons grated Romano cheese (optional)

The dough should be made, but not yet set to rise. Grease a 13- by 9-inch pan with margarine.

Sauté the onions in the oil or margarine until they are limp and just beginning to brown. Season them with the salt and pepper and then set them aside to cool to room temperature while the dough rises.

Roll out the dough into a rectangle about 22 by 10 inches. Spread the dough with the onions, sprinkle with the Worcestershire sauce and the cheese, and roll it up to form a 22-inch-long log. Slice crosswise into about 18 slices, using a dull table knife or kitchen spatula. Arrange the slices, cut side down, in the pan. Let rise about 1½ hours, until double.

Bake in an oven preheated to 350° for 35 to 40 minutes.

MAKES ABOUT 18 ROLLS.

Hot Cross Buns

Wonderful soft, raisiny buns. This is one recipe for which I will go to the trouble of boiling up a small potato.

½ cup mashed potatoes
6 tablespoons margarine
½ teaspoon ground
   cinnamon
¼ teaspoon ground
   nutmeg
½ cup raisins
¼ cup chopped mixed
   candied fruit, or a
   combination of
   candied pineapple and
   citron

¾ cup lukewarm water
2 packages active dry
   yeast
½ cup sugar
¾ teaspoon salt
2 eggs
About 4 cups flour

If you use a mashed freshly boiled potato, stir the margarine into the still-hot potato, to melt the margarine and cool the potato. If you have leftover potato, melt the margarine and stir the cold mashed potato into it; this will cool the margarine and loosen up the potato. Stir the spices, the raisins, and the candied fruit into the potato-margarine mixture and set the whole thing aside.

If you have some water in which potatoes were boiled, use it in this recipe; yeast doughs love potato water.

Put the warm water in a warmed mixing bowl and sprinkle the yeast over the water. Let set a bit to proof the yeast, then add the sugar, the salt, the eggs, and the potato mixture. Beat in 2 cups of flour.

Work in the rest of the flour gradually to form a rather soft dough. Knead about 5 minutes, until smooth. Like potato doughs in general, this one will not get very stiff, nor should it. Cover the dough with the inverted mixing bowl and let rise until double, about 1 to 1½ hours.

Knead the dough down and shape it into 24 balls. I usually do this by cutting the dough into halves and then each half into thirds. I then divide each piece of dough into quarters, making 24 little rolls in all. Set the balls of dough either slightly apart on a lightly greased baking sheet or touching each other on a lightly greased 10- by 15-inch baking pan. Let rise until double, about 1 hour.

Bake in a preheated oven at 325° about 30 minutes. While the buns are still warm, form a cross on top of each with the following:

Icing

> ½ cup confectioners' sugar
> ½ teaspoon vanilla
> 1 or 2 teaspoons water

Mix the sugar with the vanilla and enough water to make a spreadable icing.

The buns are good at room temperature, but they are even better when served warm.

MAKES 24 HOT CROSS BUNS.

Bath Buns

Similar to hot cross buns, but bigger and less rich. They are named for the English town of Bath.

1½ cups mashed potato	2 packages active dry
½ cup margarine	yeast
¼ cup raisins	1 teaspoon salt
½ cup chopped mixed	½ cup sugar
candied fruit	1 egg
1½ cups warm water	About 7 cups of flour

If the potatoes are freshly boiled and hot, stir chunks of the cold margarine into them and let set to melt the margarine and cool the potatoes. If you are using leftover mashed potatoes, melt the margarine and stir it into the potatoes to loosen them and warm them up. Stir the raisins and the candied fruit into the potatoes.

Put the warm water into a large warmed mixing bowl and sprinkle the yeast over it; add the salt and sugar and let set for a short time to proof the yeast. Stir in the potato mixture and the egg, plus 2 cups of flour. Knead in as much of the remaining flour as it takes to get a soft, nonsticky dough and continue kneading until the dough feels elastic, about 5 minutes. The dough should stay fairly soft. Round the dough up into a ball on the counter, cover with the inverted mixing bowl, and let rise until double, about 1 to 1½ hours.

Knead the dough down and shape it into 24 rolls. Set them a little bit apart on 2 greased baking sheets, and let rise until double, about 1 to 1½ hours.

Bake in an oven preheated to 325° for about 25 minutes.

Glaze

2 cups confectioners' sugar
1 teaspoon vanilla
About 2½ tablespoons water

Mix the confectioners sugar and vanilla with enough water to make a glaze. Spread glaze over the tops of the buns while they are still warm.

MAKES 2 DOZEN BUNS.

When making one of the following recipes that use a half recipe of basic roll dough, you might consider making a full recipe of dough; use half of it for sweet rolls, and the other half for dinner rolls, which freeze beautifully.

Swedish Tea Ring

Pretty, and easy to shape.

½ recipe Basic Sweet
  Roll Dough (page
  229), or Refrigerator
  Roll Dough (page 230)
  or a full recipe of
  White Bread dough
  (page 219)
1½ to 2 tablespoons
  softened margarine

⅓ cup brown sugar,
  loosely packed, or
  ¼ cup white sugar
¼ teaspoon ground
  cinnamon
¼ cup raisins or chopped
  nuts, if desired

Grease a cookie sheet.

Dust the countertop lightly with flour, and roll the dough out to form a rectangle about 25 inches long by 7 inches wide. Spread dough with margarine and sprinkle with the sugar and cinnamon, and the raisins or nuts, if used.

Using a flexible long spatula, loosen one long edge of the dough from the countertop and roll the rectangle up into a 25-inch log. Lifting it carefully by both ends, remove the log to the greased baking sheet and form it, seam side down, into a large ring; push the ends up against each other. It is okay to stretch the log a bit while you do this, to make a larger circle. Using heavy kitchen scissors, cut almost through the dough at intervals of about 1 inch. Then pull each semi-detached slice to the outside a little and twist it so that a cut edge faces up. Let rise in a warm place until double, about an hour.

Bake in an oven preheated to 325° until done, about 25 minutes. While the ring is still warm, frost it with the following:

Icing

1 cup confectioners' sugar
½ teaspoon vanilla
About 4 teaspoons water

Mix the sugar, vanilla, and water together to make a smooth, rather thin icing.

Tea ring is good served at room temperature, very good served warm.

MAKES 1 TEA RING ABOUT 11 INCHES IN DIAMETER.

Cinnamon Rolls

The basic sweet roll, always well liked.

Grease a 9- by 9-inch baking pan. Proceed as for Swedish tea ring, except that after you have formed the dough into a log, cut it into 1½-inch-thick slices. You don't have to be very exact, anywhere from 15 to 24 slices is just fine. Place them cut side down in the prepared pan and let rise until double, about 1 hour.

Bake in preheated 325° oven for about 40 minutes, until done. If you like the sugar to melt into a glaze while baking, bake at 375° for a shorter time. Ice while warm with the same icing used for Swedish tea ring.

MAKES ABOUT 18 TO 24 ROLLS.

Rum Buns

Make cinnamon rolls, but use this icing to make rum buns:

1 cup confectioners' sugar
4 or 5 teaspoons rum

Mix together well to make a thin icing.

Lemon Rolls

3 teaspoons grated
lemon rind (rind from
1 lemon)
¼ cup sugar
½ recipe Basic Sweet
Roll Dough (page
229), or a full recipe
of White Bread dough
(page 219)

1 tablespoon softened
margarine
2 tablespoons chopped
almonds (optional)

Grate the outermost yellow part of the lemon rind and mix about 2 teaspoons of it with the sugar. Cover the remaining grated peel with the confectioners' sugar to be used for icing, and set it aside.

Grease a 9- by 9-inch square baking pan.

Roll the dough out to a rectangle about 25 inches long by about 7 inches wide. Spread it with the margarine and sprinkle with the mixture of sugar and grated lemon rind. Strew with the chopped almonds, if used. Loosen one long edge of the dough with a flexible kitchen spatula and roll the dough up to form a log about 25 inches long. Again using the spatula, cut the log crosswise into about 16 slices. Transfer the slices carefully to the pan or pans. Let rise until double, about 1 hour.

Bake about 35 minutes in an oven preheated to 325°.

While warm, frost with the following:

Icing

Reserved grated lemon peel
¾ cup confectioners' sugar
About 1 tablespoon orange juice

Mix these ingredients smooth; use just enough juice to make an icing that spreads easily.

Orange Rolls

Follow the recipe for lemon rolls, but substitute 1½ tablespoons grated orange rind (½ orange) for the lemon rind. For the icing, use about ⅓ of the grated rind of the orange instead of the grated lemon rind.

Yeast-raised Apple Cake

A good, fruity coffee cake, less sweet than others of its kind.

½ cup warm water
1 package active dry
    yeast
2 tablespoons sugar
¼ teaspoon salt
1 egg
2 tablespoons melted
    margarine

1¾ cups flour
2 tablespoons apricot,
    raspberry, or other
    jam of your choice
2 medium-sized tart
    apples, to give about
    2 cups of apple slices

Grease an 8- by 8-inch baking pan. (If you double the recipe, bake it in a 9- by 13-inch pan.)

Put the warm water into a warmed mixing bowl. Sprinkle the yeast over the water, add the sugar and salt, and let set for a minute or two to proof the yeast. Add the egg, melted margarine, and 1 cup of flour and beat well until smooth and sticky. Add enough of the rest of the flour to make a soft dough, and knead it for a few strokes.

Put the dough into the prepared pan and pat it out to fill the pan; make the edges a little higher than the center. (You may want to dip your fingers in flour before you do this.) Spread the jam on the dough. Peel, core and slice the apples and arrange them on the jam.

Topping

⅓ cup flour	⅛ teaspoon ground
⅓ cup white sugar or	nutmeg
loosely packed brown	⅛ teaspoon ground
sugar	cinnamon
⅛ teaspoon salt	3 tablespoons margarine

Cut all ingredients together with a pastry blender. Sprinkle this topping over the apples and let the cake rise in a warm place until almost double, about 1 hour.

Bake in preheated 375° oven for about 40 minutes. Test the cake with a skewer to be sure it is done; insert the skewer into the center of the cake, and pull it out. If any dough clings to the skewer, bake a little longer. Let the cake cool for half an hour or longer before serving.

MAKES ONE 8-INCH SQUARE CAKE.

Stollen

This traditional German Christmas bread is popular at holiday buffets, and makes a wonderful Christmas morning breakfast. This version is not so rich as most.

¼ cup margarine	¾ cup raisins
1 cup warm water	½ cup (3 ounces)
1 package active dry	chopped mixed
yeast	candied fruit
⅓ cup sugar	About 4 cups flour
¾ teaspoon salt	1 tablespoon extra
⅔ cup almonds, chopped	margarine, soft
coarsely	enough to spread
2 teaspoons freshly	easily
grated lemon rind	
1 egg (if you double the	
recipe, use 3 eggs)	

Melt ¼ cup margarine. Put the warm water into a large, warmed mixing bowl, and sprinkle the yeast over it. Sprinkle the sugar and the salt over the yeast, and let the mixture set and get bubbly while you chop the almonds and grate the lemon rind.

Stir the margarine, egg, lemon rind, raisins, almonds and candied fruit into the dough. Gradually add as much of the flour as necessary to get a dough that can be kneaded. Turn it out onto a well-floured countertop and knead it until springy, about 5 minutes. As you knead, add just enough flour to keep the dough from being sticky.

Round the dough into a ball on the countertop and upend the mixing bowl over it; let rise for about 1½ hours, or until the dough seems puffy. For some reason, stollen dough doesn't seem to rise as much as other doughs, although when baked it will be light enough.

Grease a baking sheet. Knead the dough for a few strokes, then roll it out to form an oval about 14 inches long by 10 inches wide. Spread the top of the dough with the softened margarine, then fold it in half the long way, to give a loaf about 5 inches wide by about 14 inches long. (If you prefer, divide the dough in half and roll it out to two ovals, each 7 inches wide by 10 inches long, for 2 small stollen.)

Put the stollen on the prepared baking sheet, pulling the ends back as you do so to form a crescent shape. With the heel of your hand, press firmly along the fold of the dough. Stollen will sometimes spring open while baking; spreading the dough with margarine and pressing down on the fold will usually prevent this. Let rise until the dough seems light—about 1½ hours.

Preheat the oven to 350° and bake the stollen for about 40 minutes for a large stollen, about 35 minutes for a small stollen. Stollen is done when a skewer inserted into it comes out clean.

Glaze for 1 large stollen

    1 cup confectioners' sugar
    ½ teaspoon vanilla
    2 or 3 teaspoons water
    Candied fruit and blanched almonds for decorations
      (optional)

When the stollen has cooled, glaze it with the confectioners' sugar mixed with the vanilla and enough water to make a thin frosting. Decorate it, if you like, with the almonds and candied fruit. (To glaze 2 small stollen you will need 1½ cups confectioners' sugar, ¾ teaspoon vanilla, and 3 or 4 teaspoons water.)

Stollen is best if served within a day of baking.

MAKES 1 LARGE OR 2 SMALL STOLLEN.

Quick Breads and Coffee Cakes

Corn Bread
Blueberry Cake
Crumb Cake
Boston Baked Bread
Banana Bread
Cranberry Bread
Zucchini Bread
Strawberry-Oatmeal Bread
   Peach-Oatmeal Bread

Mincemeat Coffee Loaf
Blueberry Buckle
Strawberry Coffee Cake
   Peach Coffee Cake
Apple Coffee Cake
   Plum Cake

Corn Bread

This is Northern-style corn bread, made with yellow cornmeal and sweetened with sugar. Serve it hot with margarine and jam.

2 tablespoons margarine	½ teaspoon salt
¾ cup cornmeal	1 cup water
1½ cups flour	2 eggs
¾ cup sugar	
2¼ teaspoons baking powder	

Put the margarine into a 9- by 9-inch square baking pan, and set the pan in the oven while you preheat it to 400°.

Sift the dry ingredients into a mixing bowl. Mix the water, eggs, and melted margarine together. (Tip the pan to all sides before you pour the margarine into the eggs so that the bottom of the pan is greased.) Pour the liquid ingredients all at once into the sifted dry ingredients and stir until everything is well combined. Turn the batter into the baking pan. Bake for about 25 minutes.

Blueberry Cake

Old New England cookbooks call this blueberry cake; it is really a blueberry bread.

3 tablespoons margarine	2 cups (1 pint) blueberries, fresh or frozen
3 cups flour	
⅔ cup sugar	1½ cups water
3½ teaspoons baking powder	2 eggs
¾ teaspoon salt	

247

Put the margarine into a 9- by 13-inch pan and set it in the oven while it preheats to 400°. Sift the dry ingredients together into a mixing bowl; stir in the blueberries.

Tip the baking pan to all sides to grease the bottom of the pan thoroughly. Mix the water, eggs, and melted margarine together. Mix the liquid ingredients briefly into the dry ingredients, then pour the batter into the prepared pan.

Bake about 35 minutes if you use frozen blueberries, about 25 minutes for fresh berries.

Crumb Cake

This Pennsylvania Dutch specialty was traditionally served for Sunday breakfast at my college. With soup or salad, it makes an excellent light lunch. Crumb cake is usually served at room temperature, and it's good that way, but it's even better when still warm from the oven.

2 cups flour	1/4 cup chopped almonds
1 1/4 cups sugar	(optional)
1 teaspoon baking	1/4 teaspoon ground
powder	nutmeg or cinnamon
3/4 teaspoon salt	3/4 cup water
1/3 cup margarine	1 egg

Preheat the oven to 350° and grease a 9-inch round cake pan. Sift the flour, sugar, baking powder, and salt together into a bowl. Cut in the margarine until the pieces are about the size of peas. Remove a handful (about 1/3 cup) of these crumbs to a small bowl and mix in the almonds (if used) and the spice, to make the topping for the cake.

Mix the egg and water together and stir into the batter, until all of the dry particles are moistened; it's okay if the batter is lumpy. Pour into the greased pan and sprinkle with the topping mixture.

Bake for 30 to 35 minutes.

Boston Baked Bread

Good warm or at room temperature, this goes well with baked beans.

1 cup white flour
¼ cup sugar
2 teaspoons baking
   powder
½ teaspoon baking soda
½ teaspoon salt
1 cup whole wheat flour
⅓ cup wheat germ

¼ cup margarine
½ cup raisins
¼ cup chopped nuts
   (optional)
2 eggs
1¼ cups water
½ cup molasses

Preheat the oven to 350° and grease a 9- by 5-inch loaf pan. Sift the white flour, sugar, baking powder, baking soda, and salt into a bowl. Stir in the whole wheat flour and wheat germ. Cut in the margarine until the pieces are the size of small peas, then stir in raisins and nuts.

Mix the eggs, water, and molasses together; stir into the dry ingredients just until everything is moistened. Turn into the prepared loaf pan. Bake for about 55 minutes.

Banana Bread

3 or 4 very ripe bananas
½ cup margarine
1 cup sugar
3 eggs
2⅔ cups flour

2 teaspoons baking
   powder
1 teaspoon baking soda
¾ teaspoon salt

Preheat the oven to 375° and grease a 9- by 5-inch loaf pan. Peel and mash (with a fork or in a blender) enough ripe bananas to give 1½ cups mashed banana.

Cream the margarine, sugar, and 2 of the eggs very well. Sift the flour, baking powder, baking soda, and salt together. Add the third egg to the batter, and beat briefly; stir in the sifted dry ingredients and the mashed banana; keep on stirring just until the batter is well mixed. Turn into the greased loaf pan.

Bake about 55 minutes, or until the bread appears done; a skewer inserted into the middle will come out not quite clean. Remove from the pan to cool before serving.

Cranberry Bread

Cranberry bread is very good when freshly baked, but it will slice much more easily when a day old.

⅓ cup nuts	1 cup sugar
1¾ cups (about 6 ounces) raw cranberries	2 teaspoons baking powder
	½ teaspoon baking soda
1 orange and its juice, plus more juice to give ¾ cup	¾ teaspoon salt
	¼ cup vegetable oil
2 cups flour	1 egg

Preheat the oven to 350° and grease a 9- by 5-inch loaf pan. Chop the nuts and set them aside.

Rinse the cranberries, drain them well, and chop them. If you use a knife, you will find cranberries in remote corners of your kitchen for weeks to come; they fly about in a most amazing way. Better to do the job with a blender, food processor, or meat grinder fitted with a coarse blade. To avoid pureeing the cranberries, turn off the blender or food processor as soon as they are chopped.

Wash and dry the orange and grate the colored part of the rind; you will get about 2 to 3 teaspoons. Squeeze the juice into a measuring cup, adding enough extra orange juice to give ¾ cup total, and set this aside.

Sift the flour, sugar, baking powder, baking soda, and salt into a large mixing bowl. Stir in the nuts, cranberries, and grated orange rind.

Stir in the oil, egg, and orange juice together briefly and then stir this liquid into the flour–cranberry mixture, stirring just until the dry particles are moist. Turn the batter into the prepared pan.

Bake for about 1 hour, or until a skewer inserted into the middle comes out clean. Serve at room temperature.

Zucchini Bread

This moist, green-flecked bread is a good use for some of those August zucchini.

1½ cups grated zucchini (about ½ pound)
2 cups flour
1 cup sugar
1 teaspoon baking powder
½ teaspoon baking soda

½ teaspoon ground cinnamon
½ teaspoon salt
2 eggs
½ cup vegetable oil
½ cup water
½ teaspoon vanilla

Scrub the zucchini and grate it coarsely; you should have 1½ cups of lightly packed grated zucchini. Preheat the oven to 350° and use solid shortening to grease a 9- by 5-inch loaf pan.

Sift the dry ingredients together into a large bowl; stir in the grated zucchini.

Mix the eggs, oil, water, and vanilla together in another bowl; stir this all at once into the dry ingredients, and continue to stir just until all of the dry particles are moistened. Turn the batter into the prepared loaf pan.

Bake for about 1 to 1¼ hours. Let cool in the pan; serve at room temperature.

Strawberry-Oatmeal Bread

2 cups flour
3/4 cup sugar
1 teaspoon baking
  powder
3/4 teaspoon baking soda
1/2 teaspoon ground
  cinnamon
1/2 teaspoon salt

1 cup rolled oats
1 1/2 cups crushed
  strawberries (about
  1 pint)
1/3 cup vegetable oil
1 egg
1/2 teaspoon vanilla

Preheat the oven to 350° and use solid shortening to grease a 9- by 5-inch loaf pan.

Sift together into a large bowl all the dry ingredients except for the oatmeal; stir that in.

Crush the strawberries in a blender, with a potato masher, or with a fork; add the oil, egg, and vanilla, and mix well. Add these liquid ingredients all at once to the dry ingredients, mix well, and pour into the prepared loaf pan.

Bake for about 1 hour, or until the bread shrinks slightly from the sides of the pan, and a skewer inserted in the center comes out clean. Serve at room temperature.

Peach-Oatmeal Bread

Follow the recipe for strawberry-oatmeal bread, but use peaches instead of strawberries, and add 1/4 cup water to the fruit. You will need about 4 peaches. Peel the peaches and cut them into thick slices, then cut these slices crosswise into pieces about 1/8 inch thick.

Mincemeat Coffee Loaf

Easy to make and much sweeter than other quick loaves. Although mincemeat is customarily used in mince pie, I also like it in this coffee bread. See page 316 for a description of mincemeat, always available during the Thanksgiving to Christmas season.

2 cups flour	⅓ cup margarine
½ cup sugar	1 egg
2½ teaspoons baking powder	¾ cup (about 6 ounces) mincemeat
½ teaspoon salt	½ cup water

Preheat the oven to 375° and grease well the bottom and sides of a 9- by 5-inch loaf pan.

Sift the flour, sugar, baking powder, and salt into a bowl. Cut in the margarine until the pieces are the size of small peas. Mix the egg, mincemeat, and water together; stir all at once into the flour mixture. The batter will be lumpy, but all of the dry particles should be moistened. Spoon into the prepared pan.

Bake for about 45 minutes, or until the top is brown and the cake appears done. A skewer inserted into the middle will not come out clean, but that is okay.

Glaze

¾ cup confectioners' sugar
1½ tablespoons apple cider, or 1½ tablespoons water
plus ½ teaspoon vanilla

Mix the sugar with enough cider or water plus vanilla to make a rather runny glaze; spread this over the top of the coffee cake when it comes from the oven. Let cool in the pan before slicing and serving.

The fruit coffee cakes that follow are wonderful in summer, when plenty of fresh fruit is available. Like most of the other quick breads, they don't demand much in the way of kitchen equipment and can be easily made when you are cooking in an unfamiliar kitchen.

Blueberry Buckle

Much richer than blueberry cake.

Crumb topping

⅓ cup flour
⅓ cup sugar
¼ teaspoon salt
½ teaspoon ground cinnamon
3 tablespoons margarine

Batter

2 cups flour
¾ cups sugar
2½ teaspoons baking
   powder
½ teaspoon salt
5 tablespoons margarine

2 cups (1 pint) blueberries, fresh or frozen, small blueberries if possible
1 egg
¾ cup water

Preheat the oven to 350° and grease a 9-inch square pan.

Prepare the crumb topping. Sift the flour, sugar, salt, and cinnamon together into a small bowl; cut in the margarine until the pieces are the size of small peas.

Prepare the cake. Sift the dry ingredients into a bowl; cut in the margarine until it is the size of small peas. Stir in the blueberries. Mix the egg and water together and stir into the flour mixture, then turn this batter into the prepared pan and strew the crumb mixture over it.

Bake for about 50 minutes if you used fresh berries, or about 70 minutes if the berries are frozen.

Strawberry Coffee Cake

Rather like blueberry buckle, except the strawberries are spread on top of the batter instead of being mixed into it.

Crumb Topping

⅓ cup flour
⅓ cup sugar
½ teaspoon ground cinnamon
¼ teaspoon salt
3 tablespoons margarine

Cake

1 pint strawberries
2 cups flour
¾ cup sugar
2½ teaspoons baking
   powder

½ teaspoon salt
5 tablespoons margarine
¾ cup water
½ teaspoon vanilla
1 egg

Preheat the oven to 400° and grease a 9-inch square pan. Make the topping: Sift the flour, sugar, cinnamon, and salt into a bowl. Cut in the margarine until the pieces are the size of small peas, then set the crumbs aside while you make the cake batter.

Rinse the strawberries, remove the hulls, and slice the berries if they're large.

Make the cake: Sift the flour, sugar, baking powder, and salt together into a bowl; cut in the margarine until it is the size of small peas. Mix the water, vanilla, and egg together well; stir into the flour mixture. Turn the batter into the prepared pan and top with the strawberries, and then with the crumbs.

Bake for about 40 minutes. Serve warm.

Peach Coffee Cake

Take this to a picnic. It travels well under a foil cover.

In the topping substitute firmly packed brown sugar for white sugar and reduce the cinnamon to ¼ teaspoon.

Substitute 2½ cups peach slices (about 6 peaches) for the strawberries. Dot the peach slices with about 2 tablespoons of tart jelly (such as raspberry jelly or currant jelly) before you top with the crumbs.

Reduce the baking time to about 35 minutes.

Apple Coffee Cake

Crumb Topping

¼ cup flour
¾ teaspoon ground cinnamon
⅛ teaspoon salt
½ cup brown sugar, firmly packed
3 tablespoons margarine

Cake

4 to 6 tart apples (about 4½ cups apple slices)	¾ teaspoon salt
3 cups flour	½ cup margarine
1 cup sugar	1 cup water
4 teaspoons baking powder	2 eggs
	1 teaspoon vanilla

Preheat the oven to 400° and grease a 9- by 13-inch pan or two 9-inch round pans.

Prepare the crumb topping: Sift the flour, cinnamon, and salt into a bowl; stir in the brown sugar, and cut in the margarine until the pieces are about the size of small peas.

Peel, core, and slice the apples.

Make the batter: Sift the flour, sugar, baking powder, and salt together into a bowl. Cut in the margarine until the pieces are about the size of peas.

Mix the water, eggs, and vanilla together; add them to the sifted dry ingredients and stir until all of the dry particles are moistened—the batter should still be lumpy. Spread the batter in the prepared pan, and distribute the apple slices evenly over it. Strew the crumb topping over the apples.

Bake for about 40 minutes. Serve warm.

Plum Cake

Substitute 15 or 20 oval Italian prune plums, rinsed, cut in half, and with pits removed, for the apple slices. Lay the plums cut side down on the batter.

Muffins and Biscuits

Muffins
  Date Muffins
Apple-Spice Muffins
Blueberry Muffins
Cranberry Muffins
Prune Muffins
Cornmeal Muffins
Whole Wheat Muffins
Apple Whole Wheat
  Muffins
Bran Muffins
Seven-Grain Muffins
Popovers
  Yorkshire Pudding

Biscuits
Whole Wheat Biscuits
Potato Biscuits
Squash Biscuits
Stovetop Biscuits
Breakfast Buns

Muffins

Muffins are easy to make, and cook quickly—a useful sort of bread. Muffin batter is supposed to be lumpy. If you beat it until it is smooth, the muffins will be tough.

2 cups flour	⅔ cup water
¼ cup sugar	2 eggs
1 tablespoon baking powder	2 tablespoons extra sugar (optional)
½ teaspoon salt	
6 tablespoons vegetable oil	

Preheat the oven to 375° and use solid shortening to grease 12 muffin cups.

Sift the flour, sugar, baking powder, and salt into a bowl; form a well in the center.

Mix the oil, water, and eggs together, pour them into the well, and stir just until all of the flour is moistened. Spoon the batter into the prepared muffin cups and sprinkle the tops lightly with the extra sugar, if desired.

Bake for about 15 to 20 minutes, or until lightly browned and done.

MAKES TWELVE 2½-INCH MUFFINS.

Date Muffins

Stir ⅔ cup chopped dates into the flour before adding the liquids.

Apple-Spice Muffins

½ cup coarsely grated
  apple (1 small apple)
⅛ teaspoon ground
  cinnamon
Pinch of ground nutmeg
¼ cup plus 1 tablespoon
  sugar
1¾ cups flour
¼ cup sugar

2 teaspoons baking
  powder
½ teaspoon salt
1 egg
6 tablespoons vegetable
  oil
½ cup water
¼ cup raisins, if desired

Preheat the oven to 400° and grease 12 muffin cups thoroughly.

Peel and core the apple, and grate it coarsely. Make spiced sugar by stirring the cinnamon and nutmeg into 1 tablespoon sugar. Reserve.

Sift the flour, remaining ¼ cup sugar, baking powder, and salt together into a bowl. Mix the egg, oil, water, and grated apple together; stir them all at once into the sifted dry ingredients, mixing just until all of the flour is moistened. Stir in the raisins, if used.

Divide the dough among the muffin cups and sprinkle the tops of the muffins with the spiced sugar.

Bake for about 15 minutes, until done.

MAKES TWELVE 2½-INCH MUFFINS.

Blueberry Muffins

Either fresh or frozen blueberries can be used in this recipe. If you use frozen berries you will need to cook the muffins about 5 or 10 minutes longer.

1¾ cups flour
¼ cup sugar
2 teaspoons baking
   powder
½ teaspoon salt
¾ cup blueberries,
   preferably small ones
1 egg

6 tablespoons vegetable
   oil
½ cup water
1 tablespoon sugar
   (optional)
⅛ teaspoon ground
   cinnamon (optional)

Preheat the oven to 400° and use solid shortening to grease 12 muffin cups.

Sift the flour, sugar, baking powder, and salt together into a bowl. Stir in the blueberries. Mix the egg, oil, and water together; stir them all at once into the flour-blueberry mixture, continuing to stir just until all of the dry particles are moistened.

Divide the batter among the 12 prepared muffin cups, and sprinkle the tops of the muffins with the sugar flavored with cinnamon if desired.

Bake for 15 to 20 minutes.

MAKES TWELVE 2½-INCH MUFFINS.

Cranberry Muffins

Make these in autumn, when fresh cranberries are available in the market. Or freeze cranberries for later use—just rinse them, drain until dry, bag them, and store in your freezer.

3/4 cup cranberries
1 3/4 cups flour
6 tablespoons sugar, plus 1 tablespoon (optional)
2 teaspoons baking powder
1/4 teaspoon ground allspice
1/2 teaspoon salt
1 egg
6 tablespoons vegetable oil
1/2 cup water

Preheat the oven to 400° and grease 12 muffin cups with solid shortening.

Rinse the cranberries and chop them in a blender, food processor, or meat grinder until the pieces are about the size of rice grains.

Sift the flour, the 6 tablespoons sugar, baking powder, allspice, and salt together into a bowl; stir in the cranberries. Mix the egg, oil, and water together, then stir all at once into the flour mixture. Stir just until all of the dry bits are moist; do not beat. Spoon the batter into the prepared muffin pans, and sprinkle the tops with the remaining tablespoon of sugar if desired.

Bake for 15 to 20 minutes.

MAKES TWELVE 2½-INCH MUFFINS.

Prune Muffins

These are sweeter than most muffins. They're delicious, and a good use for cooked prunes.

⅔ cup pitted cooked
   prunes
¼ cup margarine
¼ cup white sugar
⅓ cup brown sugar,
   packed firm
1 egg

2 cups flour
1 tablespoon baking
   powder
¼ teaspoon ground
   nutmeg
½ teaspoon salt
1 cup water

Preheat the oven to 400°. Grease 18 muffin cups.

Using strong kitchen scissors, cut through the prunes in the cup a number of times in order to chop them up into pieces of a size you would be pleased to meet in a muffin.

Cream the margarine and sugars together well and beat in the egg until the mixture is light and fluffy. Sift the dry ingredients together, then mix them gently into the batter along with the water and the prunes. Spoon into the prepared muffin cups.

Bake for about 20 minutes.

MAKES EIGHTEEN 2½-INCH MUFFINS.

Cornmeal Muffins

1 cup flour
¼ cup sugar
1 tablespoon baking
   powder
½ teaspoon salt

1 cup cornmeal
6 tablespoons margarine
⅔ cup water
2 eggs

Preheat the oven to 375° and grease 12 muffin cups. Sift the flour, sugar, baking powder, and salt together into a bowl and then stir in the cornmeal. Cut in the margarine until the pieces are the size of split peas.

Using a fork or a teaspoon, beat the water and the eggs together briefly; stir this mixture into the dry ingredients just until all of the particles are moistened. Divide the batter among the prepared muffin cups.

Bake for about 20 minutes, or until the muffins are cooked and lightly browned. Serve hot.

MAKES TWELVE 2½-INCH MUFFINS.

Whole Wheat Muffins

A good tender muffin, made with more whole wheat flour than most. You can omit the cornmeal if you wish, and use 2 extra tablespoonsful of whole what flour instead.

½ cup white flour
¼ cup sugar
1 tablespoon baking powder
½ teaspoon salt
1⅓ cups whole wheat flour

2 tablespoons cornmeal
⅔ cup raisins, chopped dates, or nuts
⅔ cup water
6 tablespoons vegetable oil
2 eggs

Preheat the oven to 375° and grease 12 muffin cups.

Sift the white flour, sugar, baking powder, and salt together into a mixing bowl. Stir in the whole wheat flour, cornmeal, and fruit or nuts.

Mix the water, oil, and eggs together; add them all at once to the dry ingredients and stir just until the dry ingredients are moistened. Spoon into the prepared muffin cups.

Bake for about 20 minutes.

MAKES TWELVE 2½-INCH MUFFINS.

Apple Whole Wheat Muffins

About ⅓ cup grated
  apple (1 small tart
  apple)
½ cup white flour
1½ teaspoons baking
  powder
½ teaspoon salt

½ cup whole wheat
  flour
⅓ cup water
3 tablespoons vegetable
  oil
3 tablespoons honey
1 egg

Preheat the oven to 375° and grease with solid shortening eight 2½-inch muffin cups. Peel and core the apple, then grate it coarsely.

Sift the white flour, baking powder, and salt into a mixing bowl. Stir in the whole wheat flour and the grated apple. Mix the water, oil, honey, and egg together well; stir this mixture all at once into the dry ingredients, stirring just until all of the dry bits are moistened. Spoon into the prepared muffin cups.

Bake about 20 minutes.

MAKES EIGHT 2½-INCH MUFFINS.

Bran Muffins

A good, light whole-grain muffin.

3 tablespoons bran flakes
¾ cup boiling water
¼ cup white flour
2 teaspoons baking
  powder
¼ teaspoon salt
¾ cup whole wheat
  flour

1 tablespoon wheat germ
⅓ cup raisins (optional)
3 tablespoons vegetable
  oil
3 tablespoons molasses
1 egg

In a small bowl stir the boiling water into the bran flakes. Set the oven to 400°. Use solid shortening to grease twelve 2½-inch muffin cups.

Sift the white flour, baking powder, and salt into a bowl. Stir in the whole wheat flour, the wheat germ, and the raisins, if desired. Stir the oil, molasses, and egg into the bran flakes, in that order. (The molasses will be easier to get out of the measuring cup if you use it to measure the oil first.) Stir everything together just until mixed, then spoon the batter into the prepared muffin cups.

Bake for 15 to 20 minutes, or until a skewer inserted into the center of a muffin comes out clean.

MAKES TWELVE 2½-INCH MUFFINS.

Seven-Grain Muffins

Coarse, crunchy, good.

½ cup seven-grain cereal
¾ cup boiling water
¼ cup brown sugar,
   firmly packed
⅓ cup raisins
¾ cup flour

2 teaspoons baking
   powder
½ teaspoon salt
3 tablespoons vegetable
   oil
1 egg

Preheat the oven to 400° and grease twelve 2½-inch muffin cups.

Whirl the cereal in a blender for a minute or two, until its texture resembles that of corn meal. Soak the cereal in the boiling water for about 10 minutes, then stir in the brown sugar and the raisins.

Sift the flour, baking powder, and salt together. Mix the oil and egg with the soaked cereal, then stir the two mixtures together. Pour into the prepared muffin tins.

Bake about 20 minutes.

MAKES TWELVE 2½-INCH MUFFINS.

Popovers

American popovers are very much like English Yorkshire pudding, except they are baked in individual pans and served with butter or margarine and jam.

> 1 cup flour
> 1 tablespoon sugar
> 1/4 teaspoon salt
> 1 cup water
> 3 eggs

Preheat the oven to 400° and thoroughly grease 9 muffin cups with solid shortening. Special pans are available for baking popovers, but they aren't necessary; ordinary muffin pans or glass baking cups do very well.

Sift the flour, sugar, and salt together into a mixing bowl. (Popovers need no baking powder.) Add the water and the eggs, and beat briefly using a rotary egg beater; it is okay to leave some lumps. Fill the prepared muffin cups about 3/4 full with this batter.

Bake until well puffed and light brown—about 40 minutes. Serve immediately as popovers tend to deflate.

MAKES 9 POPOVERS.

Yorkshire Pudding

Pour the popover batter into a 9- by 9-inch square pan containing about 1/4 cup of the drippings from a just-cooked standing rib roast of beef.

Turn the oven up to 450° and bake until the Yorkshire pudding puffs up and browns, about 25 to 30 minutes. Serve hot as an accompaniment to the roast.

MAKES 9 SERVINGS.

A Word or Two about Biscuits . . .

Everybody likes biscuits, and they can be made and cooked very quickly. Light, tender biscuits are wonderful things. However, if the dough isn't handled carefully, they can be very tough little breads; practice will teach you what biscuit dough should feel like, and then you can make good biscuits quite reliably—although no two batches will ever be exactly the same.

Batches of biscuit dough are variable mainly because the proportion of liquid to flour is critical: A teaspoonful more liquid in the dough means you must add about a tablespoon more flour. Measuring cups just aren't made to be read that accurately. Also, the apparently dry flour with which you start will already contain more water or less, depending on how humid the air has been lately. This is why you must learn what biscuit dough should feel like, rather than depending on careful measuring as you can with most baking powder breads.

You begin by sifting the dry ingredients into a bowl and then cutting in the shortening with a pastry blender. The fat should be cool, and solid. I use margarine, but many people like to use vegetable shortening.

The amount of water specified in the recipe is usually enough. Mix it in rapidly, and all at once. If the dough refuses to cling together in a ball, mix in a little more water. If the dough is too sticky, a little more flour is in order. You should handle the dough as quickly and as lightly as possible; kneading a few strokes just before rolling out the dough improves it, but squeezing it will make the biscuits heavy.

Biscuits are usually cut out with circular cutters. For big biscuits I use an old tunafish can, well washed and with holes punched in the bottom. For small biscuits my cutter is an old tomato paste can, similarly treated. A clean drinking glass makes good medium-sized biscuits.

Biscuits

It was a pleasure to discover that my favorite buttermilk biscuit recipe is just as good when water and extra baking powder are substituted for the buttermilk and baking soda.

Peanut butter and honey spread is wonderful on hot biscuits. To make it, just mix equal quantities of peanut butter and honey together in a bowl.

2 cups flour, plus extra
flour for rolling out
biscuits
1 tablespoon sugar
1½ teaspoons baking
powder
¼ teaspoon salt

1 tablespoon wheat germ
(optional)
3 tablespoons margarine
or vegetable
shortening
About ¾ cup water

Preheat the oven to 475° and grease a baking pan or baking sheet. Sift 2 cups flour, sugar, baking powder, and salt into a bowl. Stir in the wheat germ if desired, then cut in the shortening until the pieces are about the size of small peas. Add the water; stir just until well mixed.

Turn the dough out onto a floured countertop and knead for a few strokes before rolling it out about ¾ inch thick. Cut out biscuits and place on the prepared baking pan.

Bake about 15 minutes. Serve hot.

MAKES SIX 2¾-INCH BISCUITS.

Whole Wheat Biscuits

1⅓ cups white flour,
  plus extra flour
1 tablespoon sugar
1½ teaspoons baking
  powder
¼ teaspoon salt
⅔ cup whole wheat
  flour

1 tablespoon wheat germ
1 tablespoon bran
3 tablespoons margarine
  or vegetable
  shortening
About ⅔ cup water

Preheat the oven to 475° and grease a baking pan or baking sheet. Sift 1⅓ cups white flour, sugar, baking powder, and salt into a bowl; stir in the whole wheat flour, the wheat germ, and the bran. Cut in the shortening until the pieces are the size of small peas. Stir in the water just until the dough is well mixed.

Spread some more flour on a clean countertop, turn the biscuit dough out onto it, and knead for a few strokes. Roll the dough out about ¾ inch thick, and cut out the biscuits. Place them on the prepared pan. Bake for 15 to 20 minutes. Serve hot.

MAKES SIX 2¾-INCH BISCUITS.

Potato Biscuits

Soft biscuits, with good flavor.

1 cup flour, plus extra
  flour
2 teaspoons baking
  powder
¼ teaspoon salt

2½ tablespoons
  margarine
½ cup mashed potato
½ cup water

Preheat the oven to 450° and grease a baking pan or baking sheet. Sift 1 cup flour, baking powder, and salt into a bowl. (Use less salt if the potatoes were salted.) Add the margarine and cut it in with a pastry blender until the particles are the size of small peas. Mix the mashed potato and the water together and stir them into the dough.

Knead the dough for a few strokes on your lightly floured countertop, then roll it out about ¾ inch thick. Cut out the biscuits and place them in the prepared pan.

Bake for about 20 minutes. Serve hot.

MAKES SIX 2½-INCH BISCUITS.

Squash Biscuits

Beautiful golden biscuits to make in fall or winter and serve with soup.

¼ cup margarine	1 tablespoon sugar
¾ cup cooked, mashed winter squash	1 tablespoon baking powder
2 tablespoons water	¼ teaspoon salt
1½ cups flour, plus extra flour	

Preheat the oven to 450° and grease a baking tin or baking sheet. Melt the margarine, add the squash and water, and mix well.

Sift 1½ cups flour, sugar, baking powder, and salt together, add the squash mixture, and stir just until well combined. Sometimes cooked squash is dry and sometimes it is moist, so you may need to add a little more water or a little more flour to get the biscuits to a consistency that will roll out easily; 2 tablespoons water is usually about right.

Knead the dough for a few strokes on a floured countertop, then roll it out about ¾ inch thick and cut out with a biscuit cutter.

Bake on the prepared tin for about 20 minutes. Serve hot.

MAKES FOUR 3¼-INCH BISCUITS.

Stovetop Biscuits

These are a first cousin, or perhaps a grandmother, to scones. Stovetop biscuits do not need an oven; they are "baked" on a frying pan.

1 ⅓ cups flour, plus
  additional for rolling
¼ cup sugar
1 tablespoon baking
  powder

½ teaspoon salt
¼ cup margarine or
  vegetable shortening
1 egg mixed with water
  to measure ½ cup

Preheat a frying pan on medium to low heat, and grease it lightly. If using an electric skillet, set it to 375°. You will need a cover for the pan.

Sift 1 ⅓ cups flour, sugar, baking powder, and salt together into a mixing bowl. Cut in the shortening until the particles are quite fine, like large grains of rice. Break the egg into a measuring cup and add water to produce ½ cup liquid. Mix the egg and water very well together. Stir this mixture briefly into the flour until all of the dry bits are moistened.

Turn the dough out onto a floured countertop and knead it for a few strokes, then roll it out about ½ inch thick. Cut out into biscuits.

Sauté the biscuits on your lightly greased skillet about 6 minutes on each side. Cover the pan while the biscuits are cooking on the first side. Serve hot.

MAKES EIGHT 2½-INCH BISCUITS.

Breakfast Buns

These cinnamon rolls are made with biscuit dough instead of the more usual yeast-raised dough, so they are quick to produce. Good for weekend breakfasts.

2 cups flour, plus extra
    flour
2 tablespoons sugar
1½ teaspoons baking
    powder

¼ teaspoon salt
3 tablespoons margarine
¾ cup water

Preheat the oven to 400° and grease an 8-inch round pan. Sift 2 cups flour, sugar, baking powder, and salt together into a bowl; cut in the margarine until the pieces are about the size of lentils. Stir in the water.

Knead the dough on a floured countertop for a few strokes, and then roll it out into a rectangle about 7 inches by 20 inches.

Topping

3 tablespoons sugar
⅛ teaspoon ground cinnamon
¼ cup raisins

Sprinkle the sugar, cinnamon, and raisins over the dough. Using a flexible kitchen spatula to free the rectangle from the countertop, roll the dough up to form a 20-inch log. Cut this log crosswise into 12 slices, and arrange the slices cut side down in the prepared baking pan.

Bake for about 25 minutes, or just until browned.

Icing

> ³/4 cup confectioners' sugar
> 1 tablespoon rum, or
>   1 tablespoon water
>   plus ½ teaspoon vanilla

Mix the rum (or the water and vanilla) into the confectioners' sugar, using just enough liquid to make a rather runny icing. Drizzle this icing over the buns as soon as they come from the oven. Serve immediately, with margarine.

MAKES 12 BUNS; SERVES 3 OR 4.

Doughnuts

Funnel Cakes
Potato Doughnuts
Raised Doughnuts
Jelly Doughnuts

About Doughnuts . . .

The most important thing about making doughnuts is the temperature of the fat in which you fry; it must be between 370° and 390° and at least 2 inches deep. If you don't have a deep-fat fryer, use a good deep kettle to keep the splattering down, and a candy or deep-fat thermometer. If the fat is too hot, the doughnuts will be scorched on the outside before the insides are cooked; if the fat is too cool, the doughnuts will absorb too much fat and be greasy.

Funnel cakes are an exception. They can be cooked quite well in an ordinary electric skillet, and are not quite so fussy about cooking temperature.

Doughnuts get very hard and tough if the dough is handled too much, or made stiff with too much flour. You want to handle the dough as little and as lightly as possible, and to use only enough flour to make the dough easy to roll out.

Use a slotted spoon or a long-handled fork to handle frying doughnuts. If you use a fork, be careful not to pierce the doughnuts with it.

Cooked doughnuts freeze well. Before serving them, thaw and then warm them in a slow (about 300°) oven for 10 minutes.

If your local department store or hardware store can't supply you with a doughnut cutter, you may well be able to find one at a flea market or antique shop.

Fat for deep-frying can be saved and reused. When the fat is cool enough to handle easily, strain it through 3 or 4 layers of cheesecloth. Store it closely covered in a cool place or the refrigerator. You can reuse the fat if it smells fresh and good when reheated, and is still reasonably pale in color.

Funnel Cakes

These are often made and sold at fairs in my part of the country. They are the easiest and quickest of the doughnut tribe to make.

For frying, about 4 pounds vegetable shortening	1 teaspoon baking powder
1 cup flour	¼ teaspoon salt
3 tablespoons sugar	1 egg
	¾ cup water

Heat 1½ inches of fat in a hot (400°) automatic frying pan. Just how much fat this will take depends on the size of your frying pan.

Sift the dry ingredients together in a bowl. Mix the egg and water together and beat in quickly, just until any lumps are gone.

Put one finger over the narrow end of an ordinary kitchen funnel, to act as a stopper; pour batter into the funnel, then test it by letting some drop through the funnel back into the mixing bowl. If the batter doesn't run smoothly out the end of the funnel, beat in a few additional teaspoons of water to thin it. When the batter is right, pour some slowly out of the narrow end of the funnel into the hot fat in a close spiral pattern. Fry until brown and crisp, about 2 or 3 minutes, turning once. Serve hot with confectioners' sugar or cinnamon sugar.

MAKES ABOUT TEN 5-INCH FUNNEL CAKES.

Potato Doughnuts

These are easier to make than plain cake-type doughnuts, and have a good flavor.

½ cup mashed potatoes
3 tablespoons margarine
2 cups flour
⅞ cup sugar (1 cup less 2 tablespoons)
1 tablespoon baking powder
¼ teaspoon ground nutmeg

½ teaspoon salt
¼ cup water
1 egg
For frying, about 6–8 pounds of vegetable shortening

If the potatoes are cold, melt the margarine and stir in the potatoes to warm them and loosen them up; if the potatoes are hot, stir in the solid margarine to melt the margarine and cool the potatoes down.

Sift the flour, sugar, baking powder, nutmeg, and salt together into a bowl. Add the water and egg to the potato mixture and beat briefly to mix. Add the liquid mixture all at once to the sifted dry ingredients, and stir just until thoroughly blended. Chill for about 2 hours in the refrigerator.

Baking powder doughnuts need careful handling, as they can easily become hard and heavy; "sinkers," these are called. Keep the dough as moist as you can without having it too sticky to roll and cut out, and handle it as lightly as possible. Chilling the dough helps make the doughnuts tender, as does using mashed potato in the recipe.

Heat several inches of fat to 380° in a deep-fat fryer or a kettle. Just how much fat you'll need depends on the size of your pan.

Roll the chilled dough out ½- to ⅝-inch thick on a well-floured countertop and cut it with a doughnut cutter.

Fry the doughnuts, 3 or 4 at a time, in the hot fat. This will take about 3 minutes per batch; turn the doughnuts once while they cook. Remove the doughnuts from the fat, draining them very well as you do so, and place them on several layers of paper towel to cool. Roll them in plain sugar or in sugar flavored with a little ground cinnamon.

MAKES ABOUT TWELVE 2½-INCH DOUGHNUTS.

Raised Doughnuts

½ cup lukewarm water
1¼ teaspoons
   (½ package) active dry
   yeast
½ teaspoon salt
⅔ cup sugar
About 2 cups flour
2 tablespoons soy flour
   (optional)

1 egg (optional)
2 tablespoons melted
   margarine
For frying, about 6–8
   pounds of vegetable
   shortening

Put the warm water into a warmed mixing bowl and sprinkle the yeast over it. Add the salt and ⅓ cup sugar and stir well, then add 1 cup flour and beat until smooth. Set in a warm place to rise until light, about 30 minutes.

Add the remaining ⅓ cup sugar, soy flour and egg, if using, margarine, and ½ cup of the remaining flour to the batter, beat it well, and let rise again until light, about 30 minutes.

Turn the dough out of the mixing bowl onto a floured countertop and knead for a few strokes, adding just enough of the remaining flour to make it possible to knead and roll the dough— keep it quite soft.

Roll the dough out about ½ inch thick and cut it with a doughnut cutter. Let the doughnuts rise on a greased baking sheet for about 1 hour, or until doubled in bulk.

Heat several inches of fat to 380° in a deep-fat fryer or a large kettle. The size of your pan determines how much fat you'll need. Test the fat by frying a couple of doughnut holes in it if you're not sure of the temperature.

Fry 3 or 4 doughnuts at a time for about 3 minutes, or until done, turning the doughnuts once during cooking.

Drain the cooked doughnuts well, then set them to cool on a baking sheet covered with several layers of paper towel. While they are still warm, roll the doughnuts in plain granulated sugar, confectioners' sugar, or sugar to which a little ground cinnamon has been added.

MAKES ABOUT A DOZEN 2½-INCH DOUGHNUTS.

Jelly Doughnuts

Cut the dough out with an ordinary round cutter that does not cut a central hole. When the fried doughnuts are cool, cut a short slit in the side of each, and insert a teaspoonful of jelly.

Fruit Desserts and One Mousse

Honeyed Fruit Mélange
Honeyed Pears
Strawberry-Orange-
Pineapple Jelly
Apricot-Raspberry Jelly
Strawberry Shortcake
Peach Shortcake
Smooth Applesauce
Chunky Applesauce
Fruit Soup
Fruit Cream
Coconut Soufflé
Prune Soufflé
Apricot Soufflé
Chocolate Mousse
Baked Apples
Apple Brown Betty
Apple Crisp

Rhubarb Betty
   Rhubarb Crisp
Pear Crumble
Pineapple-Apricot Cobbler
   Peach-Cherry Cobbler
Blueberry Slump
   Apple Jack

How to Choose Fruit

Fresh fruits in season are not only one of the world's great delicacies, they are also a bargain, easy to prepare, and very healthful.

You can wash the fruit or peel it and eat it whole, or slice it and serve with honey, sugar, wine or fruit juice, or cook it in pies and other desserts. Mashed or finely cut-up fruit adds flavor and moisture to cakes and cookies. Strawberries can be dipped into confectioners sugar or into melted semisweet chocolate.

Although supermarkets often have a good selection of fresh fruits, the best usually come from specialty fruit stores or from farm stands.

Many fruits are sold fully ripe and ready to use, but there are exceptions. Bananas, kiwi fruit, melons, nectarines, peaches, pears, and plums bruise easily when ripe, and so are usually picked and shipped green (not ripe). Ripen them for a few days on your kitchen windowsill or countertop until they are fragrant, have lost their greenish color (in most cases), and are a little soft to the touch. Ripe melons sound hollow when you knock gently on them.

Pineapples are often, but not always, sold underripe. Buy the ripest you can find. When the fruit is ready to eat, the body of the pineapple will usually be more yellow than green and a leaf will pull easily from the center top of the pineapple.

A ripe peach is a wonderfully sweet and juicy thing but if the peach was picked too green, it will turn spongy but never ripen. Most peaches peel very easily when ripe—you just start a piece of skin with a knife, then pull off a strip.

Apples, cherries, grapes, grapefruit, and oranges are usually sold fully ripe and can be used right away. Berries (blackberries, raspberries, strawberries) are also sold fully ripe but they are very fragile and should be refrigerated at once, then used within a few days. Blueberries are less perishable and will keep longer. With blueberries and strawberries, smaller is better—with a richer flavor, too. Big blueberries are apt to have tough skins, and don't distribute themselves quite so well in baked goods as the smaller ones do.

Tart, firm apples are best for cooking. If you're able to buy your apples at an orchard, the people there will be happy to advise you about the best apple for what you have in mind. Some of my favorite cooking apples are Northern Spy, Smokehouse, Jonathan, and Winesap. If you buy your apples at a supermarket, the Granny Smiths are quite good for baking, as are the Greenings. On the other hand, many people would find the Granny Smiths and the Greenings too tart for eating raw. McIntosh apples will do in a pinch; I avoid Red Delicious apples.

Honeyed Fruit Mélange

I improvised this version of a fine old recipe to use up some fruit that was getting too ripe.

> 4 cups cut-up fresh ripe fruit such as nectarines, Bing cherries, seedless grapes, blueberries
> 2 tablespoons honey
> 2 tablespoons fruit juice (orange juice, pineapple juice, or grapefruit juice)

Wash or peel and pit the fruit; grapes should be halved so their juices will mingle with the fruit.

Drizzle the honey and juice over the fruit, mix well, and let set for anywhere from 10 minutes at room temperature to several hours in the refrigerator before serving.

SERVES 4.

Honeyed Pears

This deceptively simple dessert or salad is a very satisfying combination, and I prepare it often in the fall when fresh pears are at their peak.

Scrub a fresh ripe pear, cut it into quarters, cut out the core, and cut it into chunks. Add 5 dates, pitted and chopped, and drizzle 1 teaspoon lemon juice and 1 tablespoon honey over the fruit. Mix well and serve. It is not necessary to chill before serving.
SERVES 2.

Strawberry-Orange-Pineapple Jelly

Desserts made with fruit juices and unflavored gelatin have a wonderful fresh flavor, very different from packaged mixes.

1 pound frozen
   sweetened
   strawberries, thawed
One 8-ounce can
   pineapple chunks
   packed in unsweetened
   pineapple juice
One 11–ounce can
   mandarin oranges

1 envelope
   (2½ teaspoons)
   unflavored gelatin
¼ cup sugar
2 tablespoons lemon
   juice
Nondairy whipped
   topping, if desired

Drain the fruit and set it aside; save the juice drained from the strawberries and from the pineapple, but not from the oranges. Measure the liquid. If it is less than 1⅓ cups, add water to bring it to that volume.

Put the 1⅓ cup fruit juices into a saucepan with the gelatin and the sugar, and bring just to a boil. Remove the pan from the heat and stir until the gelatin is entirely dissolved. Stir in the lemon juice and the fruits, pour into an attractive dish, and chill for several hours, until set. Stir the gelatin several times while it is chilling before it sets, to distribute the fruit evenly.

Serve plain or with nondairy whipped topping.

SERVES 6.

Apricot-Raspberry Jelly

Another gelatin dessert. Good for the forgetful cook, since the frozen raspberries don't need to be thawed before use.

¼ cup orange juice
1 envelope
(2½ teaspoons)
unflavored gelatin
One 1-pound can pitted
apricots in heavy
syrup

2 tablespoons sugar
Pinch salt
One 10-ounce package
frozen, sweetened
raspberries
Nondairy whipped
topping, if desired

Put the orange juice into a cup, and sprinkle the gelatin over it to soften.

Drain the apricots; saving 1 cup of the juice, and set the fruit aside. If there is not 1 cup of juice, add a little water or extra orange juice to make up the difference. Combine the apricot juice, the sugar, and the salt in a saucepan and bring to a boil; stir in the softened gelatin until it is completely dissolved. Stir in the raspberries and, when they are thawed, stir in the apricots.

Chill for several hours, until set. Serve plain or with nondairy whipped topping.

SERVES 5 OR 6.

Strawberry Shortcake

This is the classic New England shortcake; the berries and biscuit dough are a wonderful combination. In strawberry season we feast on this by serving it as a main course preceded by deviled eggs. If you crave shortcake and strawberries are not in season, use two 13-ounce packs of frozen strawberries instead of the quart of fresh berries.

1 quart fresh strawberries	1/4 teaspoon salt
1/3 cup sugar, plus 2 tablespoons sugar	3 tablespoons margarine
1 1/2 cups flour	3/4 cup water
1 1/2 teaspoons baking powder	Nondairy whipped topping, if desired

Rinse the strawberries in a sinkful of cool water and remove the hulls; put the hulled berries into a large bowl. Sprinkle them with about 1/3 cup sugar, or to taste. Let the berries and sugar set to draw the juices while you make the shortcake.

Preheat the oven to 375°, and grease an 8-inch round cake pan.

Sift the flour, 2 tablespoons sugar, baking powder, and salt into a bowl; cut in the margarine until the pieces are about the size of small peas. Stir in the water quickly to make a soft dough, then spread this dough out in the greased pan.

Bake for about 30 minutes, or until done and just a bit brown on top.

Split the hot shortcake in half, to make two thin 8-inch round layers. Spread the cut side of each with more margarine, if desired. Set the bottom piece on a large plate.

Crush the berries with a potato masher. Put about half the berries on the bottom layer of shortcake. Top with the second piece of shortcake, cut side up, and finish off with the rest of the berries. Add the nondairy whipped topping if desired, and serve immediately.

SERVES 4 (2 AS A MAIN COURSE).

Peach Shortcake

Substitute about 6 medium-sized peaches, peeled, sliced, and sweetened with about ⅓ cup of sugar. Or use blueberries, blackberries, or nectarines.

Smooth Applesauce

Fresh warm applesauce makes a wonderful dessert if you sprinkle the top with sugar and cinnamon, and serve it with oatmeal cookies (page 341).

> Apples, any number
> Water or cider
> Sugar (optional)
> Ground cinnamon (optional)

Scrub the apples, cut them in quarters, and cut out the stem and blossom ends; it is not necessary to peel or core them. Put them in a saucepan, add about 1 inch of water or cider, cover the saucepan, and simmer until the apples are very tender, about 10 minutes more or less, depending on the kind and number of apples.

Cool the apples a little, then use the heel of a spoon to press them through a coarse sieve or use a Foley food mill. Do this in batches, getting rid of the peels and seeds occasionally.

Taste the applesauce, then stir in a little sugar and/or cinnamon to taste.

Chunky Applesauce

The unsieved version of "regular" applesauce; the texture will depend partly on the kind of apple.

Quarter the apples, remove the stem and blossom ends, and peel them. If you elect not to peel the apples, scrub them well. Cut out the cores and cut the apples into chunks.

Simmer with a little water or cider in a covered saucepan until tender. This will take just a few minutes; use only enough liquid to keep the apples from sticking to the pan.

Sweeten if desired, add a little cinnamon if you like it, and serve warm or cold.

Fruit Soup

A Finnish neighbor taught me this easy, traditional wintertime dessert. The lemon and the cinnamon can be omitted.

> 12 ounces mixed dried fruits
> 1/3 cup sugar
> 1/2 lemon, sliced thin and seeded
> One 5-inch stick cinnamon
> 1 tablespoon potato flour or cornstarch

Put the dried fruits into a saucepan with the sugar, lemon, and cinnamon stick, and 3 cups water. Cover the saucepan and simmer gently for about 1 hour, until cooked. Check the fruit sometimes to make sure it isn't boiling dry.

Mix the potato flour or cornstarch with an additional 1 or 2 tablespoons cold water and stir it into the soup. Simmer for about 1 minute, or until the liquid appears clear and is slightly thickened. Serve at room temperature.

SERVES 4 TO 6.

Fruit Cream

Peach cream, strawberry cream, raspberry cream . . . this simple, versatile dessert is easy to make. It can be served freshly made or chilled, as a pudding or a frozen dessert that tastes like a very rich, very fruity ice cream. You can also use it as a sauce or topping in place of whipped cream or nondairy whipped topping.

> 1 egg white (see warning on page 4)
> 1¼ cups sugar
> 1¼ cups crushed strawberries or other fruit

This is the basic recipe, but I have had good results with as little as 1 cup strawberries and ½ cup sugar per egg white. One cup peaches, ½ cup sugar, and 1 egg white is one good combination; so is 1 cup raspberries and 1 cup sugar with one egg white. Make it with either a manual egg beater or an electric model. Although it will not whip up quite as high when done by hand, it only takes about 5 or 10 minutes.

Beat the egg white until foamy, then beat in about ½ cup of the sugar. Add the rest of the sugar and about ½ cup of the fruit, and beat well. Gradually beat in the rest of the crushed fruit, and continue to beat until the mixture is very thick and creamy, about 5 minutes. Chill.

Serve as a dessert, with crisp cookies on the side.

To freeze the fruit cream, pile it into a freezing container and freeze for about 4 hours—it does not get very hard, but stays creamy.

YIELDS 6 CUPS FRUIT CREAM; SERVES 6 TO 8 AS CHILLED OR FROZEN DESSERT; SERVES ABOUT 12 AS DESSERT TOPPING.

Coconut Soufflé

Soufflés are lovely, delicate, sophisticated desserts and are much easier to make than most people believe. They may fall when they are taken from the oven and are set on the table, but this is perfectly all right; just be sure to serve the soufflé hot, as soon as it comes from the oven.

2 tablespoons margarine	2½ tablespoons sugar
2 tablespoons flour	Pinch of salt
½ cup unsweetened coconut milk	½ cup dry, unsweetened coconut
2 eggs	¼ teaspoon vanilla

Preheat the oven to 350° and have ready, but do not grease, a 6-inch round soufflé dish or similar ovenproof dish that holds about 6 cups. Set a pan of hot tap water in the oven; the pan should be about 2 inches wider than your dish, and should contain about ½ inch of hot water.

Melt the margarine in a small saucepan and remove it from the heat. Using a flat-bottomed whisk, stir in the flour and the coconut milk; keep stirring until the mixture is smooth, then return it to moderate heat. Stir constantly as it thickens, comes to a boil, and simmers gently for about 2 minutes. Remove the pan from the heat.

Separate the eggs. Put the whites into a bowl, and the yolks into a cup or other small container. Beat the egg whites with a rotary beater until they are stiff.

Stirring constantly, add the sugar, salt, and egg yolks to the flour mixture; stir vigorously until it becomes smooth. Stir in the coconut and vanilla. Fold the coconut mixture carefully into the egg whites.

Turn the soufflé into the soufflé dish, then set it in the pan of hot water in the oven. Bake for about 40 minutes, or until the soufflé is puffed and golden. A double recipe baked in an 8-inch soufflé dish will cook in about 45 minutes. (To ensure height for a soufflé, add an extra egg white.) Serve immediately with jam sauce (page 410).

SERVES 3.

Prune Soufflé

This soufflé and its following variation do not use flour or whole eggs.

1 cup prune pulp,
  chopped (8 ounces
  uncooked prunes with
  pits yields 1 cup prune
  pulp)
3 egg whites

¼ cup sugar
¼ teaspoon ground
  cinnamon (the pungent
  kind, if you have it)
Pinch of salt

Preheat the oven to 350° and have ready (but do not grease) a 6-inch round soufflé dish or similar ovenproof dish holding about 6 cups, and a baking pan about 8 by 8 inches in size.

Drain the prunes and remove the pits. Pack 1 cup of prunes into a measuring cup and slice through them several times with kitchen scissors to cut them into pieces.

Beat the egg whites until foamy; beat in the sugar, cinnamon, and salt and keep beating until stiff. Beat in the prune pulp.

Turn prune mixture into the soufflé dish. Place the dish in the ovenproof pan, put both in the oven, and pour about 1 inch of boiling water into the pan around the soufflé dish.

Bake for 35 to 40 minutes, until done. Serve hot, topped with nondairy whipped topping or jam sauce (page 410), or else pass crisp cookies to eat with the soufflé.

SERVES 4.

Apricot Soufflé

Substitute well-cooked dried apricots for the prunes. After they are cooked sweeten the apricots with about ⅓ cup sugar.

Chocolate Mousse

A rich, continental-style dessert best served in tiny portions. Very good even without the usual whipped cream.

½ cup (3 ounces) semisweet chocolate bits
3 tablespoons margarine
1 tablespoon amaretto liqueur or a fruit liqueur (raspberry, orange, or apricot)

3 eggs, at room temperature, separated (see warning on page 4)
Pinch of salt
2 tablespoons toasted almonds, chopped into slivers (omit if using a fruit liqueur)

Melt the chocolate in a small bowl set into a larger pan of simmering water. Be careful that no water splashes into the chocolate or it will stiffen up. When the chocolate is melted remove it from the hot water and stir in the margarine, 1 tablespoonful at a time. Stir in the liqueur.

Beat the egg whites with the salt until stiff, and set them aside.

Beat the egg yolks until creamy and light. Mix the chocolate thoroughly into the egg yolks. Using about ⅓ of the chocolate mixture at a time, fold it thoroughly into the egg whites. Do this carefully, so that the egg whites will not lose any of the air you beat into them. Spoon the mousse into a decorative serving dish or into individual dessert dishes and top with the almonds.

Chill until about half an hour before you wish to serve the mousse, then remove it from the refrigerator to come to room temperature before serving.

SERVES 6.

Baked Apples

These can share the oven with a main dish such as roast meat or baked beans, and can then accompany that dish or be enjoyed for dessert.

> 4 apples
> ¼ cup brown sugar
> About 2 tablespoons raisins
> Ground cinnamon

Wash the apples and core them, leaving the fruit whole. It is okay to cut completely through the apple. Set the apples in a baking dish, then fill the center of each apple with about a tablespoonful of brown sugar, 4 or 5 raisins, and a dash of cinnamon. Pour half an inch of water into the baking dish, cover it, and set it in the oven. The apples will cook in about 25 minutes at 400°, or in an hour and a half at 275°. The baking time is not critical. Serve hot.

SERVES 4.

Apple Brown Betty

One of the best late autumn desserts. Use good tart cooking apples like Staymans, Smokehouse, Greenings, Northern Spies, Cortlands, or Granny Smiths. Delicious apples are too bland; McIntosh will do.

> 6 tablespoons brown
>   sugar, firmly packed
> ¼ cup regular rolled oats
> ¼ cup flour
> ¼ teaspoon ground
>   cinnamon
> ⅛ teaspoon ground
>   nutmeg
>
> ⅛ teaspoon salt
> 2 tablespoons margarine
> 5 medium apples, peeled,
>   cored, and sliced
>   (about 3½ cups)
> 2 tablespoons rum, apple
>   juice, or water

Preheat the oven to 350° and grease a 1-quart or larger casserole.

Put the sugar, rolled oats, flour, spices, and salt in a bowl; add the margarine and cut in with a pastry blender until the particles are the size of large peas.

Peel, core, and slice the apples. Put half the sliced apples into the prepared casserole. Top with half of the crumbs. Repeat these layers with the rest of the apples and crumbs. Sprinkle the liquid over all.

Bake uncovered for about 1 hour. If the betty is brown and bubbling and the apples feel soft when you poke a skewer into the middle of the dish, it is done. Different varieties of apples need different cooking times. Serve very warm, perhaps topped with vanilla tofu-based ice cream substitute.

SERVES 2 OR 3.

Apple Crisp

The same as apple brown betty, except that because you use a large shallow casserole and only one layer of apples topped with one layer of crumbs, the top becomes crisp. Bake for a shorter time, about 45 minutes.

SERVES 2 OR 3.

Rhubarb Betty

A good dish for spring, when there's plenty of fresh rhubarb, or use frozen rhubarb any time.

½ cup brown sugar,
  packed firm
¾ cup white sugar
½ cup flour
½ cup regular rolled oats
½ teaspoon ground
  allspice
⅛ teaspoon salt

⅓ cup margarine
¼ cup chopped almonds
  (optional)
1 pound rhubarb stalks,
  washed and cut in
  1-inch lengths (4 cups)
¼ cup orange or apple
  juice

Preheat the oven to 375° and grease a 1-quart casserole.

Put the sugars, flour, rolled oats, allspice, and salt in a mixing bowl; cut in the margarine until the pieces are the size of large peas. Stir in the almonds, if used.

Put half the rhubarb into the prepared casserole; sprinkle half of the crumbs over the rhubarb, and repeat with the rest of the rhubarb and crumbs. Drizzle the orange juice over the top.

Bake uncovered for about 55 minutes. Serve warm, either plain or with tofu-based ice cream substitute.

SERVES 4 OR 5.

Rhubarb Crisp

Follow the recipe for rhubarb betty, except use a shallow casserole of about 7 inches by 12 inches. Top one layer of rhubarb with one layer of crumbs, and bake for about 45 minutes.

SERVES 4 OR 5.

Pear Crumble

Pears baked under a brown sugar topping with wine and spices. A good finish to a company meal, this is also easy to prepare.

3 large, firm pears
½ cup brown sugar, firmly packed
⅓ cup flour
½ teaspoon ground cinnamon
½ teaspoon ground nutmeg
¼ teaspoon ground ginger
¼ teaspoon ground cloves
⅛ teaspoon salt
3 tablespoons margarine
¼ cup port or sherry

Preheat the oven to 375° and grease an attractive shallow baking dish about 8 inches by 10 inches.

Quarter the pears lengthwise, peel, and remove the cores. Arrange the pear slices attractively in the baking dish.

Mix the dry ingredients together in a bowl and cut in the margarine, using a pastry blender, until the pieces are about the size of shelled peanuts. Spread this over the pears, and sprinkle with the port or sherry.

Bake for about 30 minutes, or until the pears are tender when pierced with a skewer. Serve warm, plain or with vanilla tofu-based ice cream substitute.

SERVES 4.

Pineapple-Apricot Cobbler

A really good hot dessert for a cold day. This is made with convenient canned fruit from your pantry shelf.

Pastry

1 cup flour	¼ teaspoon salt
2 tablespoons sugar	2½ tablespoons
1½ teaspoons baking	margarine
powder	6 tablespoons water

Preheat the oven to 400° and get out a 2-quart casserole; you don't need to grease it.

Sift the flour, sugar, baking powder, and salt into a bowl. Cut in the margarine until the pieces are fine as cornmeal. Set it aside while you prepare the fruit.

Filling

One 20-ounce can pineapple chunks, in unsweetened pineapple juice

Orange juice or extra pineapple juice, if needed

1/4 cup sugar

1 1/2 tablespoons cornstarch

1/4 teaspoon ground cinnamon

One 16-ounce can apricot halves, drained

Drain the juice from the canned pineapple and measure it; if there is not enough, add orange juice or more pineapple juice to make 1 cup of liquid.

Mix the sugar, cornstarch, and cinnamon in a saucepan off the heat. Slowly add the juice, and stir until well mixed.

Over medium heat, bring to a boil, stirring constantly, and boil for 1 or 2 minutes or until the liquid is thick and clear. Add the drained apricots and the pineapple to the hot juice and heat the mixture through but do not let it boil.

Stir the 6 tablespoons of water into the pastry mixture just until all of the dry particles are moistened. Knead the dough lightly once or twice, then roll it out on a floured countertop to fit the top of your casserole. Turn the hot fruit into the casserole. Cover the fruit lightly with the rolled-out dough and bake for about 25 minutes, until brown and bubbly. Serve very warm.

SERVES 4 TO 6.

Peach-Cherry Cobbler

Another good pantry-shelf dessert using frozen fruit instead of canned.

Use for the filling:
 ¼ to ½ cup sugar
 2 tablespoons cornstarch
 ¼ teaspoon ground
  cinnamon
 Pinch salt
 ¾ cup orange or
  grapefruit juice
 ¼ cup water
 12 ounces (2¼ cups)
  frozen unsweetened
  pitted cherries
 16 ounces (4 cups)
  frozen unsweetened
  peach slices

Proceed as for the preceding cobbler. The fruit can still be frozen when you add it to the hot cornstarch mixture, but you should make sure it has thawed and heated through before you turn it into the casserole.

Blueberry Slump

The secret of making a slump topping light is to roll out the biscuit dough and lay it over the hot berries.

Dough

 ⅔ cup flour
 1½ tablespoons sugar
 1½ teaspoons baking
  powder
 ⅛ teaspoon salt
 2 tablespoons margarine
 ¼ cup water

Preheat the oven to 450° and have ready a 1½-quart casserole. Sift the flour, sugar, baking powder, and salt together. Cut in the shortening until the pieces are the size of large peas, then set the mixture aside.

Filling

> 3 cups blueberries
> 1/4 cup sugar
> 1/4 teaspoon ground cinnamon
> Pinch of salt
> 2 tablespoons water

Mix the blueberries, sugar, cinnamon, salt, and water in a saucepan; bring to a boil, stirring occasionally. When this has boiled for a minute or two, pour it into the casserole.

Stir the 1/4 cup of water into the reserved dough mixture, turn it out onto a lightly floured countertop, and knead for a few strokes. Roll the dough out to a size that will fit the top of your casserole, then lay it gently over the hot berries. Cut a few slits in the topping.

Bake until the crust is lightly browned, about 15 minutes. Serve warm, with hard sauce (page 414).

SERVES 4.

If you prefer to drop dumplings onto a slump or cobbler instead of rolling out a top crust, use more water for the dough: 1/2 cup water instead of the 6 tablespoons in pineapple–apricot cobbler or 1/3 cup instead of 1/4 cup in blueberry slump. Drop the dough by tablespoonsful over the hot fruit just before putting it in the oven to bake.

Apple Jack

Quarter, peel, core, and coarsely chop enough apples to give about 3 cups. Substitute these apples for the blueberries. Use 1/4 cup of water and add a little ground nutmeg.

Pies

Pie Crust
  Single-crust Pie Shell
  Prebaked Pie Shell
  Double-crust Pie
  Lattice-topped Pie
Apple Pie
Peach Pie
Blueberry Pie
Rhubarb Pie
  Strawberry-Rhubarb Pie
  Blueberry-Rhubarb Pie
Cherry Pie
Mincemeat Pie
Plum Pie
  Summer Pie
Squash Pie
Pecan Pie
"Butter" Tart

Fresh Strawberry Pie
Fresh Peach Pie
Fresh Blueberry Pie
Lemon Meringue Pie
Apple Dumplings

About Making Pie . . .

Making good pie crust takes practice, but it's a skill well worth mastering. The basic American pie crust recipe given here is similar to French pâte brisée.

There are many opinions about the proper shortening to use for pie crust. Margarine, lard, hydrogenated vegetable shortening, and goose or duck fat all have their devotees; many people like to use a combination of two different fats. Probably the lightest, flakiest crusts are made from hydrogenated vegetable shortening or from duck or goose fat.

The fat should be as cold as possible (never melt shortening for pie crust). Keep it in the refrigerator until the last minute and cut it into the flour with a pastry blender.

To measure shortening more easily, do the following. If you want ⅔ cup of fat, put ⅓ cup water into a measuring cup and then spoon in fat until the water reaches the 1-cup mark. Pour out the water and use the fat.

Crust is affected by humidity, as well as other factors, so you may need to add a little more water than indicated in the recipe to get the dough to cling together well enough to roll out. It is important to handle pie crust as little as possible and with a light hand. If you squeeze the crust, you may make it tough.

For an 8-inch pie, use ⅔ or ¾ of the recipe for the filling for a 9-inch pie. For a 10-inch pie, use 1½ times the recipe for a 9-inch pie for both crust and filling.

Use some sort of drip catcher under pies as they bake, especially under fruit pies. There is a circular tray with raised edges made for the purpose or make your own square drip catcher from aluminum foil. Tear off a sheet of foil and bend up the edges to make a raised lip about ½ inch high all around the outside. Set the pie directly on the drip catcher when you put it in the oven.

Plain fruit pies (apple, peach, rhubarb, and so on) are done when the crust is brown and juice begins to leak from the slits you cut in the top crust. If you are in doubt, insert a skewer into the middle of the pie; if it is cooked, the filling should be soft.

If you use already prepared frozen pie shells from the super-market, or use disposable aluminum pie plates, you should be aware that they are not as large as homemade pie shells made in nondisposable pie plates. The recipes in this book were developed using homemade crust and nondisposable pie plates.

Freezing Pies

I was called away from the house one day while a pie was in the oven, and discovered this very useful strategy.

Two-crust fruit pies can be made and frozen in the pie pan before being baked. The frozen pie can be baked without prethawing and will taste just like a freshly made pie, if you use the following method.

Line the pie pan with aluminum foil, and make your pie in it as usual. Freeze the unbaked pie, then remove it from the pan and cover it with another square of aluminum foil; fold both pieces of foil securely together all around the edge of the pie to seal them to each other. Store the pie in the freezer.

When you are ready for the pie, preheat the oven to 400°. Remove the foil from the frozen pie and place it in a pie pan. Cut slits in the top crust.

Bake the still-frozen pie for 30 minutes and then turn off the oven, but don't remove the pie. Leave the pie in the oven for about 2 hours. Turn the oven back on (you can leave the pie inside while it heats) and bake at 400° for about 30 minutes more, or until the top is browned and juice bubbles through the slits in the top crust.

Pie Crust

If you've never made pie crust before, or aren't pleased with the ones you've made, please read the introduction to this section before proceeding.

The amounts given below will make enough crust for a 9-inch two-crust pie, or for two 9-inch single-crust pies; the amounts in parentheses are for an 8-inch two-crust pie or for two 8-inch single-crust pies.

> 2 cups flour (1½ cups) plus extra flour for rolling out
>   the pie crust
> ½ teaspoon salt (¼ teaspoon)
> ⅔ cup cold shortening (½ cup)
> ¼ cup water (3 tablespoons)

Sift the flour and salt together into a bowl, then cut in the cold shortening until the pieces are the size of large peas. Stir in the water briefly, just until all of the flour is moistened. You will need to add a tablespoon or so more flour if the dough is too sticky, or a couple of teaspoons of water if it is too dry to cling together. In any case, handle the dough as little and as lightly as possible.

Single-crust Pie Shell

Turn the dough out onto a floured countertop and knead it for a few strokes, then roll out half of it to make a circle about 12 inches (11 inches) in diameter. Using a long, flexible kitchen spatula, carefully free half of the circle of dough from the countertop and fold it gently over the other half. Free the rest of the pie crust from the counter, and fit it gently into a 9-inch (8-inch) pie plate. Ease it into place with your fingers. Trim the dough so that it hangs about ½ inch over the lip of the pan. Once the crust is in the pan, patch small holes and tears with scraps of rolled-out dough. Select a piece slightly larger than the hole to be patched, moisten one side with water, and press it into place.

Tuck the loose edge of dough underneath itself so that this doubled edge sticks out no farther than the rim of the pie plate. Flour your fingers so that the dough won't stick to them and then pinch a piece of the edge between the thumb and first finger of one hand and the thumb of your other hand. Work around the edge of the pie, pinching the edge up into decorative scallops. Use a fork to prick tiny holes all over the bottom and sides of the crust.

The pie shell is now ready to be filled or prebaked. You can also freeze it for later use. I usually make 2 pie shells at a time and freeze the one that isn't used right away. The frozen shell can be used just as you would a freshly made one; no need to thaw it first.

Prebaked Pie Shell

This is used for some pies such as lemon meringue pie or fresh strawberry pie in which an already-cooked filling is poured into the crust.

Preheat the oven to 450°.

Roll out half a recipe of pie crust, and fit it into a pie plate, trim, flute, and prick it according to the instructions on page 309 and above.

Grease one side of a square of aluminum foil and fit it loosely, greased side down, into the pie shell. Pour into the foil 2 cups of uncooked dry beans or rice, and distribute them evenly over the foil to hold the crust in place while it bakes.

Bake the pie shell in the preheated oven for about 8 minutes, or until the edge of the crust just begins to show color. Remove the foil and the beans or rice (cool these to save and reuse with another pie shell), return the pie shell to the oven, and continue to bake at 450° for about 7 minutes more, until the whole pie shell is pleasingly browned.

Remove the shell from the oven and cool it before pouring in the filling.

Double-crust Pie

Roll out half the dough following the instructions for a single-crust pie shell on page 309, but trim off the rim of dough even with the edge of the pie pan.

Roll out the other half of the dough, fold it in two and free it from the countertop as you did the first half, then let it rest.

Fill the pie shell. Top the pie with the second crust, and trim off its edges to about ½ inch over the lip of the pan. Fold the edge of the top crust under the edge of the bottom crust and seal with a fork or with your fingers. You can make one sort of decorative edge by pinching the rim repeatedly between the thumb and first finger of one hand and the other thumb. Or, you can press down repeatedly all around the edge of the pie with the tines of a fork. Prick or cut slits in the top crust to let steam escape. Set the pie on a large pan to catch the drips, and bake as directed.

Lattice-topped Pie

Lattice tops are handsome, and are not complicated to make.

Prepare the pastry for a 2-crust pie of the desired size. Line your pie pan with half the pastry, as described on pages 309–10. Roll out the rest of the pastry as if for a regular top crust. Using a dull table knife, a kitchen spatula, or a pastry-cutting wheel, cut the pastry into strips about ¾ inch wide. You will need 10 strips for an 8-inch or 9-inch pie, 14 for a 10-inch pie.

Fill the lined pie pan with the filling, which should be at room temperature. Lay one of the longest pastry strips across the center of the pie. Lay 2 more strips, one on each side of the center strip and parallel to it, ¾ inch or a little more away from the center strip. Lay 2 of the shorter strips between these 2 side strips and the edge of the crust, again, about ¾ inch or a little more away from the nearest strip, and parallel to it. Space the strips evenly but don't worry about it; this is, after all, a handmade pie, not a machine-made one.

Lay the remaining strips of dough across these first ones, weaving as you go. In other words, take the longest remaining strip of dough and prepare to lay it across the center of the pie, at a right angle to the rest of the strips. Holding the strip in one hand and starting at the edge of the pie, lay it over the first strip you come to; with your other hand, raise the second strip you come to and lay it gently over the strip you are holding. Put the strip you're holding over the third strip (the center one), under the fourth strip, and over the fifth. Now take one of the longer remaining pastry strips and lay it parallel to the one you just put down, but this one should go under the first, third, and fifth strips and over the second and fourth strips. Continue weaving in this way with the rest of the strips. When you are finished, pinch the ends off the pastry strips so that they stick out about ½ inch beyond the rim of the pie, tuck the ends under the edge of the crust, and press the tines of a fork all around the rim of the pie to seal the crusts together and make a decorative edge.

Apple Pie

In New England a hundred years ago, apple pie was served for breakfast. Flavorful, tart apples are important if you want to have a good pie. Granny Smiths, Jonathans, Greenings, Smokehouse, and Northern Spies all make excellent pie; avoid Red Delicious and other mild apples.

Pastry for a 9-inch 2-crust pie
6 cups fresh, tart apple slices (about 6 medium apples)
1 cup sugar
½ teaspoon ground cinnamon
¼ teaspoon ground nutmeg

Preheat the oven to 425°. (Or you can turn the oven on when you put the pie in to bake and add about 5 minutes to the baking time.) Line a 9-inch pie pan with half the pastry and roll out the other half for a top crust.

Peel, core, and slice enough tart, juicy apples to give you about 6 cups of sliced apples. This is most easily done if you cut each apple into quarters, cut out the core, cut off the skin, and then slice. Pile the apple slices into the prepared pie shell, strew with the cinnamon, sugar and nutmeg, and cover with the top crust. Seal the edges of the crusts together and cut slits in the top crust to let steam escape. Set the pie on a drip catcher and bake about 50 minutes. Serve warm or at room temperature.

Peach Pie

Good in August, when farm stands have ripe peaches.

Pastry for a 9-inch
  2-crust pie
2 tablespoons cornstarch
1 cup sugar
½ teaspoon ground
  cinnamon

Pinch of salt
5 cups sliced ripe
  peaches (about 12 to
  15 peaches)

Preheat the oven to 425° or start the pie in a cold oven and add 5 minutes to the baking time.

Line a 9-inch pie plate with half the pasty. Roll out the rest of the pastry for a top crust, and set it aside. Sift the cornstarch, sugar, cinnamon, and salt together.

Peel the peaches (if they are ripe, the skins will slip off very easily). Slice them and pile them into the prepared pie shell, occasionally sprinkling some of the sugar mixture over the fruit. When all of the peach slices have been used, top with the last of the sugar mixture.

Place the top crust gently on top of the pie, trim it, and seal it to the bottom crust. Cut a few slits in the top crust.

Set the pie on a drip catcher and bake for about 45 minutes. Serve warm or at room temperature.

Blueberry Pie

Pastry for a 9-inch 2-crust pie
2 tablespoons flour, or 1 tablespoon cornstarch
¾ cup sugar
½ teaspoon ground cinnamon
5 cups blueberries, rinsed and drained

Preheat the oven to 425°. Line a 9-inch pie plate with half the pastry; roll out the rest of the pastry for a top crust, and set it aside.

Sift the flour or cornstarch, sugar, and cinnamon together. Pile the berries into the pie shell, and top with the sugar mixture. Lay the top crust over the pie, seal it to the bottom crust around the edges, and cut a few slits in the top to let steam escape. Set the pie on a drip catcher and bake for about 40 minutes, or until the pie is nicely browned and juice leaks out through the slits.

Rhubarb Pie

Pastry for a 9-inch 2-crust pie
⅓ cup flour
2 cups sugar
5 cups rhubarb, scrubbed and cut in 1-inch lengths

Line a 9-inch pie pan with half of the pastry, and roll out the other half for a top crust. Preheat the oven to 425°.

Sift the flour and sugar together. Put half the fruit into the lined pie pan and sprinkle with half of the flour and sugar mixture; repeat with the rest of the fruit and the flour and sugar.

Cover with the top crust, seal the edges, and prick the top well. Set the pie on a drip catcher and bake for about 50 minutes.

Strawberry-Rhubarb Pie

Milder than rhubarb pie.

Follow the method for rhubarb pie, but use instead:
4 cups rhubarb
1 pint strawberries, rinsed and hulled
3 tablespoons cornstarch
1¾ cups sugar

You can use 1 pound frozen unsweetened rhubarb and ½ pound frozen unsweetened strawberries for this recipe. Thaw the fruit before making the pie.

Blueberry-Rhubarb Pie

Substitute 1½ cups blueberries for the strawberries in strawberry-rhubarb pie.

Cherry Pie

¼ cup cornstarch	1¼ cups cherry juice,
⅔ to 1 cup sugar	drained from cherries
½ teaspoon ground	⅛ teaspoon almond
cinnamon	extract
Two 1-pound cans sour	Pastry for a 9-inch
cherries, water pack	2-crust pie

Off heat stir the cornstarch, sugar, and cinnamon in a saucepan until there are no clumps of cornstarch. Gradually stir in the 1¼ cups cherry juice. (You may need to add some water to get 1¼ cups of juice.) Bring the sugar mixture to a boil over medium-high heat, stirring constantly, and continue to boil and stir for about 1 minute or until the juice is thick and clear. Remove from heat and stir in the almond extract and the well-drained cherries. Let cool while you make the pastry.

Preheat the oven to 425°.

Line a 9-inch pie pan with half the pastry and roll out the rest of the pasty for a top crust. Pour the cherry mixture into the bottom crust and cover with the top crust; seal the edges of the pie, and cut a few slits in the top crust. Set the pie on a drip catcher and bake for about 40 minutes, or until the top is nicely browned and juice bubbles through the slits in the top crust. Serve warm or at room temperature.

Mincemeat Pie

Mincemeat is a mixture of preserved fruits. It usually contains apples, raisins, sugar, orange peel, and spices. It may also include finely chopped meat, suet (kidney fat from beet or lamb), and brandy or another liquid. You can use mincemeat just as it comes from the jar or you can add your own selection of spices, sugar, molasses, rum, or grated apple. Here is my favorite pie mixture.

Pastry for a 9-inch
 2-crust pie
One 28-ounce jar
 mincemeat
1 apple, grated
1/4 teaspoon ground
 allspice

1/8 teaspoon ground
 cloves
1 tablespoon brandy or
 rum

Preheat the oven to 425°. Mix extra ingredients of your choice into the mincemeat in a bowl. Line a 9-inch pie pan with half the pastry, then spoon in the mincemeat and top with the rest of the pastry. Seal the top crust to the bottom crust, prick holes in the top crust, and set the pie on a drip catcher (not as essential for this pie as it is for most). Mincemeat pies are often made with a lattice crust.

Bake for about 30 minutes, or until the pastry is nicely browned. Serve at room temperature.

Plum Pie

Prune plums are the small, oval, dark purple plums that come to market in late summer. They're wonderful for cooking and baking. A fully ripe prune plum separates pretty easily from its seed; however, the plums cook up well even when a bit underripe.

2 teaspoons cornstarch,
   if you wish
1/3 cup sugar
3/4 cup flour
1/2 teaspoon ground
   cinnamon
1/4 teaspoon ground
   allspice

1/8 teaspoon salt
3/4 cup firmly packed
   brown sugar
6 tablespoons margarine
2 1/2 pounds ripe prune
   plums
Pastry for a 9-inch pie
   shell, unbaked

This recipe makes a rather loose pie. If you like a cut piece of pie to hold its shape, mix 2 teaspoons of cornstarch with the granulated sugar before you begin.

Preheat the oven to 400°. Sift the flour, cinnamon, allspice, and salt into a bowl; stir in the brown sugar, and cut in the margarine until the pieces are the size of peas.

Rinse the plums, cut them in half lengthwise and remove the seeds, but do not peel them. Pile the plums into the pie shell, sprinkling with the 1/3 cup sugar as you do this.

Spread the brown sugar crumb mixture over the plums and set the pie on a drip catcher. Bake for 50 to 55 minutes, or until juice leaks out around the edges and the filling feels soft when you plunge a skewer into it. Serve warm or at room temperature.

Summer Pie

I invented summer pie to use up a variety of ripe fruits that happened to be around the kitchen, but we liked it so well that since then I've made it many times.

Instead of prune plums, use:
5 cups mixed ripe fruits: peaches, nectarines, plums, strawberries, blueberries, raspberries, seedless grapes, pitted Bing cherries—almost any fruit except apples, bananas, or citrus fruit. Omit the allspice and the cornstarch.

Squash Pie

We much prefer squash pie to pumpkin pie. To make pumpkin pie, try substituting cooked pumpkin for the squash; when made this way, the pie will taste different from the usual pumpkin pie. This pie is unlike most baked goods, which are best when fresh. It tastes terrible when newly made, but is very good if allowed to sit around for three or four days. I usually make it on the Monday before Thanksgiving.

3 tablespoons margarine
1 or 2 ripe pears, enough
   to give 1 cup grated
   pulp
12 ounces (about 1 cup)
   cooked winter squash
1 tablespoon flour
1 cup sugar
½ teaspoon ground
   cinnamon
¼ teaspoon ground
   ginger
¼ teaspoon salt
2 eggs
Pastry for a 9-inch pie
   shell, unbaked

Preheat the oven to 425° and melt the margarine. Quarter the pears lengthwise, cut off the skins, cut out the cores, and grate coarsely.

Beat all the ingredients together and pour them into the pie shell.

Bake for 1 to 1¼ hours, or until the pie appears well done. The crust should be well browned, the filling should appear firm, and a skewer inserted near the center should come out clean. Let set for several days before serving.

Pecan Pie

An easy pie to make. This version replaces part of the customary corn syrup with honey.

¼ cup margarine
1 cup (about 4 ounces)
　shelled pecans
3 eggs
½ cup brown sugar,
　firmly packed

¼ teaspoon salt
½ cup honey
½ cup light corn syrup
½ teaspoon vanilla
Pastry for a 9-inch pie
　shell, unbaked

Preheat the oven to 400° and melt the margarine.

Pour the pecans into the pie shell. Beat the rest of the ingredients together and pour over the nuts.

Bake 10 minutes at 400°, then lower the oven temperature to 350° and bake about 30 minutes longer, or until the nuts are lightly browned and the pie appears done. Serve at room temperature.

"Butter" Tart

In Ontario, butter tarts are favorites; they are tiny individual pies. This is the same sort of sweet, but made as one 9-inch pie instead of many small pies. Of course, this is usually made with butter.

2 tablespoons finely ground nuts (optional)	¼ teaspoon salt
½ cup raisins (optional)	½ teaspoon vanilla
6 tablespoons margarine	3 eggs
1½ cups brown sugar, firmly packed	Pastry for a 9-inch pie shell, unbaked
½ cup white sugar	Nondairy whipped topping, if desired

Preheat the oven to 350°. Strew the raisins or ground nuts (if you use them) in the pie shell.

Cream the margarine, sugars, salt, and vanilla with 1 egg. Beat in the other two eggs one at a time, and continue beating until the mixture is light. Pour it into the pie shell.

Bake for about 40 minutes, or until browned and puffy. Serve at room temperature, either plain or with nondairy whipped topping.

The following recipes for fresh fruit pies, made with uncooked fruit and a glaze of cooked fruit, are wonderful in summer. The pies are easy to make, and the kitchen stays cool.

Fresh Strawberry Pie

1½ quarts fresh strawberries	½ teaspoon vanilla, if you use water
⅔ cup sugar	1 prebaked 9-inch pie shell (see page 310)
2 tablespoons cornstarch	Nondairy whipped topping, if you wish
Pinch of salt	
½ cup water or Chablis	

Wash, hull, and drain the berries; cut the larger ones in half. Mix the sugar, cornstarch, and salt together in a saucepan. Crush 1/2 quart of the berries and stir them in, then stir in the liquid. (Save the vanilla, if you use it, for later.) Cook over moderate heat, stirring constantly, until the mixture has thickened, come to a boil, and boiled for about 1 minute. It should be thick and clear, not cloudy. Remove it from the heat and stir in the vanilla, if used. Cool the mixture slightly.

Pile the reserved quart of berries into the pie shell and spoon the cooked mixture over them. Chill for several hours. Serve cold, with or without the nondairy whipped topping.

Fresh Peach Pie

Pile 3 or 4 cups sliced fresh peaches into the baked pie shell, and use 1 cup of mashed peaches in the cooked mixture.

Fresh Blueberry Pie

Make this when blueberries are in season.

1/2 cup sugar	2 tablespoons margarine
2 tablespoons cornstarch	1 prebaked 9-inch pie
Pinch of salt	shell (see page 310)
1/2 cup Chablis or water	Nondairy whipped
4 cups fresh blueberries,	topping, if desired
rinsed and drained	

Stir the sugar, cornstarch, and salt together in a saucepan, then gradually stir in the Chablis or water. Add 1 cup of the blueberries and cook this mixture over moderate heat, stirring constantly, until the mixture has come to a boil and simmered for 2 minutes. It should be thick and clear, not cloudy. Remove it from the heat and stir in the margarine.

Pile the remaining blueberries into the pie shell. When the glaze has cooled a little, pour it over the berries. Refrigerate the pie for several hours. Serve plain or with nondairy whipped topping.

Lemon Meringue Pie

This makes a very tart, lemony pie. If you prefer a milder pie use 1 ½ cups of water and ¼ cup lemon juice.

One 9-inch pie shell, baked and cooled

Filling

1 ½ cups sugar	3 lemons
6 tablespoons cornstarch	3 egg yolks (see
⅛ teaspoon salt	warning on page 4)
1 ⅓ cups water	2 tablespoons margarine

Stir the sugar, cornstarch, and salt well together in a saucepan, breaking up any lumps of cornstarch. Gradually stir in the water, then let it set while you wash the lemon and grate the lemon rind, being careful to only use the yellow part of the rind. Squeeze out the lemon juice and strain it. Set aside all the grated peel and ⅓ cup of the juice for the pie. Save any extra juice for another use.

Lightly beat the egg yolks in a small bowl.

Stir the water-sugar-cornstarch mixture well, then cook it over medium heat, stirring constantly, until it thickens and boils for about 1 minute. It should appear clear, not cloudy. Remove it from the heat, and stir about 2 tablespoons of the hot mixture into the egg yolks; keep stirring in more of the hot mixture until you have added about 1 cup of the hot mixture to the yolks. Add the yolk mixture to the saucepan, and return it to the heat. Stir constantly while the mixture returns to a boil and simmers gently for 1 minute.

Remove the pan from the heat and stir in the margarine, then the lemon juice and rind. Set the mixture aside to cool slightly while you make the meringue.

Meringue

> 3 egg whites
> 1/4 teaspoon cream of tartar
> 1/3 cup sugar

Set the oven to preheat to 425°.

Beat the egg whites and cream of tartar together until they are light, then gradually beat in the sugar. Beat until the mixture is quite stiff and you can no longer feel grains of sugar when you rub a little of it between your fingers.

Pour the lemon filling into the pie shell, then pile the meringue onto it, making sure to press the meringue against the edge of the crust. Bake for about 5 minutes, just until the top of the meringue begins to brown attractively. Cool the pie to room temperature, then chill in the refrigerator until serving time.

Apple Dumplings

One of my favorite cold-weather desserts. The unbaked dumplings freeze well and can be baked without thawing. Just before baking, make the syrup and pour it around the dumplings. Bake as you would the freshly made pastry, but bake for about 60 minutes instead of 50.

> 4 tart apples
> 1/4 cup sugar
> 1/4 teaspoon ground
>   cinnamon
>
> 1/8 teaspoon ground
>   nutmeg
> Pastry for a 2-crust
>   8-inch pie

Preheat the oven to 400° and have ready an 8- by 8-inch square baking pan.

Peel the apples, cut them in quarters, and cut out the cores. Mix the sugar, cinnamon, and nutmeg together.

Divide the pastry into 4 equal parts, and roll each piece out to a circle big enough to wrap an apple; 8 inches in diameter is about right. Place 4 apple quarters on each circle of pastry, sprinkle them with the sugar mixture, then push each set of 4 quarters into the form of a whole apple as you wrap the pastry around them. Place the dumplings in the baking pan as you make them.

Syrup

⅔ cup sugar
1 cup water
¼ teaspoon ground cinnamon
2 tablespoons margarine

Bring the sugar, water, cinnamon, and margarine to a boil in a small saucepan, then pour the boiling syrup around the dumplings.

Bake about 50 minutes. Serve warm, perhaps with tofu-based ice cream substitute.

SERVES 4.

Cookies

Bar Cookies

Fruit Bars
Raspberry-Almond Bars
Apricot-Oatmeal Bars
Thin Peanut Bars
Lemon Bars
Chocolate Chip Bars
Brownies
Peanut Butter Brownies
Thin Brownies

Drop Cookies

Apple Cookies
Pumpkin Cookies
Honey Ginger Cookies
Soft Ginger Cookies
Oatmeal Cookies
Oatmeal–Peanut Butter Cookies

Chocolate Chip Cookies
Chocolate Jumbles
   Rolled Chocolate Jumbles

Rolled Cookies

Sugar Cookies
Thin Ginger Cookies
Breakfast Molasses Cookies

Shaped Cookies

Sandies
Thumbprint Cookies
   Cookie-press Cookies
Peanut Butter Cookies
Molasses Sugar Cookies

Lemon Refrigerator Cookies
Chocolate Refrigerator Cookies
Honey Almond Cookies

About Making Cookies . . .

Cookies, especially bar cookies and drop cookies, are easy to make, but if you are an inexperienced baker it will help if you read the cake making information on page 359 since it applies to cookies as well as cakes.

Make sure your oven is thoroughly preheated before you begin baking. Cookie sheets are usually large in proportion to the size of the oven and tend to block the flow of heat; there should be about 2 inches of clearance on all sides of the cookie sheet when it's in the oven.

Use shiny metal cookie sheets. Cookies baked on dark cookie sheets often suffer from burned bottoms. Always use solid shortening (for example, margarine) to grease cookie sheets. If you oil the cookie sheet, the baked cookies will not come off easily; they will be glued firmly in place. Consternation!

Make sure the cookie sheet is at room temperature, not hot, before you put cookie dough on it. To cool a cookie sheet quickly, wipe its underside with a wet dishcloth.

Rolled cookie dough, like pie crust, is affected by humidity, and also by egg size and the type of flour used. You may, therefore, need to add a bit more flour, just enough so that the dough handles well but not so much that the cookies become hard.

If you don't feel like cutting rolled cookie dough into fancy shapes, roll it out directly on the greased baking sheet. Using a spatula or dull knife, cut across the dough to make strips about 2 inches wide; then cut diagonally across the strips to make diamond-shaped cookies.

Regrease cookie sheets before each use.

When baking a large batch of cookies, I use three cookie sheets. At any given time one is in the oven, one is cooling, and one is being loaded.

Remove baked cookies to a cooling rack with a spatula or pancake turner as soon as you take them out of the oven.

Fruit Bars

Some people call these cakes, some people call them cookies. They are usually made with raisins, but they're also good with currants, chopped figs, chopped dried apple, or a mixture of fruits.

6 tablespoons margarine	1/4 teaspoon salt
2/3 cup sugar	1/2 cup water
1 egg	1/2 cup molasses
2 cups flour	1 cup raisins and/or
2 teaspoons baking	chopped nuts, or any
powder	chopped dried fruits
1/4 teaspoon baking soda	

Preheat the oven to 350° and grease the bottom and sides of a 9- by 13-inch pan.

Cream the margarine, sugar, and egg well together until light and fluffy. Sift the flour, baking powder, baking soda, and salt together; add to the batter along with the water and molasses and stir just until thoroughly mixed. Stir in the fruit and/or nuts.

Spread in the greased pan and bake about 25 minutes, or until the center springs back when you touch it lightly. Spread while still warm with the following:

Glaze

1 cup confectioners' sugar
1 teaspoon vanilla
1 tablespoon water, more or less

Mix the sugar, vanilla, and water together to make a glaze about the consistency of heavy cream, then spread this on the still-warm cookies. Let the cookies cool in the pan and then cut them into bars.

MAKES ABOUT 32 BARS.

Raspberry-Almond Bars

An elegant cookie.

Base

½ cup margarine	1 egg
½ cup sugar	1½ cups flour
½ teaspoon vanilla	½ teaspoon salt

Preheat the oven to 375° and grease the bottom and sides of a 9- by 9-inch pan.

Cream together the margarine, sugar, and vanilla; beat in the egg until the batter is very fluffy. Sift the flour and salt together and stir them in.

Spread the mixture in the greased pan, and bake for 10 minutes. Meanwhile, prepare the following:

Topping

1 cup almonds	¼ teaspoon salt
2 eggs	¼ teaspoon almond
1 cup minus 2 tablespoons sugar	extract
½ teaspoon ground cinnamon	1 cup raspberry jam (8 ounces)

Grind the almonds in a blender or food processor, or chop them very fine with a knife (or use 1 cup ground almonds).

Beat the eggs and sugar together until they are light and thick. Beat in the cinnamon, the salt, and the almond extract; mix in the ground almonds.

As soon as the cookie base has baked for 10 minutes (it should be puffy but not brown), remove it from the oven and spread with the jam; keep the jam away from the edges of the pan. Top with the almond mixture, which can be spread to the edges of the pan. Bake for another 25 minutes at 375°.

Glaze

>⅔ cup confectioners' sugar
>About 2 tablespoons Curaçao or orange juice

Mix the sugar and the liquid to make a thin glaze, and spread it over the cookies while they are still warm. When the cookies are cool, cut them into bars.

MAKES ABOUT 32 BARS.

Apricot-Oatmeal Bars

A lovely rich, crunchy cookie.

¾ cup margarine	1 teaspoon salt
⅓ cup almonds, chopped	1⅓ cups brown sugar,
2 cups flour	packed firm
½ teaspoon baking soda	2 cups rolled oats
½ teaspoon ground	One 12-ounce jar apricot
cinnamon	jam (about 1½ cups)

Preheat the oven to 325°. Put the margarine in a 13- by 9-inch baking pan and set this in the oven while it preheats; this will both melt the margarine and grease the pan.

Sift the flour, soda, cinnamon, and salt into a bowl; stir in the brown sugar, rolled oats, and chopped almonds. Stir in the melted margarine. Press ⅔ of this mixture into the greased pan, then spread the jam over the crumbs, keeping it away from the sides of the pan as much as possible. Cover with the remaining crumbs, and pat them down firmly.

Bake for about 45 minutes, until lightly browned. Cool in the pan before cutting into bars.

MAKES ABOUT 32 BARS.

Thin Peanut Bars

Thin, crisp, not sweet.

2½ cups (about 12 ounces) unsalted peanuts
1 cup margarine
½ cup brown sugar, firmly packed

½ cup white sugar
1 teaspoon vanilla
2 cups flour
¼ teaspoon baking soda
¾ teaspoon salt

Preheat the oven to 350° and grease a 10- by 15-inch pan. Spread the peanuts on a cutting board and chop them with a heavy knife, rocking it back and forth on the board until the peanuts are chopped into thirds. Don't be precise about this; it should go quickly.

Cream the margarine, then add the sugars and vanilla and beat until light and fluffy. Meanwhile sift the flour, baking soda, and salt together.

Beat the sifted dry ingredients into the margarine mixture until thoroughly combined. Stir in about half of the peanuts, and spread the batter in the greased pan. Sprinkle evenly with the rest of the chopped peanuts. Cover the dough lightly with a piece of waxed paper and roll a small clean glass firmly over the paper to press the peanuts into the dough. Remove the waxed paper, and place the pan in the oven.

Bake for about 25 minutes, or just until the cookies begin to brown. Cut them into squares while still quite warm.

MAKES ABOUT 48 SQUARES.

Lemon Bars

Rich, lemony, and gooey.

Base

> 2 cups cake flour
> ½ cup sugar
> ½ teaspoon salt
> 1 cup margarine

Preheat the oven to 350° and grease a 9- by 13-inch pan. Sift the cake flour, sugar, and salt together into a bowl. Cut in the margarine until the pieces are quite small and the dough particles start to cling together. Press the dough evenly into the bottom of the greased pan, building the dough up a bit around the edges.

Bake for about 25 minutes, until the dough just begins to brown.

Filling

> ¼ cup cake flour
> 1 tablespoon cornstarch
> 1 teaspoon baking
>   powder
> ⅛ teaspoon salt
> 2 large lemons, to yield
>   about 2 tablespoons
>   grated rind and 6
>   tablespoons lemon
>   juice
>
> 4 eggs
> 1¾ cups sugar
> ¼ cup confectioners'
>   sugar

While the cookie base is baking, prepare the topping. Sift the flour, cornstarch, baking powder, and salt together. Wash and dry the lemons, and grate just the yellow part of the rinds; you should get about 2 tablespoons grated rind. Squeeze the lemons, and add more juice if you need it to make 6 tablespoons.

Beat the eggs, sugar, and lemon rind together until light and foamy. As soon as the base layer is baked, briefly beat the lemon juice and the sifted dry ingredients into the egg mixture and pour this over it.

Return the pan to the oven and bake at 350° for about 20 to 25 minutes more, just until the cookies are set and lightly browned. As soon as you remove the cookies from the oven, sprinkle them with the confectioners' sugar and cool them in the pan.

Since the lemon layer is soft, you may want to chill the cookies in the refrigerator (after they have cooled to room temperature) before cutting them into bars.

MAKES ABOUT 48 BARS.

Chocolate Chip Bars

This bar cookie version of chocolate chip cookies was quite popular around 1950. It is delicious, easy to make, and deserves a revival.

3/4 cup margarine	2 teaspoons baking
1 pound brown sugar;	powder
about 2 1/4 cups, firmly	1 teaspoon salt
packed	12 ounces chocolate bits;
1 teaspoon vanilla	or, 6 ounces chocolate
3 eggs	bits and 1 cup broken
2 3/4 cups flour	nutmeats

Preheat the oven to 325° and grease a 10-inch by 15-inch pan. Cream the margarine; beat in the sugar, vanilla, and 2 of the eggs and continue beating until the mixture is very light.

Meanwhile, sift the flour, baking powder, and salt together. Beat in the last egg briefly, stir in the flour mixture and then the chocolate bits and (if you use them) the nuts. Stir just until the mixture is uniform and all of the dry particles are moistened. Spread in the greased pan.

Bake 35 minutes, or just until done.
When cool, cut into bars.
MAKES 4 DOZEN COOKIES.

All three of these brownie recipes are easy to make with just a bowl and a spoon for mixing. The margarine-egg-sugar mixture must be beaten until fluffy but it doesn't take long, even by hand.

For brownies à la mode, cut the still-warm brownies into 3-inch squares and top each one with a scoop of tofu-based ice cream substitute and chocolate sauce (page 411).

Brownies

"Baked fudge" is an old name for brownies.

Three 1-ounce squares
  unsweetened chocolate
½ cup margarine
1½ cups sugar
1 teaspoon vanilla
3 eggs
¾ cup flour

¾ teaspoon baking
  powder
½ teaspoon salt
1 cup nuts or 6 ounces
  chocolate chips
  (optional)

Preheat the oven to 350° and grease a 9- by 9-inch pan thoroughly. Melt the unsweetened chocolate in the oven, then let cool for a minute or two before using.

Beat the margarine, melted chocolate, sugar, and vanilla together very well. Beat in the eggs; continue beating until very light and fluffy.

Sift the flour, baking powder, and salt together and stir into the batter until well mixed. Stir in the nuts or chocolate chips, if you are using them. Pour the batter into the prepared pan.

Bake for about 35 minutes. Brownies should be rather soft; you want them moist. When cool, cut into squares.
MAKES ABOUT 36 BROWNIES.

Peanut Butter Brownies

A nice variation of an old favorite. These are even better when a day old.

Three 1-ounce squares
  unsweetened chocolate
½ cup margarine
1¾ cups sugar
1 teaspoon vanilla
3 eggs
¾ cup flour

¾ teaspoon baking
  powder
½ teaspoon salt
½ cup peanut butter (the
  kind made from just
  peanuts and salt is
  best)

Preheat the oven to 350° and grease a 9- by 9-inch pan. Set the unsweetened chocolate in the oven, remove it when melted.

Beat the margarine, chocolate, sugar, and vanilla well together. Beat in the eggs, and continue beating until the batter is very light and fluffy.

Sift the flour, baking powder, and salt together; stir into the batter just until well mixed. Add the peanut butter, taking care not to stir it in very thoroughly—you want to leave streaks of peanut butter in the brownies. Pour into the prepared pan.

Bake for about 30 to 40 minutes.

MAKES 36 BROWNIES.

Thin Brownies

Brownies with lots of rich chocolate frosting.

Two 1-ounce squares
   unsweetened chocolate
6 tablespoons margarine
2 eggs
¾ cup sugar

½ teaspoon vanilla
½ cup flour
¾ teaspoon baking
   powder
⅛ teaspoon salt

Preheat oven to 350°. Grease a 9- by 13-inch pan. Melt the chocolate and margarine in a small pan in the oven. Cool the chocolate mixture slightly.

Beat the eggs well, then beat in the sugar and vanilla. Sift the flour, baking powder, and salt together. Add to the beaten eggs along with the melted chocolate and margarine; stir just enough to mix thoroughly, and spread in the greased pan.

Bake for 15 to 20 minutes, or until the brownies are done. Cool.

Frosting (see warning on page 4)

One and a half 1-ounce
   squares unsweetened
   chocolate, melted
3 tablespoons margarine
1 egg
½ teaspoon vanilla

2½ cups confectioners'
   sugar
¼ teaspoon salt
About 2 tablespoons
   water

Melt the chocolate by setting it in the oven as soon as you have removed the brownies and turned the oven off.

Beat the margarine and the melted chocolate together a little. Add the rest of the ingredients except for about ½ cup of the sugar and 1 tablespoon of water, and beat very well. Beat in the rest of the sugar and enough water to make a smooth creamy frosting; spread it over the cooled brownies. When the frosting is firm, cut the brownies into bars.

MAKES ABOUT 24 BROWNIES.

Apple Cookies

A good, soft cookie.

3 medium apples, to yield 1¾ cups grated apple	1 teaspoon baking powder
1 cup margarine	1 teaspoon baking soda
1½ cups brown sugar, firmly packed	1 teaspoon salt
½ cup white sugar	1 teaspoon ground cinnamon
2 teaspoons vanilla	¼ teaspoon ground nutmeg
2 eggs	¾ cup raisins (optional)
4 cups flour	Extra sugar (optional)

Preheat the oven to 375° and grease several cookie sheets. Quarter the apples, cut out the cores, and cut off the peels. Grate them into coarse shreds and set aside.

Cream the margarine, add the sugars and vanilla, and beat until light and fluffy. Beat in the eggs very well. Sift the dry ingredients together. Add them to the batter, together with the grated apple, and stir just until well mixed. Grated apple is moist enough to take the place of liquid in some recipes, including this one. Stir in the raisins, if you use them.

Drop the batter by tablespoonsful onto the greased cookie sheets. If you aren't going to ice them after baking, sprinkle each cookie with a little sugar.

Bake for about 10 minutes, or until very light brown, and a cookie springs back if the top is touched gently. If you like, frost the cooled cookies.

Icing

> 1½ cups confectioners' sugar
> About 2 tablespoons apple juice or rum

Measure the sugar into a bowl and stir in just enough of the liquid to moisten it to a good spreading consistency.

MAKES ABOUT 6 DOZEN COOKIES.

Pumpkin Cookies

These soft, fat little drop cookies are made without eggs.

1/3 cup margarine	1/2 teaspoon ground
1 cup brown sugar,	nutmeg
packed firm	1/4 teaspoon ground
2 tablespoons water	cloves
1 1/2 cups flour	1/2 teaspoon salt
1 1/2 tablespoons cocoa	8 ounces (about 1 cup)
1 teaspoon baking soda	canned pumpkin
2 teaspoons ground	3/4 cup raisins and/or
cinnamon	chopped nuts

Preheat the oven to 375° and grease a couple of cookie sheets.

Cream the margarine, then beat in the brown sugar and the water until the batter is light and fluffy. Sift the flour, cocoa, baking soda, spices, and salt together. Stir the pumpkin briefly into the margarine mixture. Add the sifted dry ingredients and stir just until well mixed. Stir in the raisins and/or nuts, if you use them.

Drop the dough by tablespoonsful onto the greased cookie sheets. Bake for 10 minutes, or until the top of a cookie springs back when you touch it lightly.

MAKES 3 DOZEN 2-INCH COOKIES.

Honey Ginger Cookies

An old-fashioned cookie, plain and good.

1 cup margarine
1 cup brown sugar,
    firmly packed
1 egg
4 cups flour
1½ teaspoons baking
    powder
½ teaspoon baking soda

1 tablespoon ground
    ginger
¾ teaspoon salt
1 cup honey
⅔ cup hot water
1 cup raisins (optional)
About 3 tablespoons
    sugar

Preheat the oven to 350° and grease several cookie sheets.

Cream the margarine. Add the brown sugar and egg and beat until light and fluffy. Sift the flour, baking powder, baking soda, ginger, and salt together. Add the honey and the hot water to the margarine mixture, together with the sifted dry ingredients, and stir until well mixed. Stir in the raisins, if you wish.

Drop the dough by tablespoonsful onto the greased cookie sheets. Using a teaspoon, sprinkle each cookie with a little of the granulated sugar. Bake for about 10 minutes, until the cookies are just beginning to brown.

MAKES ABOUT 5 DOZEN 2¾-INCH COOKIES.

Soft Ginger Cookies

This is another old family recipe, spicier than the preceding one. They are delicious, and keep well; however, they tend to stick together in a cookie jar, so are best served when freshly made. An excellent cookie to bake for a crowd of children.

1 cup margarine
1 cup sugar
1 egg
6 cups flour
4 teaspoons baking soda
2 tablespoons ground
   ginger (yes,
   tablespoons)

1½ teaspoons ground
   cinnamon
¼ teaspoon ground
   nutmeg
1 teaspoon salt
2 cups molasses
1 cup hot water
2 tablespoons vinegar
About ¼ cup extra sugar

Preheat the oven to 350° and grease several cookie sheets.

Cream the margarine, and beat in the sugar and egg until the mixture is light and fluffy. Sift the flour, baking soda, spices, and salt together. Add the molasses, hot water, and vinegar to the sugar mixture, together with the sifted dry ingredients. Stir until batter is well mixed.

Drop by tablespoonsful onto the greased cookie sheets. Sprinkle the top of each cookie with a little of the extra sugar.

Bake for about 10 minutes, or until the top of a cookie springs back when you touch it lightly.

MAKES ABOUT ONE HUNDRED 3-INCH COOKIES.

Oatmeal Cookies

This is an old family recipe from upstate New York. If you wish, you can omit the egg.

1 cup margarine	1/4 teaspoon ground
1 cup sugar	cloves
1 egg (optional)	1 teaspoon salt
2 cups flour	1/2 cup water
2 teaspoons baking	2 cups regular rolled oats
powder	1 cup raisins and/or
3/4 teaspoon ground	chopped nuts
cinnamon	(optional)
1/2 teaspoon ground	
allspice	

Preheat the oven to 375° and grease several baking sheets.

Cream the margarine, sugar, and egg together until they are light and fluffy. Sift together the flour, baking powder, spices, and salt. Add to the margarine mixture along with the water, and mix just until well blended. Stir in the rolled oats, and the raisins and nuts if used.

Drop onto the greased baking sheets and bake for 12 to 15 minutes, or until set and very lightly browned.

If you wish, you can substitute 1 cup packed brown sugar for the granulated sugar. If you do this, decrease the baking powder to 1 1/2 teaspoons, and add 1/2 teaspoon baking soda.

MAKES ABOUT 5 DOZEN COOKIES.

Oatmeal–Peanut Butter Cookies

The combination of honey, oatmeal, and peanuts gives these chewy cookies an unusually good flavor.

½ cup margarine
½ cup peanut butter
¾ cup brown sugar, firmly packed
½ teaspoon vanilla
1 egg
1¼ cups flour

1 teaspoon baking powder
½ teaspoon salt
¼ cup honey
¾ cup regular rolled oats
⅓ cup chopped unsalted peanuts

Preheat your oven to 350° and grease a couple of cookie sheets.

Cream the margarine, peanut butter, brown sugar, and vanilla together well; add the egg and beat until light and fluffy. Sift the flour, salt, and baking powder together; add to the dough along with the honey, and mix well. Stir in the rolled oats and the peanuts.

Drop by tablespoonsful onto the greased cookie sheets. Bake for about 12 minutes, or until the cookies are just beginning to brown. Remove them to a cooling rack.

Glaze

½ cup confectioners' sugar
2 tablespoons honey
About 1 tablespoon water

Mix the sugar, honey and water together, using just enough water to make a thick, runny glaze. Spread it on the cookies while they are still slightly warm, using a pastry brush. (You may want to put waxed paper under the cookie racks to catch drips of glaze.) Let the glaze dry for several hours, or overnight.

MAKES ABOUT 36 COOKIES.

Chocolate Chip Cookies

The quintessential American cookie.

1 cup margarine
1 cup brown sugar,
    firmly packed
1/2 cup granulated sugar
1 teaspoon vanilla
2 eggs
2 1/4 cups flour
3/4 teaspoon baking soda

1/2 teaspoon salt
12-ounce package
    chocolate chips, or
6-ounce package
    chocolate chips and
1 cup nuts

By Hand or with an Electric Mixer: Preheat the oven to 350°, and grease a couple of cookie sheets. Cream the margarine, the sugars, and the vanilla well together. Beat in the eggs, one at a time, until the mixture is light and fluffy. Sift the flour, baking soda, and salt together; stir into the batter just until mixed. Stir in the chocolate chips, and the nuts if you use them.

Drop by tablespoonsful onto the greased cookie sheets. Bake for 10 minutes or until lightly browned.

MAKES ABOUT 4 DOZEN COOKIES.

Using a Food Processor: Preheat the oven to 350°, and grease a couple of cookie sheets. Fit the processor with the steel blade. Cut the margarine into chunks of about 2 tablespoons each, and put it into the workbowl together with the sugars and the vanilla; process with on-off turns until the margarine and sugar are well mixed. Add the eggs, and process the batter until it is light and smooth; you may want to pause and scrape the bowl once or twice. Sift the flour, baking soda, and salt together. Add them to the work bowl and process with a few on-off pulses just until well mixed. Stir in the chocolate chips and, if you use them, the nuts.

Drop by tablespoonsful onto the prepared cookie sheets. Bake for about 10 minutes, until the cookies are done and very lightly browned.

MAKES ABOUT 4 DOZEN COOKIES.

Chocolate Jumbles

Mother invented this recipe as a bride, and it's been a family favorite ever since.

Two 1-ounce squares
  unsweetened chocolate
½ cup margarine
1 cup brown sugar,
  firmly packed
1 egg
1½ cups flour

½ teaspoon baking
  powder
¼ teaspoon baking soda
¾ teaspoon ground
  cinnamon
½ teaspoon salt
⅓ cup water

Preheat the oven to 375° and melt the chocolate in the oven. Grease a couple of cookie sheets.

Cream together the margarine, brown sugar, and melted chocolate; add the egg and beat until very fluffy. Sift the dry ingredients together and add them, with the water, to the batter; mix just until all of the ingredients are combined and the batter is smooth.

Drop the dough by tablespoonsful onto the greased cookie sheets. Bake for about 10 minutes, or until a cookie springs back when you touch it lightly in the center. When the cookies are cool, frost them with chocolate frosting I (page 399).

MAKES ABOUT THIRTY 2¼-INCH COOKIES.

Rolled Chocolate Jumbles

Chocolate jumbles can also be made as a rolled cookie, in which case you would add about ½ cup additional flour to the preceding recipe, just enough to make the dough almost stiff enough to roll out.

Refrigerate the dough for 2 hours or more, then roll it out about ⅜ inch thick or a bit thicker, cut it out with a doughnut cutter, and proceed as above.

MAKES ABOUT FIFTEEN 3¼-INCH COOKIES.

Sugar Cookies

Thin, crisp, and sweet; these are easier to make than the usual sugar cookies since the dough is drier and you handle it as you would pie crust. You can either sprinkle sugar on the cookies before baking or glaze them after you take them out of the oven.

2½ cups cake flour, plus extra flour to roll out cookies

1½ cups sugar, plus ⅓ cup to sprinkle on cookies

½ teaspoon baking powder

¾ teaspoon salt

1 cup margarine

1 egg

2 tablespoons water

1 teaspoon vanilla

½ teaspoon lemon extract

Preheat the oven to 375° and grease several baking sheets.

Sift the flour, sugar, baking powder, and salt together into a bowl; cut in the margarine with a pastry blender until the pieces are about the size of rice grains. Stir the eggs, water, vanilla, and lemon extract together and mix them into the flour all at once. Handle the dough lightly, as you would pie crust. It is important not to handle the dough more than necessary, nor to work in too much flour, as the cookies will be tough and hard if you do. If the dough is too dry and refuses to cling together, add a few drops of water; if it is moist and sticky, add a little flour.

Flour the countertop well, and roll out half of the dough about ⅛ inch thick. Cut it with cookie cutters and place the cookies on greased baking sheets. Brush each cookie lightly with water and then sprinkle it with a little of the extra sugar, or leave the cookies plain to glaze after baking.

Bake for about 9 minutes, or until the cookies are just beginning to brown at the edges. Cool on a wire rack, and then glaze the cookies if you wish with ¾ cup confectioners' sugar mixed to a paste with 2 teaspoons water and ¾ teaspoon vanilla.

MAKES ABOUT 5 DOZEN 2½-INCH COOKIES.

Thin Ginger Cookies

This is a good, cooperative cookie dough; the unbaked cookes are easy to handle, and the cookies hold their shapes very well while baking. Here is the dough on which to try out those cookie cutters with the interesting shapes—the ones you couldn't resist in the store. If you use a skewer to make a tiny hole near the top of each cookie before it is baked, you can use a needle to thread string through it afterward and hang the cookies on your Christmas tree.

½ cup honey
¼ cup molasses
¾ cup sugar
1½ teaspoons ground
    ginger
½ teaspoon ground
    allspice
¼ teaspoon ground
    cloves

½ teaspoon salt
2 teaspoons baking soda
¾ cup margarine
1 egg
5 cups flour,
    approximately

Put the honey, molasses, sugar, spices, and salt into a medium-large saucepan and bring just to a boil. Remove immediately from the heat, and stir in the baking soda. Add the margarine, stir, and let set until the margarine is melted and the mixture is warm but not hot.

Preheat the oven to 350° and grease several baking sheets.

Into the batter in the pan stir 2 cups of the flour, and the egg; mix well with a spoon, not electric beaters. Stir in another 2½ cups of flour, then mix in the last ½ cup with your clean hand—no spoon. Mix it well, adding just enough flour so that the dough feels rather like modeling clay. The dough can be used immediately; chilling isn't necessary.

Roll out the dough. You can use a bare, floured countertop, but I usually use a pastry cloth for these cookies. My pastry cloth is a heavy cotton tablecloth folded in quarters. Into this cloth I rub about ¼ cup of flour. Using a third of the dough at a time, roll it out as thin as conveniently possible; this is usually about ⅛ inch thick, or a little less.

Cut out the dough with fancy cutters and place the cookies on the prepared cookie sheets. Bake for about 10 minutes, until the cookies just begin to brown. Remove them to a cooling rack.

Scrape any bits of clinging dough off your pastry cloth and shake the flour out of it before you either fold it up and put it away in a plastic bag or wash it.

MAKES ABOUT 150 COOKIES, DEPENDING ON THE SIZE OF YOUR COOKIE CUTTERS.

Breakfast Molasses Cookies

This very old Cape Cod recipe was given to me by a relative who learned to make the cookies as a bride, for her husband's breakfast. They were originally made with a circular cutter; however, the dough also makes excellent gingerbread men.

¼ cup margarine	¼ teaspoon salt
2¾ cups flour	¾ cup molasses
¾ teaspoon baking soda	3 tablespoons water
1 teaspoon ground	Extra flour to roll out
ginger	the dough

Preheat the oven to 375° and grease a couple of baking sheets. Melt the margarine.

Sift the flour, baking soda, ginger, and salt together into a bowl. Mix the melted margarine with the molasses and water; add this liquid mixture to the sifted dry ingredients and stir until well blended. The texture should be a little like modeling clay and should just escape being sticky.

The cookies will get hard if they are handled too much, or rolled too thin, or baked too long, or if too much flour is added.

On a floured surface roll the dough out pretty thick for a rolled cookie, about ⅜ inch thick. Cut it with cookie cutters, and place the cookies on greased baking sheets. Bake for about 8 minutes, or until the cookies just begin to brown on the bottom. Store in a closely covered container.

MAKES ABOUT FIFTEEN 2½-INCH ROUND COOKIES.

Sandies

These cookies go by many names: snowballs, Russian tea cakes, kipfels, Mexican wedding cake, and so on. They are rich, nutty little balls, covered with confectioners' sugar.

1 cup nuts (pecans,
  almonds, or walnuts)
¾ cup margarine
½ cup confectioners'
  sugar plus up to 1 cup
  additional for rolling

1 teaspoon vanilla
2 cups cake flour
¾ teaspoon salt

Preheat the oven to 325° and have a couple of cookie sheets ready; it isn't necessary to grease them. Chop the nuts to the size of rice grains in a food processor or blender, or use a knife and chop them until they are quite fine. The biggest pieces should be no larger than lentils.

Cream the margarine, ½ cup confectioners' sugar, and vanilla. Sift the flour and salt together; add to the dough along with the chopped nuts, and stir until the dough is well mixed and clings together.

Using your clean hands, pinch off pieces of dough and roll them between your palms to shape them into 1-inch balls. If the dough is crumbly, press it into balls. Set the cookies on the cookie sheets. Since the dough does not spread during baking, they can be quite close together; about 1 inch apart is fine. Bake until the bottoms of the cookies just begin to brown, about 20 minutes.

Have the extra confectioners' sugar ready in a bowl or small paper bag. As soon as the cookies come from the oven, put them— a few at a time—into the sugar, roll them around until they're well coated, and set out on a rack to cool. If you wear rubber gloves while doing this, it will protect your hands from the hot cookies.

When the cookies are cool you can roll them again in confectioners' sugar, if you like, before storing or serving them.

MAKES ABOUT 3 DOZEN 1-INCH COOKIES.

Thumbprint Cookies

Pretty, rich little cookies.

1 cup margarine	½ teaspoon salt
½ cup sugar	¼ cup jelly
1 teaspoon vanilla	
2½ cups cake flour	

Preheat the oven to 350°. You do not need to grease the cookie sheets.

Beat the margarine, sugar, and vanilla together until fluffy. Sift the cake flour and salt together; stir into the margarine and sugar, mixing until well blended and the dough clings together.

Using your hands, form the dough into 36 balls about 1¼ inches in diameter. As you shape them, put the cookies onto the cookie sheets. Flour your thumb and use it to make a well most of the way into the center of each one but not all the way through to the pan. If you poke all the way through the cookie, the jelly will glue the cookie to the baking sheet. Into each well put ¼ teaspoon of jelly. It is better to use too little jelly than too much, as the jelly in an overfilled cookie will overflow.

Bake the cookies for about 12 minutes, until the bottoms just begin to color.

MAKES ABOUT 3 DOZEN 2-INCH COOKIES.

Cookie-press Cookies

These are sometimes called spritz cookies.

Add 1 egg to the recipe for thumbprint cookies, and shape the dough by putting it through a cookie press. The dough will keep its shape better if you make these on a cool day.

Bake the cookies in an oven preheated to 350° for about 12 minutes, or until the bottoms just begin to brown. Brush the cooled cookies with vanilla glaze, if you'd like to.

MAKES ABOUT 4½ DOZEN COOKIES.

Peanut Butter Cookies

½ cup margarine
1 cup sugar
1 cup brown sugar,
  firmly packed
1 cup peanut butter,
  either smooth or
  chunky
1 teaspoon vanilla

1 tablespoon water
2 eggs
2½ cups flour
1 teaspoon baking soda
1 teaspoon salt
½ cup chopped unsalted
  peanuts (optional)

Preheat the oven to 350°. It is not necessary to grease cookie sheets, as the dough is quite rich.

Cream the margarine, sugars, peanut butter, vanilla, and water together thoroughly. Beat the eggs in well. Sift the flour, soda, and salt together and add to the dough along with the chopped peanuts; mix well.

Shape the dough by hand into balls about 1¼ inches in diameter and place these balls on the cookie sheets about 1 cookie diameter apart. Flatten each cookie with the back of a fork to make them about ½ inch thick. Bake for 11 minutes, or until the cookies are lightly browned.

MAKES ABOUT 5 DOZEN 1¾-INCH COOKIES.

Molasses Sugar Cookies

Handsome round cookies with crackled tops—mild gingersnaps. The dough can be made ahead of time and baked later.

1½ cups flour
¾ cup sugar, plus about
    ¼ cup additional sugar
    for rolling
1½ teaspoons baking
    soda
1 teaspoon ground
    ginger

½ teaspoon ground
    cinnamon
½ teaspoon ground
    allspice
½ teaspoon salt
½ cup margarine
¼ cup molasses
1 egg

Sift the dry ingredients into a bowl, then cut in the margarine until the pieces are quite small, about the size of lentils. Stir the molasses and egg together with a fork until well blended; add to the sifted dry ingredients, and mix thoroughly. You may need to finish the mixing with your hand instead of a spoon.

Cover the bowl and set it in the refrigerator for an hour or two, or for a couple of days. If the dough is not too sticky and is easy to handle, you can skip the chilling and shape and bake the cookies right away.

Preheat the oven to 375°, and grease a couple of baking sheets.

Form the dough into small balls (about 1¼ inches in diameter, or whatever you prefer) and roll them in the extra sugar, which has been put into a soup plate or other shallow bowl. Place the cookies on the prepared cookie sheets—it isn't necessary to flatten the cookies. Bake about 10 to 12 minutes.

MAKES ABOUT THIRTY 3-INCH COOKIES.

Lemon Refrigerator Cookies

A crisp, delicate cookie. The dough should be made ahead of time and kept in the freezer. Just slice off rounds and bake them as needed.

1 tablespoon freshly grated lemon rind (the grated rind of 2 lemons)
2 teaspoons lemon juice
¾ cup margarine
1 cup sugar

½ teaspoon lemon extract
1 egg
2 cups flour
½ teaspoon baking powder
½ teaspoon salt

Wash and dry the lemons, then grate off just the yellow part of the rinds. Squeeze out 2 teaspoons of juice.

Beat the margarine well; beat in the lemon rind, lemon juice, sugar, and lemon extract. Beat in the egg very well, until the mixture is quite light. Sift the flour, baking powder, and salt together; beat into the margarine just until the dough is well mixed and uniform in appearance.

Tear off 2 sheets of waxed paper, each about 15 inches long. Spoon half the dough onto a sheet of waxed paper, and form the dough into a roll about 7 inches long and 1¾ inches in diameter. Fold the paper over the dough, and then repeat this process with the other sheet of waxed paper and the other half of the dough. Set these logs of cookie dough in the freezer for 2 hours or more to stiffen. If you are going to leave the dough in the freezer for more than about a day, put the rolls into a plastic bag and seal the opening.

When you are ready to bake, heat the oven to 375° and grease several cookie sheets. Unwrap the cookie dough and place it on a cutting board. Using a thin, sharp knife, cut the dough into rounds about 1/8 inch thick. Put these slices onto the cookie sheets.

Bake just until well browned at the edges, about 10 minutes. These cookies should be allowed to cool for a minute or two on the cookie sheet before being removed to the usual wire rack for cooling.

MAKES ABOUT 5 DOZEN 2½-INCH COOKIES.

Chocolate Refrigerator Cookies

Crisp, not sweet, and very chocolate.

Four 1-ounce squares
   unsweetened chocolate
1/2 cup margarine
1 cup sugar
1/2 teaspoon vanilla
1 egg

1½ cups flour
1/2 teaspoon baking
   powder
1/2 teaspoon baking soda
1/2 teaspoon salt

Melt the chocolate and cool it briefly. Cream the margarine, chocolate, sugar, and vanilla together. Beat in the egg, and continue beating until the mixture is quite fluffy. Sift the flour, baking powder, baking soda, and salt together; stir into the creamed mixture until the dough is well blended and uniform.

Set out 2 pieces of waxed paper, each about 15 inches long. Spoon half of the dough onto each piece of paper, and (flouring your hands first) shape each piece of dough into a log about 9 inches long and 1½ inches in diameter. Wrap the waxed paper around the dough and freeze for 2 hours or more. If you don't plan on baking the cookies within a day or so, put the wrapped rolls of dough into a plastic bag and tie the bag firmly shut.

When you are ready to bake the cookies, preheat the oven to

325° and get out several baking sheets—it is not necessary to grease them.

Cut the logs of dough into slices about ⅛ inch thick. Set the slices on the cookie sheets. Bake for about 12 minutes, until the cookies are done but not browned.

MAKES ABOUT 6 DOZEN 2-INCH COOKIES.

Honey Almond Cookies

Crisp and slightly spicy, this is another cookie that can be kept in the freezer until you are ready to bake.

½ cup almonds
½ cup margarine
½ cup brown sugar, firmly packed
¼ cup honey
1¾ cups flour
¼ teaspoon baking soda
½ teaspoon ground ginger
½ teaspoon ground cinnamon
½ teaspoon ground allspice
½ teaspoon salt
2 tablespoons water

Grind the almonds fine. Cream the margarine, add the brown sugar and honey, and beat until light and fluffy. Sift the flour, baking soda, spices, and salt together. Add the water, then the sifted dry ingredients, and then the chopped almonds to the dough, and stir just until thoroughly mixed.

Get ready 2 sheets of waxed paper, each about 12 inches long. Using your hands, shape the dough into 2 rolls, each about 2 inches in diameter, and place each roll on a sheet of waxed paper. Wrap each roll securely in the waxed paper and freeze it for 2 hours or longer. If the dough is to be kept in the freezer for more than about a day, put the rolls into a plastic bag and close it tightly.

When you are ready to bake, heat the oven to 350°. Unwrap

the dough and put it on a cutting board. With a thin, sharp knife cut off rounds about ⅛ inch thick and place these slices on baking sheets, which need not be greased. Bake for about 11 minutes, until the cookies are lightly browned.

MAKES ABOUT FORTY 2-INCH COOKIES.

Cakes

Yellow Cake
Egg White Cake
Egg Yolk Cake
Golden Cake
Applesauce Spice Cake
Banana Cake
Pumpkin Cake
Prune Cake
Candied Ginger Cake
Eggless Spice Cake
Chocolate Cake
Chocolate Date Cake
Quick Chocolate Cake
Sachertorte
Graham Cracker Torte
Carrot Cake
Easy Apple Cake
Sponge Cake
Silver and Gold Cake

Cherry Pound Cake
  Pound Cake
Rum Cake
Pineapple Upside-down Cake
  Douglas's Upside-down
  Cake

About Making Cakes . . .

You must follow a few simple rules in making cakes.

Careful measuring is important. A meat dish may turn out well if you add a handful of this and a dash of that, but a cake won't. It will probably fall.

When the recipe calls for margarine, always use solid margarine sold in sticks. If you are using a pastry blender or food processor to make the cake, the margarine can be cold and straight from the refrigerator; if you are using a mixer, the margarine should be at room temperature so it will cream easily.

Most cakes are made by a standard method: cream the shortening and sugar together, then beat in the eggs until the batter is light and fluffy. Next add the previously sifted dry ingredients along with the liquid, and stir everything together just enough to mix. The initial beating of the eggs, shortening, and sugar, and the sifting of the flour help make a light cake with good texture.

Some cakes when made without milk turn out better if they are made by the cut-in-the-shortening method more commonly used for biscuits and other quick breads. That is why I use this unusual method for some cakes.

Most cookbooks tell you to sift flour before measuring; however, I get good results by just fluffing up the flour with a spoon before measuring. (Sifting flour gives it greater volume.) If—for any recipe in this book—you sift the flour before measuring it, you will be using too little flour.

After you add the dry ingredients and the liquid, stir just until the batter is well mixed; it should have no lumps, but overbeating will toughen the cake. Turn the batter into the prepared cake tin, and bake immediately.

The recipes in this book are written for shiny metal pans. If you use glass or black metal baking pans, reduce the oven temperatures given by 25 degrees.

A cake is done when it is lightly browned, and a thin skewer inserted into its center comes out clean; the cake will usually shrink slightly from the sides of the pan.

I often frost a cake in the pan and serve it right from the pan, family style. If you plan to remove a thin cake such as a layer cake from the pan before icing it, let it cool for about 10 minutes. Then, loosen it from the sides of the pan by working around the edge of the cake with a blunt knife, loosening and pushing the cake carefully away from the sides of the pan. Place a clean plate or your outspread hand (if the cake is cool enough) over the cake; invert the pan and shake it gently to dislodge the cake. If you have turned the cake out onto your hand, you then put a plate over the cake and turn everything right side up on the counter, with the plate underneath, where it belongs.

Upside-down cake should be turned out of the baking pan directly onto a serving plate as soon as it comes from the oven, to avoid having the topping remain behind in the pan when you turn the cake out.

Usually a large, deep cake like a pound cake is allowed to cool completely in the pan before being removed. Sponge cakes and angel-food cake should always be allowed to cool completely in the pan.

Cupcakes

Use any plain cake recipe like yellow cake, chocolate cake, or applesauce spice cake, but not recipes for Sachertorte or for pound cake.

A recipe for a 9-inch round or 8-inch square cake will make about 12 cupcakes, if you use 2½-inch round cups.

Either grease well and flour your cupcake tins, or put ungreased paper liners in them. It helps to grease the top of your cupcake tin, so that "hangovers" will release from the pan easily. Fill each cup about ⅔ full.

Set the oven hotter than you would for the basic recipe; 400° is usually right. Bake the cupcakes for about 15 minutes, or until a skewer inserted into the center of a cupcake comes out clean.

Cool the cupcakes for 3 or 4 minutes before turning them out of their baking tin and putting on a wire rack to cool before frosting. If you didn't use paper liners for the cupcake tins, you will probably need to ease the cupcakes out by lifting carefully around the edges with a blunt table knife; slide the knife carefully all around the outside of each cupcake first.

Yellow Cake

A plain, basic cake. The lack of milk makes this light cake a little drier than usual.

½ cup margarine	2½ cups cake flour
1½ cups sugar	1½ teaspoons baking
1 teaspoon vanilla	powder
½ teaspoon lemon	¾ teaspoon salt
extract (optional)	¾ cup water
2 eggs	

Preheat the oven to 375° and grease and flour the bottoms (not the sides) of three 8-inch round, two 9-inch round, or one 10- by 15-inch oblong cake pan(s).

Cream the margarine, sugar, and vanilla and lemon extracts well together; add the eggs and beat until very light and fluffy. Sift the flour, salt, and baking powder together.

Add the water to the batter along with the sifted dry ingredients, and stir only until well mixed. Turn the batter into the prepared cake pans.

Bake until done; the layers take about 25 minutes, the oblong cake takes about 30 to 35 minutes.

Egg White Cake

This light cake is good with mocha (pages 398–99) or raspberry (page 397) frosting.

½ cup margarine
1¾ cups sugar
1 teaspoon vanilla
5 egg whites or 3 egg
   whites plus 1 whole
   egg
2½ cups cake flour

1 tablespoon baking
   powder
¾ teaspoon salt
1 cup water

Preheat the oven to 350°. Grease and dust with flour the bottoms of two 8-inch round cake pans or one 13- by 9-inch oblong pan.

Cream together the margarine, sugar, and vanilla; add 3 of the egg whites and beat until very light and fluffy. Sift the dry ingredients together. Add the 2 remaining egg whites or the whole egg to the margarine mixture and beat briefly.

Add the sifted dry ingredients and the water to the batter, mix thoroughly, and then pour into the prepared cake pan(s).

Bake the 8-inch layers for about 25 to 30 minutes. The oblong cake will bake in about 35 minutes.

Egg Yolk Cake

Rather like a sponge cake. Dress up a two-layer cake with apricot filling (page 405) and boiled frosting (pages 402–3), or use peanut-coconut broiled icing (page 402) for the single-layer cake.

½ cup margarine
1¼ cups sugar
1 teaspoon vanilla
6 egg yolks or 4 egg
   yolks plus 1 whole
   egg

2 cups cake flour
4 teaspoons baking
   powder
¾ teaspoon salt
1 cup water

Preheat the oven to 350° and grease and flour the bottom(s) of two 9-inch round pans or one 10- by 15-inch oblong pan.

Cream the margarine; beat in the sugar and vanilla very well. Beat the egg yolks (and the egg if you use it) in gradually and continue beating until the mixture is very light and fluffy.

Sift the dry ingredients together and add them with the water to the batter; stir just until well mixed. Turn into the prepared pan or pans.

Bake about 25 minutes for the round layers, or about 35 minutes for the oblong cake.

Golden Cake

This simple cake uses no eggs and is very easy to make. Good with coffee, or as dessert. Sprinkle confectioners' sugar over the top while the cake is still hot, or spread it with vanilla glaze (page 404) to which you have added about 3 tablespoons of raisins.

1 1/4 cups flour	3/4 cup applesauce
2/3 cup sugar	1/3 cup vegetable oil
3/4 teaspoon baking soda	1/2 teaspoon vanilla
1/4 teaspoon salt	

Preheat the oven to 350° and grease either a 9-inch round or an 8-inch square pan.

Sift the flour, sugar, soda, and salt together. Mix the applesauce, oil, and vanilla in a bowl; add the dry ingredients and stir just until all of the flour is moistened. Spread the batter in the prepared pan.

Bake for 30 minutes, or until done.

Applesauce Spice Cake

Fill a two-layer cake with plum jam and ice it with seafoam frosting (page 403); spread a single-layer cake with plain "butter" frosting (page 396), or dust it with confectioners' sugar.

3/4 cup margarine
1 1/4 cups brown sugar, firmly packed
2 eggs
2 3/4 cups flour
1 1/2 teaspoons baking soda
1 1/2 teaspoons ground cinnamon
1/2 teaspoon ground nutmeg
1/2 teaspoon ground allspice
3/4 teaspoon salt
1 cup applesauce
1/2 cup raisins
1/2 cup chopped nuts (optional)

Preheat the oven to 350° and grease, then dust with flour, the bottom(s) of one 9- by 13-inch oblong pan or two 8-inch round pans.

Cream the margarine and sugar well together; add the eggs, one at a time, and beat until the mixture is light and fluffy.

Sift the dry ingredients together; add to the batter together with the applesauce, and stir only until well mixed. Briefly stir in the raisins and nuts. Turn the batter into the prepared pans.

Bake about 40 minutes for the oblong cake, about 30 minutes for the 8-inch round layers.

Banana Cake

The single-layer cake is good with rum frosting (page 398) or "butter" frosting (page 396), or bake the cake as two layers and use peach jam as a filling. Dust the top of the layer cake with confectioners' sugar. This is a good use for bananas that are beginning to get too ripe.

1¼ cups mashed banana (3 medium-sized very ripe bananas)
½ cup margarine
1 cup brown sugar, firmly packed
½ cup white sugar
1 teaspoon vanilla
2 eggs
2 cups flour
2 teaspoons baking powder
¾ teaspoon baking soda
1 teaspoon salt

Preheat the oven to 350° and prepare a 9- by 13-inch pan or two 8- or 9-inch round pans by greasing and flouring only the bottoms.

Mash the bananas well, either with a fork or in a blender; set aside. Cream the margarine, the sugars, and the vanilla well; add the eggs one at a time and beat until very light and fluffy. Meanwhile, sift the flour, baking powder, baking soda, and salt together.

Add the sifted dry ingredients and the mashed banana to the batter; stir just until thoroughly mixed. Turn the batter into the prepared pan or pans.

Bake the layers for about 30 minutes; the oblong for about 40 minutes.

Pumpkin Cake

A good autumn cake. Finish it with orange (page 398) or nutmeg (page 396) frosting.

½ cup margarine
1 cup sugar
½ teaspoon vanilla
   (optional)
2 eggs
2 cups flour
1 teaspoon baking
   powder
½ teaspoon baking soda
1 teaspoon ground
   cinnamon

½ teaspoon ground
   nutmeg
½ teaspoon ground
   allspice
1 teaspoon salt
¼ cup molasses
¼ cup water
8 ounces (1 cup) canned
   pumpkin
½ cup raisins

Preheat the oven to 350°. Grease and flour the bottoms of two 8-inch round cake pans.

Cream the margarine, sugar, vanilla (if you use it), and eggs well. Sift the flour, baking powder, soda, spices, and salt together. Mix the molasses with the water and the pumpkin.

Add the sifted dry ingredients and the pumpkin mixture to the batter at the same time; beat briefly, until the batter is nearly smooth. Stir in the raisins, and divide the batter between the two cake pans.

Bake for about 30 minutes, until a skewer inserted into the center of a layer comes out clean.

NOTE: A double recipe of this cake can be baked in a 10- by 15-inch pan; it will take about 40 minutes.

Prune Cake

This is a milk-free version of a cake that has been a family favorite for many years. Plain "butter" frosting (page 396) or seafoam frosting (page 403) is good on this. Double the recipe for a layer cake.

½ cup cooked prunes, drained and cut up
⅓ cup margarine
1 cup brown sugar, firmly packed
2 eggs
1 cup flour
½ teaspoon baking powder

¼ teaspoon baking soda
1 teaspoon ground cinnamon
½ teaspoon ground nutmeg
½ teaspoon ground allspice
½ teaspoon salt
½ cup water

Preheat the oven to 350°. Grease and flour a 9-inch round or 8-inch square pan on the bottom only.

Measure the prune pulp, and cut through it several times with kitchen scissors to cut up the fruit into small pieces.

Cream the margarine, sugar, and 1 egg; beat very well, until they are light and fluffy. Meanwhile, sift the dry ingredients together.

Beat the remaining egg into the creamed mixture; add the dry ingredients and the water, and mix just until smooth. Stir in the prune pulp, and pour the batter into the prepared pan.

Bake for about 40 minutes.

Candied Ginger Cake

The grated pear adds richness to the cake, but its mild flavor is masked by the candied ginger and grated chocolate. A wonderful combination—please try it!

⅓ cup nuts
3 tablespoons crystallized ginger
Two 1-ounce squares semisweet chocolate
2 large pears, ripe but still firm, to give 1 cup grated pear
½ cup margarine
½ cup sugar
½ cup brown sugar, firmly packed

1 teaspoon vanilla
2 eggs
2 cups flour
1½ teaspoons baking powder
¼ teaspoon baking soda
¾ teaspoon salt
2 tablespoons confectioners' sugar

Preheat the oven to 350° and grease, then dust with flour, the bottom and sides of a 9- by 13-inch pan.

Chop the nuts, then cut the ginger into pieces about the size of dried peas. Chop the chocolate coarsely into pieces about the same size as the pieces of ginger. Cut the pears into quarters, cut off the peels, cut out the cores, and grate the flesh coarsely.

Cream the margarine, sugar, brown sugar, and vanilla together; add the eggs and beat until fluffy. Sift the flour, baking powder, baking soda, and salt together.

Add the sifted dry ingredients to the batter together with the grated pear, and mix just until uniform. Stir in the nuts, ginger, and chocolate. Spoon the batter into the prepared pan.

Bake for about 30 minutes, or until the top is lightly browned and a skewer inserted into the middle of the cake comes out clean. As soon as the cake comes from the oven, dust it with the confectioners' sugar. Serve warm or at room temperature.

Eggless Spice Cake

A spicy, dark cake with good flavor. Keeps well, is easy to make, and travels well for car trips or picnics. Ice the cooled cake with nutmeg frosting (page 396), or glaze it with a mixture of 1 cup confectioners' sugar and 2 tablespoons apple juice.

1½ cups raisins
½ cup dates
2 cups brown sugar, firmly packed
1½ teaspoons ground cinnamon
1 teaspoon ground allspice
¼ teaspoon ground cloves
1 teaspoon salt
¾ cup vegetable oil
2 cups water
4 cups flour
2 teaspoons baking soda
1½ cups nuts, chopped

Put everything but the flour, baking soda, and nuts into a big saucepan; bring to a boil, boil for 1 minute, and let cool to room temperature.

Preheat the oven to 350°. Grease the bottom of a 13- by 9-inch oblong pan.

Sift the flour and baking soda together and stir them into the batter along with the nuts. Turn into the prepared pan.

Bake for about 45 minutes.

Chocolate Cake

Three 1-ounce squares unsweetened chocolate
½ cup margarine
1 pound (2¼ cups, firmly packed) brown sugar
1 teaspoon vanilla
3 eggs
2½ cups sifted cake flour
1½ teaspoons baking powder
1½ teaspoons baking soda
¾ teaspoon salt
1½ cups water

Preheat the oven to 375°. Put the chocolate into a small oven-proof dish and set it in the oven to melt—it should take 5 to 10 minutes. Grease and dust with flour only the bottom(s) of two 9-inch round pans or one 9- by 13-inch oblong pan.

Beat the margarine, melted chocolate, and brown sugar together; add the vanilla and 2 of the eggs, and continue beating until very light and fluffy. Sift the cake flour before measuring; sift it again with the baking powder, baking soda, and salt.

Beat the last egg into the batter. Add the sifted dry ingredients and the water and mix well, then turn the batter into the prepared pan(s).

Bake the oblong cake for about 45 minutes; the layers take about 35 minutes.

Chocolate Date Cake

This European-style dessert is a sophisticated cousin of eggless spice cake (see page 369).

3/4 cup dates
3/4 cup hot water
1 teaspoon baking soda
2 large pears, ripe but still firm, to give 1 cup grated pear
1/2 cup margarine
1 cup sugar
1 teaspoon vanilla
2 cups flour
2 tablespoons cocoa

1 teaspoon baking powder
1 teaspoon ground cinnamon
3/4 teaspoon ground cloves
1/2 teaspoon salt
1/2 recipe Chocolate Glaze (page 404), or about 1/3 cup confectioners' sugar

Preheat the oven to 350° and grease and flour the bottom of a 9- by 9-inch pan.

Cut up the dates, pour the hot water over them, sprinkle the baking soda over the water, and let stand while you make the cake. Quarter, core, and peel the pears; grate enough of the flesh on a coarse grater to give 1 cup grated pear.

Cream the margarine, sugar, and vanilla together, then beat in about ¼ cup of the pear pulp until the mixture is quite fluffy. It is okay if the batter curdles.

Sift the flour, cocoa, baking powder, spices, and salt together. Stir the remaining pear pulp into the dates, and add this to the batter together with the sifted dry ingredients. Stir just until well mixed. Spoon into the prepared pan.

Bake for about 45 minutes, or until the cake shrinks slightly from the sides of the pan and a skewer inserted into the middle comes out clean. While the cake is still warm, drizzle a half recipe of chocolate glaze over it in a lacy free-form pattern. Or, if you prefer, sift confectioners' sugar over the cake instead.

Quick Chocolate Cake

This recipe uses no eggs, and is very quick and easy to make. Either chocolate frosting I (page 399) or peanut-coconut broiled icing (page 402) is good on this cake, or you can simply dust the top with a little confectioners' sugar.

1½ cups flour	⅓ cup vegetable oil
¼ cup unsweetened cocoa powder	1 cup water
	½ teaspoon vanilla
1 teaspoon baking soda	2 tablespoons almond
¼ teaspoon salt	liqueur (optional)
¾ cup brown sugar, firmly packed	

Preheat the oven to 350° and grease a 9-inch round or an 8-inch square pan.

Sift the flour, cocoa, baking soda, and salt together into a bowl. Measure the brown sugar and add it. (If the brown sugar is very lumpy, you may want to break the clumps up with your fingers.) Stir the dry ingredients well. Mix the oil, water, and vanilla together, then add them to the dry ingredients and stir just until all of the dry bits are wet. Turn the batter into the prepared pan.

Bake the cake for 30 minutes.

Sachertorte

This is a classic Viennese dessert.

6 ounces German's sweet
  chocolate
6 eggs, separated, at
  room temperature
3/4 cup sugar
1/2 cup margarine, at
  room temperature
1 cup flour

1/4 teaspoon salt
9 ounces raspberry or
  apricot jam
1 tablespoon almond
  liqueur (optional)
Glossy Chocolate Icing
  (page 400)

Cut circles of waxed paper to fit the inside bottoms of two 8-inch round cake pans. I do this by fitting a square of waxed paper into each cake pan and then running the tip of a sharp knife around the edge where the side meets the bottom of the pan, to mark the paper. It is then easy to cut the papers to the right size. Grease the inside bottom of each cake pan, line it with a circle of waxed paper, and grease the top of the waxed paper.

Preheat the oven to 350°. Set the chocolate in a small heatproof dish and melt it in the oven while the oven preheats, about 5 or 10 minutes.

Beat the egg whites until foamy, then beat in the sugar and continue beating until stiff.

Cream the margarine well, beat in the melted chocolate, and gradually beat in the egg yolks. Sift the flour and salt together, and beat them briefly into the margarine and chocolate, just until well mixed.

Using a rubber spatula, mix some of the egg whites into the chocolate mixture to lighten it. Then fold the chocolate mixture gradually into the egg whites just until the two are thoroughly combined. Divide the batter between the two cake pans.

Bake for about 25 minutes.

When the cakes have cooled to room temperature, turn one of them out upside down on a plate, peel off the waxed paper, and cover the top surface, not the sides, of this layer with the jam. (You are going to put the two layers together bottom to bottom.) The torte will be even better if you sprinkle this bottom layer with some almond liqueur before spreading it with jam. Top with the second layer and let set a bit before icing with glossy chocolate icing.

Graham Cracker Torte

Fill with apricot jam and top the torte with sifted powdered sugar or with whipped nondiary topping. Or use chocolate frosting instead of the filling and topping.

¼ cup margarine	6 full-size oblong
1 cup flour	graham crackers
1 cup sugar	(about 1¼ cups when
2½ teaspoons baking	crushed)
powder	1 cup water
⅛ teaspoon salt	2 eggs

Cut circles of waxed paper to fit two 8-inch round baking pans. (See directions given with the recipe for Sachertorte on the preceding page.) Be sure to grease the inside bottom of each pan as well as the top of each piece of waxed paper.

Preheat the oven to 375° and melt the margarine in the oven while it preheats.

Sift the flour, sugar, baking powder, and salt together into a bowl. Crush the graham crackers with a rolling pin or in a blender or food processor and add the crumbs to the dry ingredients. Mix the water, egg, and margarine in another bowl; add the liquids gradually to the dry ingredients, stirring as you do this. Pour the batter into the prepared pans.

Bake for about 35 minutes. When the layers are cool, put together as a layer cake.

Carrot Cake

Glaze this with 1 cup of confectioners' sugar to which you have added enough orange or pineapple juice to make it runny.

Carrots—to give
1½ cups grated carrots
3 eggs
1¼ cups sugar
½ teaspoon vanilla
2 cups flour
1¼ teaspoons baking powder
¾ teaspoon salt
1 teaspoon ground cinnamon
½ teaspoon ground nutmeg
½ teaspoon ground cloves
½ cup vegetable oil
¾ cup canned crushed pineapple (most of an 8-ounce can), undrained
½ cup raisins

By Hand or with an Electric Mixer: Preheat the oven to 350°. Thoroughly grease and lightly flour a 13- by 9-inch baking pan. Grate the carrots.

Beat the eggs, sugar, and vanilla together well. Sift the flour, baking powder, salt, and spices; add them to the egg mixture along with the oil, the canned pineapple with its juice, the grated carrots, and the raisins; beat or stir together just until mixed.

Pour into the prepared pan and bake for about 45 minutes.

Turn the cake out of the pan after it has cooled for about 15 minutes, and glaze it.

Using a Food Processor: Many cakes, including this one, can be made with a food processor. Peel the carrots by hand and grate them coarsely with the grating disk. Remove the carrots from the work bowl, and replace the grating disk with the steel blade. Process the eggs, sugar, and vanilla until they are light and thick. Sift the flour, baking powder, salt, and spices together. Add these sifted dry ingredients to the egg mixture along with the oil and the canned pineapple with juice; process very briefly. Stir in the raisins and the grated carrots, or process them into the dough with just one or two quick pulses. Or make an interesting variation by processing the batter until it is nearly smooth after you add the carrots, but before you add the raisins. Bake and glaze.

Easy Apple Cake

This is a good cake to know about. Not only is it delicious, you can make it with very little equipment—you don't even need a pastry blender. Serve plain; it needs no embellishment.

About 4 cups thin apple slices (4 medium apples)
3¼ cups flour
2½ cups sugar
3½ teaspoons baking powder
1 teaspoon salt
½ cup orange juice

1 cup vegetable oil
2 teaspoons vanilla
4 eggs
¼ teaspoon ground nutmeg
¼ teaspoon ground cinnamon
2 tablespoons honey

Preheat the oven to 350° and set the oven shelf a little lower than usual (this is a tall cake). Grease thoroughly a 10-inch round tube pan or bundt pan.

Prepare your apples: Cut them in quarters from stem end to blossom end, peel, cut out the cores, and slice.

Sift the dry ingredients into a large bowl. Put the juice, oil, vanilla, and eggs into another bowl and beat them briefly with a fork until they are well mixed. Make a well in the center of the dry ingredients, pour in the liquids, and stir with a spoon just until the mixture appears uniform.

Put half this batter into the prepared pan, and cover with half the apple slices. Spread the rest of the batter carefully over them, and top with the remaining apple slices. Sprinkle the nutmeg and cinnamon over the top of the cake, and drizzle with the honey.

Bake for about 1½ to 1¾ hours, until a skewer run into the cake comes out clean. Turn the cake out of the pan while still a little warm.

Sponge Cake

Adapted from a handwritten recipe in my great-grandmother's cookbook. The egg yolks provide the only fat in this cake. Ice with mocha frosting (pages 398–99), raspberry frosting (page 397), or pass a bowl of sweetened sliced peaches or strawberries to spoon over the cake.

3 eggs
1 cup sugar
1 cup cake flour
1½ teaspoons baking
  powder
¼ teaspoon salt
¼ cup water

½ teaspoon vanilla
  extract
¼ teaspoon lemon
  extract
Few drops almond
  extract

Preheat the oven to 350° and grease and flour just the bottom of a 9- by 9-inch square pan.

Separate the eggs, and beat the egg whites until stiff. In another bowl, beat the egg yolks briefly with the sugar until light in color. Sift the flour, baking powder, and salt together and add to the egg yolks along with the water and extracts; beat well for 5 minutes. Fold in the egg whites, and turn the cake into the prepared pan.

Bake for about 30 minutes. Cool completely in the pan. Ice the cake when cool.

Silver and Gold Cake

A pretty, lemon-flavored marble cake made with angel-food and sponge cake batters.

9 egg whites
5 egg yolks
3/4 teaspoon cream of
  tartar
1 3/4 cups sugar
1 1/2 teaspoons vanilla
  extract
1/2 teaspoon lemon
  extract

1 1/2 cups cake flour
2 teaspoons baking
  powder
1/4 teaspoon salt
2 tablespoons water

Preheat the oven to 375°. Move the oven shelf down to make space for baking this tall cake. Have ready an angel food pan (a 10-inch tube pan with a removable bottom). Do not grease the pan; you want the batter to cling to the sides of the pan, to help make it a very high, light cake.

Beat the egg whites and the cream of tartar together until they are foamy but not stiff. Beat in 1 cup of sugar gradually and continue beating until the egg whites stand in stiff peaks when you lift up the beaters. Beat in the vanilla and lemon extracts.

Sift the flour, 3/4 cup sugar, baking powder, and salt together. Working by hand, fold this gradually into the beaten egg whites, just until they are thoroughly combined.

Beat the egg yolks and water well together in a medium-sized bowl. Add half the egg white mixture to the yolks, and fold by hand just until thoroughly blended. You now have a yellow sponge cake batter and a white angel food cake batter. Drop alternate tablespoonfuls of the two batters into the tube pan until they are used up. Smooth the top of the cake gently.

Bake for about 45 minutes, or until a skewer poked into the middle of the cake comes out clean. Turn the pan upside down (making sure that there is space for air to circulate underneath) as soon as it comes from the oven, and leave it that way for several hours, until completely cooled.

Remove the cake from the pan and set it on a large plate. You will have to use a dull knife to cut the cake carefully away from the sides and then from the bottom of the pan.

Glaze

> 1 cup confectioners' sugar
> 1 tablespoon lemon juice
> ½ teaspoon lemon extract
> 1 tablespoon water

Mix the sugar, lemon juice, and lemon extract together with enough of the water to make a glaze about the thickness of heavy cream. Drizzle it over the cake, encouraging some to run down the sides. Smooth the glaze over the top of the cake.

Cherry Pound Cake

This is a real old-style pound cake, and it's delicious. Pound cake keeps well.

½ pound margarine	3 eggs
2¼ cups confectioners' sugar	1½ cups cake flour
½ teaspoon vanilla	¼ teaspoon salt
¼ teaspoon almond extract	4 ounces candied cherries, chopped

All the ingredients should be at room temperature. Preheat the oven to 350° and grease both the bottom and sides of a 9- by 5-inch loaf pan very well; dust with flour.

This cake has no leavening agent, so it depends on sifting and lots of beating for its light, delicate texture. Cream the margarine, then beat in the confectioners' sugar; add the vanilla and almond extracts, and an egg, and beat until very light and fluffy. Beat in another egg, and again beat well until light and fluffy; beat in the third egg. You should beat this batter for 5 to 10 minutes.

Sift the flour and salt together and stir them gently into the batter. Stir in the cherries, then turn the batter into the prepared pan.

Bake for about 70 minutes. Cool the cake completely before serving. Serve plain, or dust the top with confectioners' sugar.

Pound Cake

Omit the candied cherries. Substitute ½ teaspoon vanilla extract, or the grated rind of ½ lemon, for the almond extract.

Rum Cake

A big pound cake, baked in a fancy pan and then soaked with rum syrup and finished with a thin frosting. Omit the syrup and the glaze if you just want a large, handsome, plain pound cake.

1⅓ cups margarine	4 eggs
3 cups confectioners' sugar	2 cups cake flour
1 teaspoon vanilla	¾ teaspoon salt

All the ingredients should be at room temperature. Preheat the oven to 325°. Grease thoroughly and dust lightly with flour a fancy ring pan (bundt pan) that holds 8 to 10 cups. As a pound cake, this depends on sifting and a lot of beating for its lightness and fine texture.

Cream the margarine. Add the confectioners' sugar, the vanilla, and one egg and beat until very light and fluffy. Beat in the other eggs, one at a time, beating after each egg is added until the mixture is very light. You should beat the mixture for 5 to 10 minutes.

Sift the flour and salt together and mix them into the batter, stirring just until it is smooth. Spoon into the prepared pan. Bake about 1 hour and 10 minutes.

Cool the cake in the pan for about 15 minutes, then turn it out onto a plate with a raised edge, which will be needed to catch the syrup.

Rum Syrup

> 1½ cups sugar
> 6 tablespoons rum
> 6 tablespoons water

Heat the sugar, rum, and water together until the sugar is dissolved, stirring constantly.

As soon as the cake comes from the pan, spoon the hot syrup very slowly over the cake, allowing it plenty of time to soak in, until all of the syrup is used up.

Frosting

> 1 cup confectioners' sugar
> About 2 tablespoons rum

Mix the confectioners' sugar with enough rum to make a thin frosting. When the cake has cooled to room temperature, spread it on the top and encourage a little to run down the outside of the cake in places. Let the cake mellow for several hours, or overnight. You may want to move it to a clean plate before serving.

Pineapple Upside-down Cake

Usually upside-down cake is made by the creaming method; however, I find that the cut-in-the-shortening method gives a better texture to this milk-free cake.

¼ cup margarine
⅔ cup brown sugar, firmly packed
⅛ teaspoon salt
One 8-ounce can pineapple slices, drained

Preheat the oven to 350°. Melt the margarine in a 9-inch square pan in the oven. Remove the pan from the oven and sprinkle the brown sugar and salt evenly over the melted margarine. Arrange the pineapple slices attractively on the sugar. Let set to cool slightly while you prepare the cake.

Cake

1½ cups flour
1 cup sugar
2 teaspoons baking powder
½ teaspoon salt
6 tablespoons margarine
½ cup water
1 teaspoon vanilla extract
1 egg

Sift the flour, sugar, baking powder, and salt together into a bowl. Cut in the margarine until the pieces are about the size of lentils. Mix the water, the vanilla extract, and the egg briefly together; stir them into the sifted dry ingredients all at once. Mix just until all of the dry particles are moistened, then spoon the batter carefully over the fruit in the prepared pan. Smooth out the batter a little, using the back of a spoon—you are doing this to cover the fruit.

Bake for about 40 minutes, or until the cake is lightly browned. Turn the cake out immediately, upside down, onto a serving plate; if you wait very long to turn the cake out, the fruit topping will stick to the pan. Serve warm or cool.

Douglas's Upside-down Cake

For the pineapple in the preceding recipe, substitute enough other fruit such as apricots, blueberries, strawberries, or water-packed canned sour cherries to pleasantly cover the bottom of the pan; about 1½ cups. If you like, sprinkle the fruit with about ½ teaspoon ground cinnamon.

Baked
and Steamed
Puddings

Cottage Pudding
Gingerbread
Autumn Apple Cake
Baked Plum Duff
Bread Pudding
Rice Pudding
Christmas Pudding
Steamed Fig Pudding

Cottage Pudding

Very plain cake like this becomes cottage pudding when you serve it hot, with a sauce such as lemon sauce (page 409), orange sauce (pages 409–10), or chocolate sauce (page 411).

1½ cups flour	6 tablespoons margarine
1 cup sugar	¾ cup water
1 teaspoon baking powder	1 teaspoon vanilla
½ teaspoon salt	1 egg

Preheat the oven to 350° and grease a 9-inch square pan. Sift the flour, sugar, baking powder, and salt into a bowl. Cut in the margarine until the pieces are about the size of peas. Stir the water, vanilla, and egg together; stir them all at once into the flour mixture, and continue stirring only until the ingredients are well blended. Spread this batter in the prepared pan.

Bake for about 35 minutes, or until a skewer inserted into the middle comes out clean. Serve hot or warm, with a sauce.

Gingerbread

Wonderful when hot from the oven, but also very good when cooled to room temperature. Grandmother's recipe, from which this is adapted, called for beef drippings instead of margarine. Serve with nondairy whipped topping or tofu-based ice cream substitute.

2 cups flour	½ teaspoon ground cloves
¼ cup sugar	½ teaspoon salt
1 teaspoon baking soda	½ cup margarine
1 teaspoon ground ginger	¾ cup molasses
½ teaspoon ground cinnamon	¾ cup hot water
	1 egg

Preheat the oven to 325° and grease a 9- by 9-inch pan.

Sift the dry ingredients into a bowl, then cut in the margarine until the pieces are the size of lentils. Mix the molasses, water, and egg together; stir all at once into the flour mixture, and pour into the prepared pan.

Bake for about 35 minutes.

Autumn Apple Cake

A very moist, fruity cake. Vanilla tofu-based ice cream substitute or nondairy whipped topping are good with it; if you really want to gild the lily, serve brandy sauce (pages 412–13) also.

2¼ cups grated apple (3 medium-sized tart apples)	¼ teaspoon ground nutmeg
⅞ cup sugar	¾ teaspoon salt
⅔ cup margarine	1 teaspoon baking soda
1 egg	¾ cup raisins
1⅓ cups flour	½ cup chopped nuts
¾ teaspoon ground cinnamon	2 tablespoons confectioners' sugar (optional)

Preheat the oven to 350° and grease a 9-inch square pan. Cut the apples lengthwise into quarters, cut out the cores and cut off the skins, and grate the apples coarsely. When you measure the grated apple, push it down a little in the cup to pack it lightly.

Fill a 1-cup measure with sugar and then remove 2 tablespoons of the sugar to give ⅞ cup. Cream the margarine, sugar, and egg together until they are light and fluffy. Sift the flour, baking soda, cinnamon, nutmeg, and salt together. Add these sifted dry ingredients, along with the grated apple, to the batter and blend well. Stir in the raisins and nuts, and turn the batter into the prepared pan.

Bake for about 45 minutes. When the cake comes from the oven, dust it with the confectioners' sugar if you wish.

Serve the cake either warm from the oven or cooled to room temperature.

SERVES 6 TO 9.

Baked Plum Duff

This is an updated version of an old-time pudding that was cooked by being tied up very tightly in a cloth bag and then boiled for several hours. Serve with hard sauce (page 414) or foamy sauce (page 414).

⅔ cup cooked prunes, drained, and pitted
3 tablespoons margarine
6 tablespoons brown sugar, firmly packed
1 egg

⅓ cup flour
¼ teaspoon baking powder
⅛ teaspoon baking soda
¼ teaspoon salt

Preheat the oven to 350° and grease 6 medium-sized (about 2½-inch) muffin cups.

Measure the prune pulp by packing in into a cup. Using heavy kitchen scissors, cut through the pulp several times to chop it into medium-sized pieces.

Cream the margarine, then beat in the brown sugar and egg until the mixture is light and fluffy. Sift the flour, baking powder, baking soda, and salt together and add to the batter along with the prunes. Mix well. Divide batter among the greased muffin tins.

Bake about 25 to 30 minutes. Serve warm or cool, upside down and topped with sauce.

SERVES 6.

Bread Pudding

A homey, old-fashioned desert. Serve it warm, with vanilla-flavored hard sauce (page 414).

1 cup coconut milk (see page 17)
3 slices white bread, to yield about 1½ cups soft bread crumbs
2 tablespoons sugar
Pinch of salt
½ teaspoon vanilla
⅛ teaspoon ground nutmeg
1 egg
½ cup raisins

Preheat the oven to 350° and grease an 8-inch round pie plate or a 6-inch round casserole.

In a saucepan bring the coconut milk just to a boil. Remove the pan from the heat and add the bread, tearing it into pieces as you do so. Make sure all of the bread is moistened, and let it set for about 5 minutes to soak.

Add the rest of the ingredients, except for the raisins, and beat a minute or two with a rotary beater. Stir in the raisins, and pour the pudding into the prepared dish.

Bake for about 45 minutes, or until the pudding is set and beginning to brown on top.

SERVES 3.

Rice Pudding

A fine old milk-based dessert, which I make with coconut milk. A double boiler will let you cook the pudding slowly, as it requires, without danger of burning it. The combination of coconut milk with almonds in this pudding is magic. Serve warm or cold with hard sauce (page 414), foamy sauce (page 414), or jam sauce (page 410).

⅓ cup unprocessed raw
  white rice
2 tablespoons sugar
¼ teaspoon salt
A generous pinch of
  ground nutmeg or
  cinnamon
¼ cup raisins or currants
  (optional)

1 tablespoon slivered
  almonds (optional)
1½ cups (12 ounces)
  coconut milk (see page
  17)
1 cup water

Bring several cups of water to a boil in the bottom half of a double boiler.

Combine all of the pudding ingredients in the top half of the double boiler. Cover closely and cook over the simmering water in the bottom half for about 1¼ hours, or until the rice is soft and creamy and the liquid has been absorbed. Stir the pudding several times during the cooking period.

SERVES 4.

About Steamed Pudding . . .

Many people think steamed puddings are difficult when they are actually one of the easiest desserts to make. They taste especially good on a cold winter evening. Remember to start cooking your pudding about 3 hours before serving time.

The length of time a steamed pudding should cook seems to be determined by the size of the pudding mold rather than by the size of the pudding. In a 6-cup mold, steamed fig pudding cooks in 2½ hours; in a 12-cup mold, a pudding of this size takes 3 hours.

If you do not have a pudding mold, clean and grease a coffee can; for a lid, use 2 layers of aluminum foil tied tightly around the can with cotton string.

If your pudding mold wants to float and tip in the simmering water, you can weight it with a small, heavy mixing bowl set upside down on top of the mold.

Test a steamed pudding for doneness the same way you would a cake, by inserting a skewer into the middle. If wet dough clings to the skewer when it is withdrawn, continue cooking the pudding for a while longer.

Christmas Pudding

Serve with hard sauce (page 414) or foamy sauce (page 414).

1½ cups flour
1 teaspoon baking
   powder
¾ teaspoon baking soda
1 teaspoon ground
   cinnamon
½ teaspoon ground
   cloves
½ teaspoon ground
   nutmeg

½ teaspoon salt
6 tablespoons margarine
½ cup raisins
½ cup chopped nuts
¾ cup chopped candied
   fruit
¾ cup molasses
¾ cup water
2 eggs

Boil several quarts of water and grease well the inside, including the inside of the lid, of a 12-cup pudding mold. Have ready a large lidded pot big enough to contain the pudding mold.

Sift the flour, baking powder, baking soda, spices, and salt into a bowl. Cut in the margarine with a pastry blender until the pieces are the size of peas. Stir in the raisins, nuts, and candied fruit. Mix the molasses, water, and eggs together; stir into the dry mixture just until it's all moistened. Turn into the prepared pudding mold, cover the mold tightly, and set it into the large pot. Set the pot on a burner, and pour in boiling water until the water comes about ⅓ to ½ way up the sides of the pudding mold; cover the pot and simmer the pudding gently for 3 hours. Check occasionally to make sure that there are still several inches of water left. If you need to add more water, use boiling water.

Unmold the pudding by upturning the pudding mold over a plate and shaking it gently. You may need to run a thin knife around the edge of the pudding first, to loosen it from the mold. Serve hot or warm with sauce.

SERVES 8.

Steamed Fig Pudding

Serve with hard sauce (page 414) or foamy sauce (page 414).

1 cup chopped dried figs
  (about ¼ pound)
1 cup flour
¼ teaspoon baking
  powder
¼ teaspoon baking soda
½ teaspoon ground
  allspice
¼ teaspoon ground
  cloves
¼ teaspoon ground
  nutmeg
¼ teaspoon salt
2 tablespoons brown
  sugar, well packed
2 tablespoons margarine
¼ cup molasses
½ cup water

First, chop the figs. Using large kitchen scissors, cut off the stem end of each fig and cut the fig into about 5 strips. Snip each strip into pieces about the size of raisins.

Set several quarts of water boiling, and thoroughly grease the inside (including the inside of the lid) of a pudding mold, preferably a 6-cup mold. Have ready a large lidded pot big enough to contain the pudding mold.

Sift the flour, baking powder, baking soda, spices, and salt into a mixing bowl. Add the brown sugar, and cut in the margarine until the particles are very fine; about the size of rice grains. Stir in the chopped figs. Mix the molasses and water together, and stir briefly into the rest of the batter. Spoon into the prepared pudding mold, cover tightly, and set into the large pot.

Set the pot on a burner, pour several inches of boiling water into the pot, cover it, and let simmer for 2½ hours. Check occasionally to make sure there is still plenty of water in the pot; add boiling water if necessary.

Unmold the pudding by first running a thin knife between the pudding and the mold, then upending the mold over a serving plate and shaking gently to dislodge the pudding. Serve hot with sauce.

SERVES 4 TO 6.

Frostings

"Butter" Frosting
   Nutmeg Frosting
   Berry Frosting
Lemon Frosting
   Orange Frosting
Rum Frosting
Mocha Frosting
Chocolate Frosting I
Chocolate Frosting II
Glossy Chocolate Icing
Rocky Road Frosting
Penuche Frosting

Peanut–Coconut Broiled Icing

Boiled Frosting
   Seafoam Frosting
   Coconut Frosting

Vanilla Glaze
Chocolate Glaze
Apricot Filling

About Making Frosting . . .

The plain so-called butter frostings consist of butter (or margarine), confectioners' sugar, a liquid, and flavoring. You beat the margarine, then add enough sugar and liquid to get it to a consistency that spreads easily but doesn't flow down the sides of the cake all by itself. You can add whatever you like as flavoring, for instance, vanilla, fruit juice, or chocolate. If the frosting is too stiff to spread easily, add a few drops of liquid and beat it a little longer; if it is too soft and runny, just beat in more confectioners' sugar. Replacing some or all of the liquid with a raw egg yolk or whole egg makes a very rich-tasting frosting, but see warning, page 4. About the only thing that can go wrong with butter frosting is that if you start with too much liquid, you may have to add too much confectioners' sugar. If this happens you can beat in more margarine, salt, and flavoring or you can drizzle the runny frosting over the cake and call it a glaze.

Lumpy confectioners' sugar makes it difficult to produce smooth frosting. Press the lumpy sugar through a sieve or whirl it in a blender.

If the frosting is lumpy, add a little liquid and beat it very well until smooth. Finish the frosting with more sieved confectioners' sugar.

Glaze is even easier to make than frosting; you just stir enough flavoring and liquid into your confectioners' sugar to make a creamy-looking liquid. Glaze is usually put on a cake while it is still warm from the oven, so that the glaze will soak in. If you wait to glaze your cake until it has cooled, you can make very attractive free-form patterns on top of the cake by drizzling the glaze on slowly from the tip of a spoon. Let some glaze run down the sides of the cake to decorate the sides as well.

When making a layer cake I usually use jam between the layers partly because it is easy. The apricot filling on page 405 is an elaborate version of plain jam filling. When you spread the bottom layer of a cake with jam or filling, let the top layer sit on it for a few minutes before frosting; the top layer will be less apt to slide around on the bottom layer.

The simplest frosting of all, and very good on a rich cake, is a light dusting of confectioners' sugar.

"Butter" Frosting

This is so easy to make, and so good, that I've never understood why people use canned frosting.

3 tablespoons margarine
1½ cups confectioners'
   sugar
⅛ teaspoon salt

½ teaspoon vanilla
   (optional)
About 2 tablespoons
   fruit juice or liqueur

In the small bowl of an electric mixer beat the margarine, 1 cup of the confectioners' sugar, the salt, vanilla, and half of the liquid. Add enough of the reserved confectioners' sugar and reserved liquid to make a smooth frosting of a spreadable consistency. If you accidentally get the frosting too liquid, add more confectioners' sugar to stiffen it up; if it's too stiff, add a few drops of liquid.

MAKES ENOUGH FROSTING FOR THE TOP OF TWO 9-INCH CAKE OR FOR A DOZEN 2½-INCH CUPCAKES. TO FROST THE TOPS AND SIDES OF TWO 9-INCH LAYERS OR A 10- × 15-INCH CAKE, USE: ½ CUP MARGARINE, 4 CUPS CONFECTIONERS' SUGAR, ½ TEASPOON SALT, 1 TEASPOON VANILLA, ABOUT ⅓ CUP FRUIT JUICE OR LIQUEUR. BEAT THE MARGARINE WITH 3 CUPS OF THE CONFECTIONERS' SUGAR TO START.

Nutmeg Frosting

Omit the vanilla and use instead ⅛ teaspoon (½ teaspoon for the larger recipe) freshly grated nutmeg. Apple juice, water, or brandy would be the best liquid to use.

Berry Frosting

Very pink, very good flavor. Raspberries, strawberries, and Bing cherries are all good in this.

Omit the vanilla and instead of the liquid use about 2 tablespoons (about ⅓ cup for the larger recipe) of whole ripe berries. It is not necessary to remove the seeds—unless, of course, you use cherries.

Lemon Frosting

3 tablespoons margarine
1½ cups confectioners' sugar
⅛ teaspoon salt
1 teaspoon freshly grated lemon rind or
½ teaspoon lemon extract

2 tablespoons water, brandy, or orange juice

In the small bowl of an electric mixer beat together 1 cup of confectioners' sugar, the salt, lemon rind (or lemon extract), and half of the liquid. Add more liquid and more confectioners' sugar as needed to get a creamy frosting that spreads easily. Lemon juice is not a good choice for the liquid, as it will make the frosting taste thin.

ENOUGH FOR ONE 8- OR 9-INCH LAYER. TO FROST THE TOPS AND SIDES OF TWO 9-INCH LAYERS, USE: ½ CUP MARGARINE, 4 CUPS CONFECTIONERS' SUGAR, ½ TEASPOON SALT, 1 TABLESPOON FRESHLY GRATED LEMON RIND OR 1 TEASPOON LEMON EXTRACT. BEAT THE MARGARINE WITH 3 CUPS OF THE CONFECTIONERS' SUGAR TO START.

Orange Frosting

Instead of lemon rind, use the freshly grated rind of ½ orange, about 2 teaspoons. (For the larger recipe, 1 to 2 oranges will give about 2 tablespoons of grated rind.) Use orange juice for the liquid. If you're in a hurry, substitute ½ teaspoon (1 teaspoon) orange extract for the orange rind.

Rum Frosting

2 tablespoons margarine
1 egg (see warning on page 4)
1 tablespoon dark rum
⅛ teaspoon salt
3 cups confectioners' sugar

In the small bowl of an electric mixer beat together until smooth all of the ingredients except 1 cup of the confectioners' sugar. Add the rest of the sugar and continue beating. If the frosting is too soft, add more confectioners' sugar; if it is too stiff, add a few drops of rum.

MAKES ENOUGH FOR THE TOP OF A 13- BY 9-INCH CAKE, OR THE TOPS OF TWO 8-INCH ROUND LAYERS, OR THE TOP AND SIDES OF A 9-INCH ROUND LAYER CAKE IF YOU USE JAM AS A FILLING.

Mocha Frosting

To melt chocolate easily, put it in an ovenproof dish in the oven (turned off, but still hot) from which you have just removed your cake. When the chocolate is melted, about 5 to 10 minutes, take it out and leave it in a warm place for up to half an hour until you are ready to use it.

2 tablespoons margarine
One 1-ounce square
   unsweetened
   chocolate, melted
⅛ teaspoon salt

½ teaspoon vanilla
2 cups confectioners'
   sugar
About 2 tablespoons
   strong cold coffee

In the small bowl of an electric mixer beat the margarine, melted chocolate, salt, vanilla, half of the sugar and half of the coffee until smooth. Add the rest of the sugar, and enough of the coffee to make the frosting easy to spread.

FROSTS THE TOP OF A 9- BY 13-INCH CAKE.

Chocolate Frosting I

This simple, light-colored chocolate frosting tastes very rich.

2 tablespoons margarine
Two 1-ounce squares
   unsweetened
   chocolate, melted
Few grains of salt
½ teaspoon vanilla

2 cups confectioners'
   sugar
1 tablespoon water,
   crème de cacao, or
   brandy
About 2 tablespoons
   water

In the small bowl of an electric mixer beat the margarine, melted chocolate, salt, vanilla, and 1 cup of the sugar together with the crème de cacao or brandy until well mixed. Add the rest of the sugar; beat well, adding water as necessary to get a good spreading consistency.

FROSTS A 9-INCH CAKE OR A BATCH OF CHOCOLATE JUMBLES (PAGE 344).

Chocolate Frosting II

Darker than chocolate frosting I.

6 tablespoons margarine
Five 1-ounce squares
  unsweetened
  chocolate, melted
⅛ teaspoon salt
2 tablespoons brandy, or
  2 tablespoons water
  plus ½ teaspoon
  vanilla

3 cups confectioners'
  sugar
Water

In the small bowl of an electric mixer beat the margarine, melted chocolate, salt, liquid, and 12 cups of the confectioners' sugar. Add the remaining sugar and water as needed to make the frosting a good consistency.

FILLS AND FROSTS A 9-INCH LAYER CAKE.

Glossy Chocolate Icing

Eight 1-ounce squares semisweet chocolate
¼ cup margarine
⅛ teaspoon salt

Set the chocolate and margarine to melt in a warm oven for 5 or 10 minutes. Add the salt and beat the frosting until it is well mixed.

ICES THE TOP AND SIDES OF A 9-INCH ROUND CAKE. HALVE THE RECIPE TO GET ENOUGH TO DO ONLY THE TOP OF THE CAKE.

Rocky Road Frosting

An old favorite—chocolate frosting with peanuts and marshmallows.

3 tablespoons margarine	3 cups confectioners'
Three 1-ounce squares	sugar
chocolate, melted	About 1/3 cup water
1/4 teaspoon salt	1/4 cup peanuts
1 teaspoon vanilla	1/2 cup tiny
	marshmallows

Beat the margarine, melted chocolate, salt, vanilla, and 1 cup of the sugar in the small bowl of an electric mixer. Beat in the remaining sugar and enough water to make the frosting a good spreading consistency. Stir in the peanuts and marshmallows.

FROSTS THE TOP OF A 9- BY 13-INCH CAKE.

Penuche Frosting

1/2 cup margarine	1/4 cup water
1 cup brown sugar,	1 teaspoon vanilla
packed firm	About 2 1/2 cups
1/2 cup white sugar	confectioners' sugar
1/2 teaspoon salt	

Melt the margarine in a saucepan over medium heat. Add the brown sugar, the white sugar, and the salt; raise the heat to high and cook, stirring often, until the mixture comes to a boil and boils for a minute and a half.

Remove the frosting from the heat and stir in the water, then return the frosting to the heat and bring it just to a boil while stirring constantly.

Remove the frosting from the heat and let it set for about half an hour, stirring occasionally, until it's cool enough so that you

can comfortably touch the outside of the pan. Add the vanilla and
1½ cups of confectioners' sugar. Beat until the frosting is quite
smooth, then beat in as much more confectioners' sugar as it takes
to make a smooth, easily spreadable frosting.

MAKES ENOUGH FOR TWO 9-INCH LAYERS, OR FOR THE TOP OF A 10-
BY 15-INCH CAKE.

Peanut-Coconut Broiled Icing

Easy to make, a little different, and very good.

> 3 tablespoons margarine
> ¼ cup peanut butter
> ½ cup brown sugar, packed firm
> ¼ cup chopped peanuts
> ¾ cup unsweetened shredded
> coconut

Melt the margarine, then mix in the remaining ingredients in
the order given.

Spread over the top of an 8- or 9-inch cake and broil just until
bubbly; 1 minute or so. Watch carefully, as the frosting will go
from nicely cooked to scorched in the blinking of an eye.

Boiled Frosting

*Sometimes called marshmallow frosting. This old-fashioned frosting is reason-
ably easy to make if you follow the instructions given, and a cake frosted with
it looks handsome. Since it's an unusual frosting, I have made the directions
very complete.*

1½ cups sugar
½ cup water
1 tablespoon light corn
  syrup

2 egg whites (see
  warning on page 4)
½ teaspoon vanilla
Pinch of salt

Put the sugar, water, and corn syrup into a saucepan large enough to keep the mixture from overflowing when it boils; 2½ quarts is a good size. Bring to a boil, and boil hard until the last drop of syrup, when dripped slowly from a metal spoon held about 12 inches above the pan, spins a very fine thread as it leaves the spoon—about 236° on a candy thermometer. While the sugar is boiling, beat the egg whites until they're stiff.

Pour the hot syrup slowly over the beaten egg whites while continuing to beat. If you do not have an electric mixer with its own stand, ask someone to help you by pouring the hot syrup. Pause two or three times while you do this to let the syrup get well beaten into the egg whites. Continue beating until the frosting is just stiff enough so that when you rotate a spoonful of it slowly, the tail of frosting that wraps around the spoon remains distinct from the rest of the frosting and does not immediately melt into it. Beat in the vanilla and the salt.

Frost the cake right away; the frosting stiffens on standing. It is usually at its best a few hours after it is made. This is a reliable frosting if you follow the directions, and measure carefully; but it is a little different each time, depending on the humidity, how long you beat it, and exactly how hot the syrup was.

FROSTS TOP AND SIDES OF A 9-INCH LAYER CAKE, IF YOU USE A JAM FILLING.

Seafoam Frosting

Especially good on spice cake.

Use ¾ cup firmly packed brown sugar and ¾ cup white sugar.

Coconut Frosting

Frost your cake with boiled frosting. Just as soon as you have done this, while the frosting is still very sticky, sprinkle the top and sides of the cake with about 1 cup of grated or flaked coconut.

Vanilla Glaze

Rum, liqueur, or fruit juice can be substituted for the vanilla and water.

> 1 cup confectioners' sugar
> ½ teaspoon vanilla
> About 2 tablespoons
>   water

Mix all together; it should be the consistency of—please forgive the expression—thick cream. Drizzle over the top of your cake.

MAKES ENOUGH FOR A 9- BY 13-INCH CAKE.

Chocolate Glaze

> 1 cup confectioners' sugar
> 2 tablespoons cocoa
> 2 tablespoons brandy
> 1 tablespoon water

Stir the sugar and cocoa well together, then stir in the brandy and water. This glaze also should be easy to pour, but not watery.

MAKES ENOUGH FOR A 9- BY 13-INCH CAKE.

Apricot Filling

The perfect filling for a plain white or yellow cake and boiled frosting.

¼ cup almonds, chopped and toasted
¼ cup dried plain cake or graham cracker crumbs, in
   pieces about the size of the chopped almonds
One 12-ounce jar apricot jam
1 teaspoon vanilla

As soon as the cake comes out of the oven, put the almonds in to toast in a small, ungreased pan for about 5 to 10 minutes. Next toast the crumbs so they are crisp but not brown. Watch them carefully; they can go from nicely toasted to burned very quickly.

When the crumbs and the almonds are cool, mix them with the jam and vanilla. Spread this filling on the bottom layer of your cooled cake; cover with the top layer and let set a while before frosting.

MAKES ENOUGH FILLING FOR A 9-INCH ROUND LAYER CAKE.

Dessert Sauces

Lemon Sauce
Orange Sauce
Jam Sauce
Chocolate Sauce
Chocolate Rum Sauce
Toasted Almond Sauce
Brandy Sauce
Marshmallow Sauce
Hard Sauce
Foamy Sauce
See also: Fruit Cream (page
   294)

Lemon Sauce

Especially good on cottage pudding (page 385). If this sauce gets lumpy after it is cooked, and hard stirring doesn't smooth it out, put it through a sieve.

Freshly grated rind of 1 lemon (1½ to 2 teaspoons)
¼ cup lemon juice
1 cup sugar
1 tablespoon cornstarch
½ cup margarine
¼ teaspoon salt
1 cup water
1 egg

Wash the lemon, dry it, and grate off just the yellow part of the rind. Squeeze out the juice, and add more if necessary to make up the ¼ cup.

Stir the sugar and the cornstarch together well.

Melt the margarine in a saucepan over medium heat. Stir in the rest of the ingredients, bring just to a boil, and boil gently for about 1 or 2 minutes, stirring constantly, preferably with a whisk. The sauce should be thick. Serve hot or warm.

MAKES ABOUT 2 CUPS; SERVES 8.

Orange Sauce

A very flavorful sauce.

Freshly grated rind of 1 orange (about 2 to 3 teaspoons)
1½ cups orange juice
½ cup sugar
1½ tablespoons cornstarch
⅛ teaspoon salt
1 tablespoon lemon juice
1 egg
1 tablespoon margarine
2 tablespoons Cointreau or triple sec (optional)

Wash and dry the orange, then grate off just the colored part of the rind. Squeeze the orange and add more juice to make up 1½ cups.

Mix the sugar and the cornstarch well in a saucepan, then gradually stir in the rest of the ingredients except for the liqueur. Bring slowly to a boil and boil gently for 1 to 2 minutes, stirring constantly; the sauce should be thickened. Stir in the liqueur, if you use it. Serve hot or warm.

MAKES ABOUT 2 CUPS; SERVES 8.

Jam Sauce

Easy to make and especially good on coconut, prune, and apricot soufflées (pages 295–296).

> ⅓ cup good-quality jam or jelly
> About 1 tablespoon fruit juice, wine, or liqueur

Some good combinations are:

> Plum jam with orange juice
> Peach jam with Curaçao
> Grape jelly with brandy

Stir the liquid into the jam or jelly, put the mixture into a small pan and heat just to the boiling point, stirring often. Serve warm or at room temperature.

MAKES ⅓ CUP; SERVES 3.

Chocolate Sauce

A thick chocolate sauce.

Three 1-ounce squares
  semisweet chocolate
3 tablespoons margarine
1½ cups confectioners'
  sugar

⅛ teaspoon salt
3 tablespoons water
¾ teaspoon vanilla

Put the chocolate and margarine in a small saucepan and set it in the oven to melt if you have just turned the oven off; if you have not, set the saucepan in a large pan of simmering water. Take care that no water gets into the melting chocolate, or it will become very stiff.

Remove the pan from the heat, and stir in the sugar, salt, and water. Set the pan over medium heat and stir the sauce constantly with a whisk just until it comes to a boil. Remove from the heat, stir in the vanilla, and serve.

MAKES 1 CUP; ENOUGH FOR A 9-INCH COTTAGE PUDDING SERVING 6.

Chocolate Rum Sauce

A slightly thinner chocolate sauce than the preceding recipe. You can substitute water and a little vanilla for the rum.

One 1-ounce square
  unsweetened chocolate
1 tablespoon margarine
Pinch of salt
1 cup sugar

2 teaspoons white corn
  syrup
2 tablespoons water
2 tablespoons rum

Melt the chocolate and the margarine together over low heat. Stir in the rest of the ingredients and simmer gently for about 2 minutes, stirring constantly. Serve hot or warm.

MAKES ABOUT 1 CUP; SERVES 4 TO 6.

Toasted Almond Sauce

Good on graham cracker torte (page 373) or tofu-based ice cream substitute.

6 tablespoons margarine	1 cup white sugar
½ cup almonds, chopped	¼ teaspoon salt
½ cup brown sugar, firmly packed	¼ cup water
	1 teaspoon vanilla

Melt the margarine in a small heavy saucepan and brown the almonds in it, stirring occasionally. Just when you think they'll never brown they do, quite suddenly. Remove the pan from the heat, and stir in the sugars, salt, and water.

Return the sauce to the heat and bring it just to a gentle boil; again remove it from the heat, and stir in the vanilla. Serve hot.

MAKES ABOUT 2 CUPS; SERVES 6 TO 8.

Brandy Sauce

A thin, brown sugar sauce for tofu-based ice cream substitute or for puddings.

2 tablespoons margarine
½ cup brown sugar, firmly packed
1 tablespoon water
Few grains of salt
¼ cup brandy

Over medium-high heat, melt the margarine; stir in the brown sugar and cook, stirring constantly, until it begins to bubble. Stir in the water and salt and keep on stirring until the sauce seems well mixed. Stir in the brandy and simmer the sauce gently for 2 or 3 minutes. (Sugar is very soluble in water, but not very soluble in alcohol. If you have trouble getting the sugar to dissolve after you add the brandy, add a teaspoon or so of extra water, then heat gently.) Serve warm.

MAKES ABOUT ⅔ CUP; SERVES 4.

Marshmallow Sauce

This is very much like boiled frosting; but with more liquid and cooked to a lower temperature. Try this on tofu-based ice cream, with crumbled fudge bits.

½ cup sugar
½ cup white corn syrup
3 tablespoons water

1 egg white (see warning
  on page 4)
Pinch of salt
½ teaspoon vanilla

Mix the sugar, corn syrup, and water in a saucepan; boil until the temperature reaches 234° on a candy thermometer (be sure the thermometer's tip is well covered with syrup when you read the temperature), or until a small amount of the syrup forms a soft ball when dropped into cold water.

Meanwhile, beat the egg white until stiff. When the syrup is done, continue beating the egg white while you pour the hot syrup into it in a thin, steady stream. This is easier if you have an electric mixer with a stand, or a helpful friend. Continue beating for a minute or two, or until the mixture appears uniform and makes soft peaks. Beat in the salt and the vanilla. If the mixture should stiffen up too much, beat in a few drops of hot water. Serve warm or at room temperature.

MAKES ABOUT 2 CUPS OF SAUCE; SERVES 6.

Hard Sauce

Wonderful on steamed puddings, and easy to make.

½ cup margarine, at room temperature
2 cups confectioners' sugar
Pinch of salt
About 3 tablespoons liquid: water with ¼ teaspoon
    vanilla, or fruit juice, brandy, rum, or whiskey

Beat all of the ingredients, except for half of the liquid, in the small bowl of an electric mixer; add enough liquid to make the hard sauce a good creamy consistency. Beat very well to make it light and fluffy. If you find you have added to much liquid, add a little more confectioners' sugar to correct the problem. The sauce only becomes hard when it is chilled. Chill until firm.

MAKES ABOUT 1⅓ CUPS, OR PLENTY FOR EITHER OF THE STEAMED PUDDING RECIPES HERE; SERVES 8 TO 10.

Foamy Sauce

Like hard sauce, this is very good on steamed puddings. I usually make a half recipe of foamy sauce to serve along with hard sauce, so that people can have a choice.

4 eggs (see warning on page 4)
1¼ cups confectioners' sugar
1 teaspoon vanilla
⅛ teaspoon salt

Using a rotary beater or electric mixer, beat the eggs until foamy. Add the rest of the ingredients and beat until light and very thick, about 5 minutes. Serve immediately with steamed pudding.

MAKES ABOUT 2 CUPS; SERVES 6.

Candy

Popcorn Balls
Peanut Brittle
Toffee Crunch
Molasses Taffy
White Taffy
Emily's Fudge Sandwiches
Divinity Fudge
Chocolate Fudge
Penuche

Please be very careful when working with hot sugar as it can cause quite a bad burn.

Exact temperatures are crucial in candy-making. When reading a candy thermometer, make sure that its bulb is well covered with the hot syrup (tip the pan slightly if necessary) or the reading will not be accurate.

Popcorn Balls

These are especially good for Halloween parties.

1 tablespoon margarine if needed for popping the popcorn	¼ cup molasses
	¼ cup light corn syrup
	½ cup sugar
¾ cup unpopped popcorn, to give about 2 quarts popped corn	⅛ teaspoon salt
	1 tablespoon additional margarine
½ cup peanuts (optional)	

If you add peanuts, use a little less popped corn.

Melt 1 tablespoon margarine in a medium-large saucepan, add the popcorn, cover the pan, and shake over high heat until the corn stops popping; remove the pan from the heat. Or pop the corn according to directions in a popcorn popper or microwave oven. Mix in the peanuts, if you use them.

Boil the molasses, corn syrup, sugar, and salt together until a candy thermometer indicates 250°. When it has reached this temperature, the syrup will form a hard ball when a little is dropped into cold water.

Remove the syrup from the heat, and stir in the additional margarine. As soon as the bubbling stops, pour the syrup slowly over the popped corn and the peanuts, mixing the syrup into the popped corn with a spoon as you pour.

Since the popcorn mixture will still be hot, you may find it easier to wear rubber kitchen gloves while you shape the balls. Grease your hands, or your gloves, and shape the mixture into balls about the size of baseballs. Set the popcorn balls on waxed paper to cool.

MAKES ABOUT 2 DOZEN POPCORN BALLS.

Peanut Brittle

1½ cups sugar
⅓ cup light corn syrup
¾ cup water
2 cups (about 10 ounces) salted peanuts

2 tablespoons margarine
1 teaspoon baking soda
¾ teaspoon vanilla

Grease a large pan, preferably one with a raised rim, about 10 inches by 15 inches. Set it on something heatproof, such as a wooden breadboard.

Mix the sugar, corn syrup, and water in a saucepan; bring to a boil, and cook to 230°, or until the mixture spins a thread when a little is dropped back into the pan from a metal spoon held about 12 to 18 inches above the surface.

Stir in the peanuts and continue to cook, stirring constantly, until the mixture just starts to darken, about 290°. Immediately remove the pan from the heat, and stir in the margarine and the baking soda. When the margarine is melted, stir in the vanilla.

Work quickly, as you don't want the candy to harden in the saucepan. Pour the peanut brittle out onto the prepared pan, spreading it thin if possible. When the candy is cool and hard, (about an hour, but it can sit whole for hours) break it into pieces.

MAKES ABOUT 1½ POUNDS OF PEANUT BRITTLE.

Toffee Crunch

1½ cups sugar
⅓ cup light corn syrup
¾ cup water
¼ teaspoon salt
1 teaspoon baking soda
2 tablespoons margarine

One 12-ounce package
semisweet chocolate
chips
⅔ cup ground almonds,
pecans, or walnuts

Grease a cookie sheet, preferably one with a raised rim, and set it on some heatproof surface such as a wooden cutting board.

Using a large saucepan, bring the sugar, corn syrup, water, and salt to 280° on a candy thermometer; a drop of the hot syrup will form a hard ball in cold water.

Remove the pan from the heat and stir in the baking soda and margarine. Turn the candy out onto the cookie sheet, encouraging it to spread thin, about ⅛ inch or a little less. Let the candy cool.

Melt half of the chocolate in a heatproof dish in a 300° oven and spread it evenly over the cooled candy. Sprinkle with half of the ground nuts, then let the chocolate harden; if you are impatient, you can set the pan in the refrigerator for a few minutes.

Lift the candy up and turn it over; a wide spatula will help. It doesn't matter if the sheet of candy breaks. Melt the rest of the chocolate and spread it on the uncoated side of the candy, then sprinkle with the rest of the nuts.

Let the toffee cool, and break it up into pieces. It will be better if left to ripen in a covered container for a day or so.

MAKES ABOUT 1½ POUNDS OF TOFFEE CRUNCH.

Molasses Taffy

Turn-of-the-century teenagers used to enjoy getting together to make this. Taffy was entertainment as well as candy. They would pair off to pull the cooling candy repeatedly into long ropes; this pulling gives taffy its distinctive color and texture. Of course they ate the candy when it was finished.

1 cup sugar	1 tablespoon vinegar
½ cup molasses	Pinch salt
¼ cup water	1 tablespoon margarine

Grease thoroughly a large baking pan or a cookie sheet with a raised rim, and set it on a heatproof surface such as a wooden breadboard. Also grease a large dinner plate and have a clean pair of strong kitchen scissors handy.

Put the sugar, molasses, water, vinegar, and salt into a saucepan that will hold at least 3 quarts, and bring to a boil. Continue cooking until the syrup reaches 250°—a drop of the syrup will form a hard ball in a cup of cold water.

Stir in the margarine, then pour the cooked candy onto the greased baking sheet and let it cool for a few minutes. Check the candy occasionally; if the edges harden before the middle does, pull them carefully in to the center. Use a spoon for this, and be careful not to burn yourself.

When the candy is cool enough to handle, grease your hands very well and start to pull it out into a long rope; fold the rope in half or thirds and pull again. Keep doing this until the taffy is light in color and getting so hard that you can't pull it any more. The candy rope should be about ½ inch in diameter when you've pulled it for the last time.

Using the strong scissors, cut the taffy up into 1-inch lengths and put the pieces on the dinner plate to cool. If the candy is not to be eaten right away, wrap the pieces individually in waxed paper.

MAKES ABOUT ½ POUND OF TAFFY.

White Taffy

Easier to make than molasses taffy. This will turn creamy and soft in a day or two.

2 cups sugar
1/2 cup water
2 teaspoons vinegar
1/2 teaspoon vanilla,
   lemon, wintergreen, or
   mint extract

A drop of food coloring
if you wish

Thoroughly grease a 10- by 15-inch baking pan or a cookie sheet with a raised rim, and set it on a heatproof surface. Have ready a piece of waxed paper about 20 inches long, and a clean pair of strong kitchen scissors.

Put the sugar, water, and vinegar into a saucepan big enough to hold about 3 quarts. Cook without stirring to 265°, or until a drop of the syrup forms a hard ball in cold water.

Pour the candy out onto the greased pan, and let cool for a few minutes. As the edges start to harden, pull them in to the still-liquid center. Use a spoon for this and be careful, as hot candy can burn you badly.

When the candy is cool enough to handle, sprinkle it with the flavoring and with the food coloring, if you use it. Grease your clean hands well, and pull the candy out into a long rope; fold the rope in half or in thirds, and pull it out again. Keep folding and pulling until the candy is creamy-looking and very difficult to stretch. The last rope you pull should be about as big around as your little finger.

Using the scissors, cut the rope up into 1-inch lengths and spread them out on the waxed paper to cool. When the taffy is completely cool, you should store it in a covered container. It isn't necessary to wrap this candy.

MAKES ABOUT 1 POUND OF WHITE TAFFY.

Emily's Fudge Sandwiches

These resemble very rich cookies. Except for melting the chocolate, no cooking is required.

Chocolate

> One 12-ounce package semisweet chocolate chips
> ½ cup margarine
> ½ teaspoon vanilla
> ¼ teaspoon salt

Melt the chocolate chips and the margarine together in a heat-proof dish in a 300° oven. When they are melted, remove them from the oven and stir in the vanilla and salt. Set aside in a warm place while you prepare the oatmeal crumbs.

Oatmeal layer

> 2 cups rolled oats
> ½ cup margarine
> 1 cup brown sugar, packed firm
> ½ teaspoon salt
> 1 teaspoon vanilla

Grease a 9- by 5-inch loaf pan, and line it (both bottom and sides) with waxed paper.

Grind the rolled oats in a blender or a hand grinder, or put them through a food processor fitted with the steel blade, to make a coarse flour. Use a food processor or a pastry blender to mix the margarine into the oats (cut it into chunks first if you use a food processor), along with the brown sugar, salt, and vanilla, until you get a grainy, dense substance. Pack half of the crumbs into the prepared pan.

Pour the melted chocolate evenly over the oatmeal layer in the pan. Crumble the rest of the oatmeal mixture over the chocolate, and pack down lightly with your hand. Refrigerate until the chocolate center is firm, and cut into small squares.

MAKES ABOUT 40 PIECES; ABOUT 2 POUNDS.

Divinity Fudge

Many people like to add candied cherries to this fudge at Christmas time.

3 cups sugar	1 teaspoon vanilla
3/4 cup water	4 ounces (about 3/4 cup)
1/2 cup light corn syrup	chopped nuts and/or
3 egg whites	candied cherries
Few grains of salt	(optional)

Grease a 9-inch square pan, or line a cookie sheet with waxed paper.

Boil the sugar, water, and corn syrup to 260°, or until a hard ball forms if a bit of the syrup is dropped into cold water. Meanwhile, beat the egg whites until stiff.

Pour the hot syrup slowly—in a thin stream—into the egg whites, while you continue beating them. This step is easier if you have either a mixer with its own stand or a human helper. Beat in the salt and the vanilla after a few minutes. Continue beating until the candy begins to lose its gloss and/or to hold its shape well. If the divinity should start to harden in the bowl, beat in a few drops of hot water right away.

Quickly stir in the nuts and/or the cherries, if you use them. Turn the candy out into the prepared pan, or drop it by tablespoonsful onto the waxed paper. When the fudge is cool and firm, cut it into squares if you made it in the pan.

MAKES ABOUT 1½ POUNDS, OR 36 PIECES OF CANDY.

Chocolate Fudge

When making fudge or penuche (page 425), it is important to get the cooking temperature right. If you don't cook it to a high enough temperature, the candy will not solidify; if this happens, you can use it as a sauce, or you can stir in enough confectioners' sugar to stiffen it up. If you overcook the candy, it is apt to harden before you can get it out of the cooking pan. If you see this happening, add a little hot water—a teaspoonful at a time—until it is just possible to spread the candy out in the pan. Be careful not to add too much water.

2 cups sugar	Three 1-ounce squares
3 tablespoons light corn	unsweetened chocolate
syrup	3 tablespoons margarine
¼ teaspoon salt	1 teaspoon vanilla
⅔ cup water plus 3	¾ cup nuts (optional)
tablespoons additional	
water	

Grease an 8-inch square pan.

Put the sugar, corn syrup, salt, and ⅔ cup water into a saucepan; boil until a candy thermometer registers 238°, or until a small amount forms a soft ball when dropped into cold water. Remove the mixture from the heat and add the chocolate and margarine.

As soon as these are melted, add 2 of the 3 additional tablespoons of water and stir well; keep stirring occasionally until the mixture starts to thicken, and then add the vanilla and the rest of the water (if it is needed) and keep on stirring until the fudge loses its gloss and becomes quite thick. (The milk usually used in making chocolate fudge seems to keep this hardening from happening quite as suddenly as it does without milk.) Add the nuts, if you use them, and spread the fudge out in the prepared pan. Cut into pieces when firm.

MAKES ABOUT 1¼ POUNDS OF FUDGE; ABOUT 36 PIECES.

Penuche

Brown sugar fudge.

2 cups light brown
  sugar, firmly packed
3 tablespoons corn syrup
²/₃ cup water

¼ teaspoon salt
3 tablespoons margarine
½ teaspoon vanilla
¾ cup nuts (optional)

Grease an 8-inch square pan.

Put the brown sugar, corn syrup, water, and salt into a saucepan; bring to a boil, and boil until a candy thermometer indicates 238°. When the syrup is ready, it will form a soft ball when a little is dropped into cold water. Remove the candy from the heat, add the margarine, and let cool for a few minutes.

When the penuche thickens or begins to turn lighter in color, add the vanilla and stir well with a sturdy spoon until the candy begins to stiffen. Immediately stir in the nuts, if you use them, and turn the candy into the prepared pan; let it cool before cutting into squares.

MAKES ABOUT 1 POUND, OR 36 PIECES.

Beverages

Favorite Punch
Sherbet-shake
Glorified Lemonade
Louise's Sun Tea
Mulled Cider
Hot Cocoa
Instant Hot Cocoa
Chocolate Coffee
James's After-dinner Coffee

Favorite Punch

This is an especially good punch to prepare for a crowd as you can chill the ingredients ahead of time and it is easy to make more punch very quickly if needed.

One 2-liter (68-ounce) bottle ginger ale or any
    lemon-flavored soft drink, cold
One 64-ounce can pineapple-grapefruit juice, cold
Ice

If you can't find pineapple-grapefruit juice, use 32 ounces each pineapple juice and grapefruit juice. Mix the soft drink and juice together, pour over ice, and serve.

MAKES 1 GALLON PUNCH; TWENTY 6-OUNCE SERVINGS.

Sherbet-shake

Lighter than a milkshake, this very cold drink is good on a hot day.

Milk-free sherbert
Lemonade
Cracked ice

Use equal quantities of all 3 ingredients. About ½ cup of each makes 1 serving.

Put the sherbet and the lemonade in a blender and run the blender briefly until you have a thick foam. Put the crushed ice in a glass, and pour the mixture over it. Serve immediately.

Glorified Lemonade

The fresh lemon gives very good flavor.

> 1 lemon
> 1 quart lemonade—I usually make it from frozen
>   concentrate
> 2 tablespoons sugar
> Plenty of ice

Wash the lemon, cut it up into 6 or 8 pieces, and remove the seeds. Put the lemon chunks, lemonade, and sugar into a jar or pitcher with a good nonleaky lid; cover tightly, and shake very hard—you're trying to bruise the lemon rind, to release its flavor. Serve over ice.

SERVES ABOUT 4.

Louise's Sun Tea

An easy way to make very good iced tea.

> Tea bags
> Water

Use 2 standard tea bags for each quart of water, or 8 for each gallon. Put the water into a glass or clear plastic jar and put the tea bags in the water; set the jar in a sunny spot until the tea is the color you like—about an hour on a hot day usually does it. Remove the tea bags, and refrigerate the tea until needed.

If you're making sun tea for just one or two people, a clean glass mayonnaise jar works very well. If you're making a large quantity of tea, use the gallon jugs of spring water available in most markets or drugstores.

Mulled Cider

This is a wonderfully warming drink for a cold day. Whole spices are much better than powdered as they don't make the drink cloudy.

1 quart apple cider
One 3-inch stick
   cinnamon, cracked
1/4 to 1/2 whole nutmeg,
   cracked

5 allspice berries
3 whole cloves
Rum (optional)

The spices listed are the ones I most commonly use, but they are only suggestions—please feel free to create your own combinations.

It is easy to crack cinnamon and nutmeg if you put them on a breadboard and hit them with the side of a meat-tenderizing hammer. Just one or two blows will do it—the spices should still be in big pieces.

Put the cider in a large saucepan. Put the spices in a big tea egg or tie them up loosely in a square of clean cheesecloth. Add them to the cider, and bring the cider just to a boil. Remove the spices just before serving—if you let them set in the hot cider for a while, it will be all the better. Add rum if desired.

MAKES 1 QUART; FOUR 8-OUNCE SERVINGS.

Hot Cocoa

Who ever heard of hot cocoa made without milk? It's not quite the same but is good, with or without the nondairy creamer, and is easy to make. You start with plain powdered cocoa, the kind sold for baking.

2 tablespoons
   unsweetened cocoa
1/4 cup sugar
Few grains salt
3 cups water

Nondairy coffee creamer
   (optional)
Few drops vanilla
   (optional)

Stir the cocoa, sugar, and salt together in a small saucepan. Add a tablespoonful or so of water and mix it with the sugar and cocoa to form a paste.

Add ½ cup of the water to the cocoa. Set the pan over medium-high heat and boil the mixture for 1 minute, stirring occasionally. Add the remaining 2½ cups of water and bring the cocoa just to a boil. Stir in the creamer and the vanilla if you use them, and serve the cocoa immediately.

SERVES 3.

Instant Hot Cocoa

You can prepare cocoa more quickly by making it directly in the mug. However, this method may leave a layer of undissolved cocoa if the water isn't hot enough.

2 teaspoons unsweetened
  cocoa
4 teaspoons sugar
Few grains salt
1 cup boiling water

1 tablespoon nondairy
  creamer (optional)
Few drops vanilla
  (optional)

First warm up your mug by filling it with very hot water, then dry it quickly with a dish towel. Stir the cocoa, sugar, and salt together in the mug. Fill the mug with boiling water, and stir well to dissolve the cocoa. Add creamer and vanilla if you wish.

SERVES 1 COLD CHILD.

Chocolate Coffee

Good in cold weather, as light dessert or snack.

4 teaspoons unsweetened cocoa
¼ cup sugar
4 cups freshly brewed hot coffee
¼ teaspoon vanilla extract
Nondairy creamer, if desired

Stir the cocoa and sugar together; add the coffee—it should be very hot—then stir in the vanilla extract. Pass nondairy creamer for those who like to use it.

SERVES 4.

James's After-dinner Coffee

This can be served as dessert and coffee, all in one.

4½ cups strong, very hot coffee, preferably European roast
¼ cup rum
½ cup crème de cacao or Tia Maria
Nondairy creamer (optional)

Stir everything but the creamer together, and serve at once. Pass nondairy creamer for those who like to use it.

SERVES 6.

Appendix

Basic Kitchen Equipment

An old-fashioned metal four-sided grater with a handle at the top will grate almost anything. The finest mesh is for grating nutmeg; the next to finest handles grated orange rind or hard cheese; the coarse side does for soft cheese, or apples, or vegetables such as onions or cabbages.

The best sort of whisk for making sauces and gravies is a flat-bottomed coil of wire attached to a handle. It will keep a sauce from sticking to the bottom of the pan, and get into corners much better than the more readily available balloon whisk.

A good electric mixer with its own stand and one or more mixing bowls helps when making cakes and cookies. It should have a reasonably strong motor and a good range of speeds. However, many of the cakes and cookies in this book can be made without a mixer.

Sharp knives not only make cooking much easier, you're less apt to cut yourself with a sharp knife than with a dull one. Buy good-quality kitchen knives, buy a sharpener for them—and learn to use it! I use a sharpening steel, and give each knife a few strokes with the steel after every time the knife is washed, and before it goes back into the knife holder.

The best place to find most of the equipment mentioned above is the cookware department of a large hardware or department store. Specialty cookware shops are great fun, but they usually don't have such a good selection of the really basic items. Sometimes a flea market will produce things the local stores don't carry.

Using a Food Processor

A food processor can substitute for an electric mixer except that it will not beat egg whites without a special attachment. The food processor can do some cutting and grating jobs better and quicker than a knife or grater; however, it is often quicker and easier to use the old-fashioned tool. It is usually easier to knead bread by hand or make pastry with a hand pastry blender. I find that handmade bread or pastry is tenderer because I can control the amount of mixing more easily.

The strength of a food processor is in pureeing, grating, or slicing, especially helpful if, for instance, you are making a big batch of coleslaw. It is very good at chopping nuts, provided you watch the machine carefully—your nuts will go from coarsely chopped to nut butter in just a few seconds. The processor will very quickly grate lemon or orange peel for use in baked goods or frosting. You simply measure the sugar specified in the recipe into the bowl of the processor, which you have fitted with the steel blade. Wash and dry the fruit, use a potato peeler to remove thin strips from just the colored part of the rind, then process these strips with the sugar until the peel is finely ground.

In general, use the food processor first for dry ingredients. Grate your lemon peel with the sugar, and set it aside; chop your nuts, and set them aside. Next, grate or chop moist things such as carrots or apples. Set them aside, and proceed as you normally would. Things that should be left as chunks (raisins or chocolate chips, for instance) are added last. If you don't mind chopping these up somewhat, you can mix them very carefully into the batter, with the steel knife still in place. Often I just use a spoon to stir in these last little bits.

See the recipes for coleslaw (pages 194–95), carrot cake (pages 374–75), and chocolate chip cookies (pages 343–44) for examples of how to adapt a recipe for use with a food processor.

Ingredients

In devising and testing these recipes, I have used the following as standard ingredients:

Apples—tart, firm apples. Jonathan, Cortland, Smokehouse, Northern Spy, Stayman, Greening, and Granny Smith. McIntosh will do, but Delicious is too bland and mealy, especially for pie or brown betty.

Brown sugar—light or medium brown; must be measured firmly packed.

Chocolate—unsweetened baking chocolate, sold as 1-ounce squares.

Cornmeal—stone ground, preferably fresh. The best comes from historic sites, from fairs where milling is being demonstrated, or from a good health-food store. Keep it refrigerated or frozen until use.

Eggs—size large.

Flour—unbleached white, not sifted before measuring.

Margarine—milk-free margarine sold in stick form. Not all margarine is milk-free (see page 16). Avoid reduced-calorie or soft margarine for any use except spreading on toast.

Molasses—unsulfured, from the West Indies. This is a mild molasses.

Oatmeal—regular or quick rolled oats but not instant rolled oats.

Sugar—white, granulated pure cane sugar.

Tomatoes—good quality Italian canned tomatoes.

Whole wheat flour—see cornmeal. Freshly ground whole wheat flour, kept properly stored in the refrigerator or freezer, is wonderful stuff and a great deal better than that usually sold in markets—try some!

Baked Goods Without Eggs

Here is a list of recipes for egg-free baked goods and desserts included in this book.

Yeast breads

Casserole Bread
Herb Bread
White Bread
Health Bread
Anadama Bread
Oatmeal Bread
Best Raisin Bread

Rolls

English Muffins
Honey Whole Wheat Rolls
Hamburger Buns
Hot Dog Rolls

The following rolls can be made without eggs if you just omit the egg from the recipe and reduce the amount of flour by ¾ cup for each omitted egg, or use the recipe for white bread as your basic dough.

Refrigerator Roll Dough
Cornmeal Dinner Rolls
Bath Buns
Pan Rolls
Crescent Rolls
Onion Rolls
Swedish Tea Ring
Cinnamon Rolls
Rum Buns
Lemon Rolls
Orange Rolls

Biscuits

Biscuits
Whole Wheat Biscuits
Potato Biscuits
Squash Biscuits
Breakfast Buns

In the recipe for raised doughnuts the egg is an optional ingredient and may be omitted.

Pancakes

All the following pancake recipes suggest using 2 tablespoons water in place of an egg if you cannot have eggs.

Pancakes
Apple Pancakes
Blueberry Pancakes
Cornmeal Pancakes
Whole Wheat Pancakes
Apple Whole Wheat Pancakes
Yeast-raised Pancakes

Fruit desserts

Honeyed Fruit Mélange
Honeyed Pears
Strawberry-Orange-
   Pineapple Jelly
Apricot-Raspberry Jelly
Strawberry Shortcake
Peach Shortcake
Smooth Applesauce
Chunky Applesauce
Fruit Soup

Baked Apples
Apple Brown Betty
Apple Crisp
Rhubarb Betty
Rhubarb Crisp
Pear Crumble
Pineapple-Apricot Cobbler
Peach-Cherry Cobbler
Blueberry Slump
Apple Jack

Pies

Apple Pie
Peach Pie
Blueberry Pie
Rhubarb Pie
Strawberry-Rhubarb Pie
Blueberry-Rhubarb Pie
Cherry Pie

Mincemeat Pie
Plum Pie
Summer Pie
Fresh Strawberry Pie
Fresh Peach Pie
Fresh Blueberry Pie
Apple Dumplings

Cakes and puddings

Golden Cake
Eggless Spice Cake
Chocolate Date Cake
Quick Chocolate Cake
Steamed Fig Pudding

Frostings

All of the frostings on pages 396–405 except for rum frosting, boiled frosting, seafoam frosting, and coconut frosting are made without eggs.

Dessert sauces

Jam Sauce
Chocolate Sauce
Chocolate Rum Sauce
Toasted Almond Sauce
Brandy Sauce
Hard Sauce

Cookies

Apricot-Oatmeal Bars
Thin Peanut Bars
Pumpkin Cookies
Oatmeal Cookies

Breakfast Molasses Cookies
Sandies
Thumbprint Cookies
Honey Almond Cookies

Candy

All of the candy recipes are made without eggs, except for the recipe for divinity fudge.

Measurements

3 teaspoons = 1 tablespoon
16 tablespoons = 1 cup
1 cup = 8 ounces
1 pint = 2 cups
4 cups = 1 quart
1 quart = 4 cups, or 32 ounces
1 gallon = 4 quarts
1 pound = 16 ounces
1 pound of margarine = 2 cups
1 stick of margarine = ½ cup

Index

Index

Index

Notes

Notes

Notes

Notes